Healing Shine

A Spiritual Assignment...

Also by Michael Johnson

The Most Special Person

Susie, The Whispering Horse

Cowboys and Angels
Best Non-Fiction 2002 Oklahoma Writers' Federation

Tad Pole and Dr. Frog

A Gift for Ida and Bell

Chicken Soup For the Horse Lover's Soul
Contributing Author

Reflections of a Cowboy
(Audio Book)

Healing Shine

A Spiritual Assignment...

Michael Johnson

First Edition

This is a work of non-fiction describing the healing of an
emotionally disturbed horse.

ISBN 9780967948355

Library of Congress Control Number: 2006935816

Designed by Darron Moore, MOORE OR LESS DESIGN

Portrait Artist Sammy Watson

Printed in the United States of America

Season of Harvest Publications
Texas

Dr. Fred Tarpley, Editor

A *note from the publisher...*

Man and horse. How many centuries have we worked
on this relationship? How many lessons have been
learned and forgotten by later generations? How many
books have been written? The relationship between
man and horse has been romanticized almost as much
as that between man and woman. Some would say it's
more complicated. Michael Johnson and I learned
about horses from our fathers, grandfathers and
uncles. We learned to break horses—that man must
dominate animals that are often five times our size.
Those methods work. Most true horsemen, however,
learn something more from their horses. Explaining
something more is another story.

   The horse training books on my shelves by
legendary horsemen are all small books. They are all
excellent, but I always found it confusing that one could
write about training horses in so few pages. Of course,
if you wrote all there is to know in one book, it would
be so big that nobody would read it. The more I learn
about riding and working with horses, the more I realize
how little I know. Horses have personalities. They do
not speak our language—or is it that we do not speak

theirs? Can we learn their language? What works for one may not work for another. Some methods seem not to be working when they really are and vice-versa. It is often darkest before the dawn; one step forward and two steps back; clichés, I know, but they apply.

It took a story, a novel made into a movie, to bring a different kind of less dominating, more patient, communing with horses into the light. Horse whispering became a popular moniker for this type of horse-human relationship building. As a novelist, I think I am pleased about that—whatever spreads the word. In *Healing Shine*, Michael Johnson tells a different kind of story. When he first told me about Shine, I did not understand—partly because his voice would crack like tempered glass a couple of sentences into it. When he wrote the whole story, I began to understand.

This is a story about one horse, one man, and their spiritual journey together. It's about healing. It's about what man can learn from horses and how we can learn to speak each other's languages. It's about listening, observing, failure, small victories followed by utter defeat, about persistence—and finally, about that *something more.*

Jim Ainsworth, Publisher

Season of Harvest

Dedication

For all the horsemen who helped Shine

Acknowledgments

I'm grateful to many who are both friends and business associates for their help in the creation of *Healing Shine*. Publisher Jim Ainsworth has been so instructive both professionally and personally. Dr. Fred Tarpley, editor of *Healing Shine*, is a master of our language and has polished this book many times. What wonderful teachers both have been for me. My gratitude to Sammy Watson for his magnificent portrait of Shine, and for his friendship.

To the horsemen and horsewomen who helped both Shine and me, know that neither of us can repay the debt we owe. Bronc Fanning has been the recipient of endless late night phone calls regarding Shine, and patient and instructive during each and every one.

Only Darrell Buzan has heard more about Shine than Bronc, and bless you both for listening.

Craig Hamilton used his skill and strangely wonderful spirit to "crack the crust" of the gray's mind, and Shine and I are both the better for it. Shine still asks about the great Craig Hamilton from time to time.

Rosie Austin expanded my thinking and stretched the corners of my mind. She did for me what great teachers do for us all – she built my confidence.

Kenneth Colson had more patience than Job with both Shine and with me. Now on some days when we rope at his arena, Shine calmly lopes after steers and turns them nicely. He's no longer sick and he's no longer afraid. And on those days, I try so hard not to weep with joy.

For all of you who helped me with Shine – thank you. What weak words to convey how I feel.

To the Shine Man - the best teacher I ever had. It's been a privilege to rope with you.

My fondest wish is that your spirit be light and for you, the Oklahoma version of the Irish blessing for good horses....

May the wind always be at your back, the Good Lord keep you in the palm of His hand and may you never come up lame.

"It was the most difficult thing I ever did. I couldn't get through to him - tried every way in the world, used everything I knew...nothing. He never improved – he was the same two years after we began even though we worked every day, and then much the same for two more - not that you could tell any difference after two years or after four. Four years and nothing. And finally after all that time, finally he started listening. It took me so long to get him to understand."

Imps Bandino Blue

Shine

Introduction

I don't know why I was the way I was about him. If I'm honest, I've done the same thing a few times before. See something or somebody and go off the deep end – just lose all common sense. I've been a fool for lesser things.

The first time I ever saw him he was standing in a stall lost in thought. When he sensed my presence, he turned his head, fixing one big soft black eye on me. He didn't say anything; he just stared. I looked back at a creature the Lord had taken His own sweet time to create. Standing just short of sixteen hands, with his blistered black mane and tail, and all those dapples shining like old silver dollars in the late afternoon sun, his body was too long, and his head was just a shade the same, but my my, did it all fit together well. As I looked down at the black stockings casing his powerful legs, I asked the ranch owner, "And how much is this one?"

"Him?" he said. "Oh, I don't think you would like him. He's been ridden only thirty days in his life, and he was two then. He's five now and been alone in the pasture for three years. I don't think you would like him," he said.

"And how much is he?" I repeated and then took

a deep breath because... *because I felt troubled. This wasn't like me. This wasn't like me at all. I was a conservative person, and not only was such a purchase out of the question – I couldn't afford horses of this quality and caliber. This man sold horses before they were even born. Just a few moments earlier, he had shown us a mare, and pointing to her swollen, very pregnant belly, casually mentioned he had just sold that unborn baby for $10,000 dollars. I could never afford the horses on this man's farm. And besides, even if I were considering it - a long discussion with myself before doing anything remotely like this would have been of paramount importance. But this time, it seemed someone else was in me, some part of me I didn't know about was saying, "It's him...he's the one." It all happened in just a few moments, but in those few moments, time seemed to slow down and stretch forever. And I knew whatever the man said, my next move would be to reach for the halter hanging on the stall door. I heard the man speak, but neither his voice nor the price he requested made its way down into the part of us that hears such things. I really didn't know what he said; I just heard him speak, and that was all I needed because whatever he said, my words had already formed, and they jumped from my mouth.*

"That's fine, I'll take him."

Years would pass before I understood why I did that. A woman explained it to me later. "I know why," she said.

"I wish you would tell me," I answered back. "Because...sometimes one just reaches out and grabs you by the heart."

Only horse people would understand that.

And I suppose that's the best explanation I will ever

hear. Walter Merrick must have felt that way the first time he ever laid eyes on Three Bars. For a man who never cursed, it was an odd statement. He said, "I don't know who owns that son-of-a-bitch, but I will." And later, he would say, "I believed in Three Bars the first time I ever saw him." I know how Walter Merrick felt. When the big gray looked at me that day, something moved inside. He was beautiful, no doubt about that, and I knew he would be a star. I knew how great we would look in the roping arena – couldn't wait. But there was something else, and that other thing was strange. Considering the circumstances of his current life and looking at the surroundings where he lived, there was no reason for me to feel the thing I felt. The man who owned him was legendary in the horse world, and his mistreatment of any animal was simply out of the question – something this man would never do. And there was no possibility the horse was suffering from anything in any way. His physical condition was perfect.

No, it wasn't the man that caused the feeling or the horse's health; it was something or someone else. When he looked at me, my spirit took note, and I remembered. I had seen this thing and felt this thing before – one other time when I was in the seventh-grade. On that occasion, this thing was in a man. Actually, he was no more than a boy then, or maybe better said, a man-child. It was in a human then, and I don't know how I knew but I knew. I felt it in the human and turned out I was right. I was right and it was real. I sensed it in a human that time, and on this day, that thing was in this horse, and it was the thing called...*greatness.*

And that's what I felt about this horse. Just standing there staring at him, knowing that anyone would have laughed had I told them, but I knew. Inside this animal was the thing called greatness. And there was something else, and that other tangible something was truly perplexing. Made no sense whatsoever. Considering this magic I felt at that moment, the other thing made no sense. At the same time, the awareness of this greatness made itself present, at that same moment...I felt sorry for him.

But I'm getting ahead of the story.

Healing Shine

A Spiritual Assignment...

Chapter One

A FOUNDATION BUILT ON SAND

All good stories begin at the beginning, so that seems a logical place to start. I was born in 1947 into a good and caring lower middle-income rural family who did everything in the world for me. If my daddy said once, "I want you to have it better than I did," he said that a hundred times. Unfortunately, I never did anything for him in return and regret that until this day. Like so many young people can be, I was an irresponsible ne'er do well – a silly and immature child, a poor student, and a youth devoid of any desire to help him. There was one thing I worked on however. Roping. I never tired of practicing on the dummy, or in the roping pen. The original "arena rat," I pushed an infinite number of calves into the chute, and after pulling the old cotton rope to release the gate, flew down the arena in hot pursuit countless times, and only regretted that we didn't have lights. Becoming proficient with the rope could not help but cause me to think I had somehow become quite a trainer of horses at a relatively early age, and that belief would stay with me for years. Considering the family I was born into, there were ample opportunities to practice those horse-training skills, but I was so wrong. As an old friend once said, "Experience ain't what it's cracked up to be."

And those opportunities and my surroundings influenced me greatly in ways that I did not know or think about. The behaviors, beliefs, and thought processes of those who raise us cannot help but become part of our psychological make-up in our treatment of others – both humans and horses. Later in life we adopt those same belief patterns without question and often become copies of the men who shaped our thinking. While this is certainly true for females modeling on women, perhaps male children are even more malleable and influenced more strongly by the desire to identify with masculine models. After all, to boys - the most important thing in the world is to become a man. And if there were ever masculine models to copy, I had them – my dad and five uncles.

Certainly there are those who would say, "Well, perhaps that's not really the model we should strive for," and that may be true. Remember, however, this was the fifties - a time of John Wayne, Gary Cooper, and Mickey Mantle when real men fought, drank, smoked cigars, and took not one single thing off of or from any other living human being. In those days, everyone unconsciously agreed on the internal mental blueprint for how and what all men should be.

My father was the original prototype of the "real man." "Cork," as he was known, was a legendary figure in our small northeast Texas community. A highly recruited running back with superior agility and speed, his feats on the football field were re-told countless times in small coffee shops, cafes, and around woodstoves in barns for decades. As a catcher, he didn't "throw" the baseball to second; he hosed it with a crackling snap from his crouched position. He didn't stand to throw; he remained in that crouch, threw to second like some mythical figure with a lightning bolt in his hand, and he was deadly. And if skill on the gridiron and diamond weren't enough, his real gift was in track and field. My father defeated all comers in the pole vault in 1936 in Austin, Texas, at a time when there were no divisions between schools. Schools from large metropolitan areas competed against all others including tiny Class B schools, and reaching the height of 13' 6" with a bamboo pole as a sophomore proved to be better than all the rest. With black curly hair, broad shoulders, and slim waist, and just plain lucky enough to be dead-ringer for Tyrone Power to boot, this blue-eyed fighter and cowboy provided what most sons would view as a perfect model to mold one's self after. And can you imagine just how impossible I felt it was to do that? In my mind, no one could be like him. No starry-eyed admiration here - there really wasn't anyone like him.

Men fought in those days. Certainly in the war, but I mean with their fists at honky-tonks, rodeos, and at impromptu games of chance. It seems to me that small caliber handguns so prominent in the news today must not have been invented in the fifties. There was almost never a story about any altercation involving firearms, and now that I think about it, there was never any news coverage of the infinite number of fights, scrapes, and brawls I witnessed in my wonder years. No reporter could have covered them all. And each and every one filled me with a sick dread.

Regardless of how many stories were told about my dad's athletic achievements, the number paled in comparison to those recounted of his prowess with his fists. I never saw him start a fight, but Lord, did I see him finish so many. I burned up my childhood days watching this man dismantle men twice his size, who committed the cardinal sin of picking on some little guy. He floated like a butterfly and stung like a 30.06. His hands were so fast when he hit someone, you simply could not see the first four punches.

I remember as a child sitting in his old truck he always drove watching the men crowded and huddled around an army blanket on the ground behind the sale barn. The cards would flutter, and the dice would click, and I knew it was just a matter of time until the inevitable disagreement came, and sure enough, the accusation of cheating or dispute of some obscure rule would result in a war. Watching with fear in my heart and certainty that surely they would kill my daddy, I would hear the first few blows from his electric fists. Then the blood would spatter, and the blood was never his. Considering his skill, he might easily have become a bully, but that was never the case. He fancied himself – and accurately so – a champion of the underdog. In all my time with him, I never saw him start a fight, but Lord, I did see him finish so many.

His masculinity needed no arrogant posing or posturing of any kind, nor did he strut his maleness. He really was a man made of saddle leather and steel, and he felt no need to convince others of anything. My uncles were just like him. If Dad's sheer granite toughness could be matched by anyone, my uncles were

right there with him. The thought comes now that some
might read these words and attribute a negative quality
to the description of these men in present times, yet in
that time long ago, these same words would have been
considered complimentary. The truth is the Lord
seemed to have made them from some alloy of steel and
stone; they were hard men. And for years, I felt a great
failure and sadness in me that I was not like them.

One might assume all this was frightening and
undesirable to a child – and sometimes - often in fact,
that was so. But on most other occasions, so much of
the time, there was just something so surpassingly
wonderful about them. There was never a group more
exciting, more fun, and more what I wanted to be than
these men. For all their rough, hard qualities, there was
this soaring magic about them – something tangible that
you could poke and feel if you had a mind to. About
their boots and leggings, about their spurs and hats, and
the way they handled dogs. Such fierce creatures these
dogs. Dogs that could grab a cow by the nose running
at full speed and flip her so fast you could hardly
believe you witnessed the feat. Dogs that could kill a
wild hog and would die for their master without
hesitation. And when these men came 'round, these
highly trained, at times lethal, fierce, and ferocious
beasts would melt. All that anger, savagery, and
aggression, all those laid back ears and bared teeth, and
all that venom would slip from their minds and bodies
into that Texas sand when these men came 'round. I
knew what it was when I saw it. It was love. The dogs
loved these men and would do anything for them. They
had a deep desire to please these men. And I was just

like them. I was just like those dogs.

There was a distinct sense of wildness about my daddy and uncles. Everything they did was in excess. Too much was never enough for any of them. Moderation was a word none of them knew or would ever use even if they did. Whether they were fishing, cooking, drinking, working cattle, or rodeoing, "just the right amount," was a phrase that never entered their minds, and "far too much" wasn't nearly enough. When they fished – always with nets – I thought of Peter and his crew who after the Lord told them "to let their nets down for a draught," could not pull the nets from the sea. When they ran their nets, the catch of buffalo would later fill the entire bed of pick-up trucks to the brim. To me it seemed they were like the Lord; they could call the fish forth from the waters.

When they worked cattle, the day would be spent doctoring, de-horning, de-worming, and inoculating two to three hundred head. Far more than you would ever expect a handful of men could do. Everything they did was like that, even when they were in the kitchen...and what masterful chefs they were. So many days began with my uncle Carroll nudging me from a sound sleep.

"Come on, son," he would say. "Breakfast in a little while." Stumbling and fumbling with my clothes, I could see the old clock in the kitchen showing just a little past four. What time they must have risen to have this much food already prepared was beyond me. Always some six to eight men came, and I would see my Uncle Ray standing over the massive cast iron skillet gently stirring two dozen farm fresh eggs mixed with some ten to twelve heavy shakes of Worcestershire, and as the eggs turned a golden and bronzy dark, he would add the sharp cheddar. Just barely done, and impossibly gooey, they are 'til this day perhaps the most delicious things I have ever eaten. Farm raised bacon and sausage seasoned with too much sage and black pepper, and cat-head biscuits dripping with honey and butter proved ample fare to hold the men – and one boy – 'til lunch.

Trucks and trailers filled with good dogs and better horses would leave the still and silent farm in single file headed to some neighbor's ranch for a day that began and ended in the dark. Arriving just as dawn was breaking, the requisite small talk with the ranch owner would be completed, the horses would be saddled, and the gathering would begin. Riding through pin oak flats, along creek bottoms and riverbanks, collecting cows with these men, horses, and dogs normally was accomplished quickly and without undue effort or a wasted minute. After crowding an impossible number of cattle into impossibly small catch pens and corrals, my uncles took up their individual posts and as they treated, castrated, de-horned, and vaccinated, finished products rolled off the assembly line. Like Sammy Kershaw says in an old song, *"...the talk was small if they talked at all."* Communication and instructions came from pointing fingers and guttural barks. On those occasions when I made a mistake, a simple steely-eyed look of disapproval would be forthcoming. When my heel loop missed the same cow more than two times, the men would step back and stare without saying a word, and I knew what that meant - words were not necessary. Those stares meant....

"Come on son, you're holding us up."

Making my loop bigger, I concentrated on keeping

7

the top strand of the rope up, and doing everything in my power to insure the bottom strand hit the ground first, and then, I would breathe a sigh of relief when the loop finally pulled tight against the cow's two back feet. The men never said a word, but their thoughts were clear in my mind. Their eyes said, *"Shoulda' done that the first time."*

Even though they did everything in excess, no waste seemed to occur, and all their efforts had a distinct sense of style and competency. You might see a pop bottle or beer can on the ground at their farm, but you could bet it wouldn't be there long. Tack, saddles, horses, feed, and all other inhabitants, both living and non, had their place on the farm. Catch pens and corrals were massive fortresses built from cross ties and oak 2 x 12's. They could hold a buffalo with ease but were rarely used. The men in my family preferred to work the cattle in the open pasture.

For all their roughness, to a man they were neat, clean-shaven, ironed jeans and pressed shirts cowboys. Any of them were likely to wrestle a 700-pound steer to the ground by the horns, but their clothes never really seemed soiled. They maintained poise without visible effort, and they bent the world to their will. Even though they would never say such a thing nor did any of them believe it, as a child, I *knew* the reason America won the war. That victory came because my daddy and all my uncles were in the 36th Division. When the Germans saw them coming, they just laid down their weapons and gave up.

They bent the world to their will.

The unspoken requirement that all things adhere to their particular plans included tractors, balers, farm machinery, hay growth, pond levels, calving dates - and wives and children. If any living animal, bolt, nut, carburetor, or irrigation ditch rebelled, these men simply re-arranged whatever was necessary for all matters to work properly, flow smoothly, and cease to cause trouble. And should any piece of matter - whether mechanical or organic - continue to resist, necessary steps would be taken, and those steps would be swift and severe. Not that they were tyrants...they were not. To describe them as mean and demanding would be not only false, but unfair. There wasn't any meanness about it all, but rather a *practicality* about it all. Whatever they deemed necessary as a collective group would in most all cases be the course of action reasonable people would agree on as the best and clearly apparent solution. And of course, they were the same with horses.

As I have been planning to share thoughts about their molding and shaping of my future relationship with horses, an awareness continues to grow that every precaution must be taken not to convey a sense of blame at their feet for the coming words. An image of one of my old aunts – one not too fond of me – haunts my study where I work. *"They taught you everything you know,"* her apparition sneers at me. *"And here you are criticizing them."*

"I'm innocent of that charge," I respond, and as her image fades not honoring my defense with even a verbal reply, her face disappears in that same old twisted disapproving sneer. But I am innocent of that charge. I blame them no more than I blame my old friend, Morris McCarty.

Michael Johnson

The Wyoming Cowboy

Morris is just a little bit bigger than life. He left by
horseback from Terry, Montana, when he was thirteen -
seventy years ago now. Cowboying southwest along the
way, he eventually settled in Meeteesee, Wyoming, at the
Larson Ranch. He's had quite a life, and just like ours,
his has been filled with joy, and sometimes –just like ours
- unbearable hardships. Much of the joy came when he
married the ranch boss' daughter, and most of the sadness
came when they would later lose a son in Vietnam.

He came to Oklahoma a couple of years ago to visit
his niece, Sharon, my neighbor and wife of my best
friend, Darrell. We sat in my barn evening after
evening for most of those two weeks and talked about
horses…and brother, did I listen. Here was a man who
had been on them for seventy years. Not some
weekend team-roper, Morris had been horseback every
day for over a half-century - in the valleys, in the
mountains, in the rivers and canyons of the real west -
and did I listen. Most everything he said is recorded
with indelible ink in my brain, but one thing more than
all the many rich conversations we had, one
conversation in particular remains.

On a cold December night huddled around my barn
stove sipping on something that warmed us more than
the stove, I began to lament my mistakes with horses in
my previous life. "It's certainly not that I've mastered
it," I began.

"None of us ever do," Morris interjected.

"Well said," I added. "But it's just that however
small my awareness is about them now, at least there is
some awareness."

"Me too," he laughed softly. "Even though it's a *small* awareness, at least I have some about them now." "Why did we do that, Morris? Why did we do that to them? I never gave them adequate time to learn even the simple things, yet in spite of all my impatience and clumsiness, they learned anyway."

He shook his head slowly and started to speak. I interrupted....

"My goodness, Morris, I've been around them all my life. Considered myself pretty handy, and then at forty-five, the crushing realization came I didn't know much about them at all."

"Well, you beat me about fifteen years," he said, finally able to get a word in.

"What?"

"I said, 'You beat me about fifteen years, Michael.' I didn't start to see it – or feel it – until I was sixty."

"Why did we do that, Morris?" Why were we that way – so blind?"

He shook his head slowly again, and took a sip and he was silent for a time. Then he said, *"It just never occurred to us."* And I suppose for all my sins with horses, that is why I committed them. A more excellent way just never occurred to me. I'm sorry about that now.

Artist Carrie Ballantyne's portrait of an old cowboy graces the cover of the November 2004 issue of *Western Horseman* magazine, and her subject is none other than Sharon's uncle and my friend, Morris McCarty. Her painting shows a weathered man in a denim jacket and leggings, holding an old well-worn saddle. "A tribute," she says, "to an eighty-three-year-old cowboy," and she perfectly captures the soul and life of a man who did what he could to live the life he loved.

That picture hangs in my den, and every time I look at it, I hear his words. The expression on his face matches perfectly with the thought in my mind and his. A deep regret that we didn't see it sooner, and no need to wonder why anymore. *"It just never occurred to us."*

That is the best explanation I will ever hear. I would never blame Morris or my dad and uncles anymore than I would blame the wind for not sending me some answers about some horses sooner. And now I know that is the place that answers - at least some answers - to some questions about horses come from...the wind. When you're working with them for long periods, and days and weeks go by with no improvement, and you're stuck on a long, flat, and windy mesa, sameness for days, weeks, and months, then suddenly the wind whispers to you, and you know what he needs. Something in your spirit tells you what he needs. You don't know how you know, but you know. You know what he needs, and what will help him.

"Why didn't you tell me sooner?" I ask the wind, and there is silence.

"If you had told me that sooner, I would have done it," I say to the Spirit.

And what I didn't know was - what Morris and I didn't see until we had lived on the earth for more than a half-century for goodness sake - the horse is saying the same thing to us.

"Oh," he says when he understands. *"If you had told me that sooner, I would have done it for you."*

That's the problem with modeling yourself after men who bent the world to their will, particularly so when dealing with horses. With so many subtle shades of behavior and others not so subtle at all, these men

12

bent both the world and horses to their will. "What's wrong with that?" one might ask. There is something wrong with that. Such a belief system is a foundation built on sand.

That's the way poor teachers think. "It's not me," they say. "It's these kids, they're not like we were." That's what poor supervisors say, "It can't be me. I'm doing the best I can. It's people these days – they don't care." And that's what the poor horse trainer says when he finds himself on one that he cannot reach, and there is something wrong with blaming the kids, and the people, and the horse.

That belief system prevents us from considering the possibility it might be us. Have we answered all the questions in our own heart that really pinpoint the center of the problem? Do we really know how to reach the kids and the people? Have we really made an exhaustive study of the way the horse communicates and how he understands? When we tell him to do something, do we in fact give him time to comply? Do we give him the same time to comply we would give a *human*? While none of us will ever be a master at any of those aforementioned tasks, at the very least, we should realize that there are others – others do exist – that know more than we do. Before we blame someone for failing to perform - horse or human - perhaps we should become what we might call a *seeker*. Then we can begin to build something of value. That something may not be much, but at least it's not built on sand.

There are a multitude of problems with the belief system inculcated in my bones regarding how I was taught to deal with horses. And inculcated it is; some geneticist peering through his electron microscope might even be able to see physical evidence on my DNA. But the most serious problem with the entire approach to dealing with horses in this old manner now haunts me every time I swing my leg up on one. This memory and this awareness sits on my shoulder tugging at my psychic sleeve saying, *"Remember, be careful. You must know the answer before you proceed...is it him or is it you?"*

If you don't think that way, you run a risk – and one I believe to be a serious and important one. The occasion may be rare – but if a horse ever comes in your life that won't bend, you will *miss* him. You will let him slip by. What if, like Ray Hunt, you come face to face with a Hondo, a horse whose will was just as strong as Ray Hunt's? The more pressure he applied, the harder Hondo bucked, the more he rebelled, the more Hondo said, *"I will not bend!"* The philosophy and belief system down inside in my male role models – the same one they transferred to the deep part of me – says, *"You make him do what you want!"* And most of the time, you win...but what if you don't? Then people who *rule* the horse – people like my father and uncles - would have an immediate response to that situation. They would say, "Well, if you have tried everything you know, and nothing has worked, then the answer is obvious. That horse is not one you want to keep...he's not a good one."

With that belief system, you can toddle merrily on your way never looking at your own behavior, never even considering the fact that perhaps the horse was not the problem, but *you* were the problem. You will never have to admit that you made a mistake. And while my daddy and uncles could do so many things – even defeat the Germans – admit to a mistake? That was the one thing they could not do.

But I don't blame them, any more than I blame Morris. I would never blame Morris or those men for not telling me any more than I would fault the wind. They were doing the best they knew how, and isn't that like all of us? We're just doing the best we can. What I didn't know was the horse feels exactly the same way. *"I'm doing the best I can,"* he says. And we don't hear him 'cause our soul is asleep.

> *"How many times does something have to happen before something occurs to you?"*

-- *Robert Frost*

"Hmmm...he probably thinks he's being a little hard on himself, but he's not being nearly hard enough. Not even close. He didn't give me time. I was a basket case in those days. High strung and afraid, but doing the best I could. For God's sake, I hadn't been ridden much at all in my life, and he knew that! Don't fall for all those flowery words – he's just like every other two-legged bastard I ever met. All of 'em in a big hurry with their calendars and wristwatches. They miss the whole point. It's like Eliza said to Colonel Pickering in Pygmalion, 'The difference between a lady and a flower girl isn't how she behaves...it's how she's treated.' Ain't it a shame he doesn't know that's true about roping horses too?"

--Shine

Chapter Two

TWO SIDES TO EVERY STORY

Things were so perfectly good on the day I brought him home. It was in May then, and life couldn't have held another single thing in her hands because they were just too full of promise. The sun was bright; the spring grass was peeking through, and me? I'm driving along in a big trailer pulling a star in the wagon behind. I unloaded him with nothing on my mind but sheer pride. In spite of every one of my very best efforts, I just could not keep my cowboy hat on my head – my head was just swelled too big. Then I unloaded him, and things got even better.

My wife came driving up the lane at that moment – the perfect moment, of course - and stepped from her car with her eyes wide as saucers and mouth open. At a loss for words, she stared silently gaping at this stunningly beautiful gray ghost, who with his flying mane and tail was so busy at the moment. So busy running up and down the fence, then dropping his butt, sliding, and throwing wonderfully beautiful chunks of mud everywhere, and then spinning and turning, and then spinning and turning and running up and down the fence again. Had someone approached me at that moment and asked, "Will you ever have another bad day?" I would have said, "Not in this lifetime I won't."

"My Lord!" she said breathlessly. "Whose horse is that?"

I can still remember the taste of the words I used to answer. They tasted like a chicken fried steak I had late one night in the small town of Post, Texas. It was almost midnight, and I couldn't believe the little diner was still open. As I went in, I noticed the key characteristic of all truly great restaurants, and that is they already have everything on the table – all the salt, pepper, ketchup, forks and knives, A-1 Sauce, Heinz 57, and Tabasco already sittin' there just in case there's anything you need. And if you dare make the mistake of asking for anything, the waitress will say, "It's right there, Shug," pointing to something right in front of you. This was that kind of place. The steak was crunchy and had this unforgettable flavor that just arc-welded itself to your taste buds. So good. The words were like that, and when I said them, I had that same taste in my mouth I did in the little town of Post long ago.

"Whose horse is that?" she said.

The words were crunchy and good and unforgettable.

"He's ours," I said.

And she began to cry. "Uh oh," I thought, remembering I should have asked her about doing such a thing. I had no defense because there was no time, but had I been given all the time in the world, I still wouldn't have been able to prepare one.

"I'm...uh, well, I'm sorry. I know I should have asked you, but...."

"No, no," she said wiping her eyes. "It's all right... really, it's all right. He's just so...he's just so *beautiful!* You had to buy him. I understand. You couldn't help it."

And she was not the only one. Poochie, the big Lab we had in those days, sat still as a stone not even wagging his tail for the first and only time in his life. He just sat and stared, and so did the barn cats, all peering around the corner with awe dripping from their whiskers. What a day. What a day it was. Did you ever have a day like that? When things were right with the world? That day everything was right with the world. In an old song, John Denver talked about a day like that one. In "Sunshine on My Shoulders," he says, "If I could give you a day, I would give you a day like that one." That's the kind of day it was. When we were young, and full of hope. I wish I could give you a day like that one. A day when the azaleas bloom, or the hummingbirds come back, or when the cardinal lights on your windowsill, and you are reminded of the Thing that made him. But I can't give you a day like that. Those days – like this one was – just come when they decide. Those days just come on their own, and this day came on its own. What a precious, wonderful, and beautiful day that really was...the day Shine came to Johnson Farms.

"I'll have him going in about a month," I said. "Maybe sixty days." I really didn't believe that last part because expert horsemen don't really need sixty days.

"Well," she said. "I know you will because you

know about horses."

"Yeah," I said, cocking my hat back on my head like Audie Murphy used to do. "That's one thing I do know about. My daddy and uncles raised me on them, and you can't help but pick up a few things," I said, trying to sound modest 'cause that's what Audie always did. And the next day we began.

I couldn't sleep much that night because I knew tomorrow was going to be better than today even though I didn't see how such a thing could be possible – but I knew it would. Cleaned up my saddle, oiled the bridle, washed the horse blankets, and re-read some old magazine articles about starting colts. Not that I needed to, you understand. Because – well, you know - after all, I was raised around them, and true, James, the man I bought him from had frowned when I asked him how much the horse would cost, and said, "Uh, I don't think you want this one, Michael. I don't think you will like him." But come on, really now…what did he know? Did he have uncles like mine? And did his uncles whip the Germans? I hardly thought so. And so I went to bed with my eye locked on the clock, and kept it there 'til about 4:30 or so, and remembered that's when my uncles rose or even before, and it was high time I started becoming more like them anyway. I went to the barn to saddle Shine. Couldn't catch him for about an hour.

Small matters never deter real cowboys. After what seemed far too long a time, Shine's first saddling at Johnson Farms was officially in the books. Stepping back to admire my work, I couldn't help but notice the saddle hung sharply almost half-way down his left side with the blanket only half under, and said blanket protruded at an awkward angle and equal distance in the opposite direction down the right side - with Shine looking somewhat like a camel saddled by two blind men. I decided to do the whole thing over again.

Having begun shortly before 5 a.m., I knew we would be pretty well worn out by 9, and that four hours would be plenty of practice for the first day. Somewhere around 9:30, I got the damn saddle on him.

"How's it going?" my wife said, walking into the barn.

"Going? How's it going? It's going fine. I'm just getting the saddle on him."

"What's taking so long? You've been out here forever."

"Worst thing you can do is rush one," said Audie. "First saddling is important, and you have to take your time."

"Four hours?" she asked.

"It takes as long as it takes," I said, parroting a line used by all great horsemen.

I had actually been on Shine before at James' farm. For just five minutes and all of that in a small round pen. James had cautioned that I should be careful as Shine had not been ridden much at all in three years, and he was uncertain of what might happen. All of his concern - while appreciated of course - was of not the slightest importance to me. Small matters never deter real cowboys. I had mounted Shine on that day at James' farm, and rather than listen to his counsel, did exactly as instructed by my uncles long ago when dealing with a spooky horse.

"Kick him pretty hard there in the side, son, and see if he'll buck."

On that day at James' I had done just that, and Shine hadn't raised an eyebrow. He responded instantly with a jerky kind of bolt, and a feeling shot through me eerily similar to the one we all feel just after we've touched an electric fence by mistake... but there was no buck in it. I could also tell he didn't like that kick. He seemed offended by it. Even though not ridden for some time, at the moment of the kick, he hopped into a soft little lollipop lope and gently made his way circling in an easy canter 'round the pen. I sat my butt down in the saddle and there was instant no motion. And at that moment, I knew we were home free.

> ***"That's what he thinks."***
>
> ***--Shine***

Now on this day at my farm, I knew the training plan I had carefully constructed the night before would work like the intricate inner mechanisms of a well-oiled machine, and I also knew there was no need whatsoever for a round pen. Even though my round pen rested only a few yards away, I knew this horse, and I knew how to help him move down the path. I didn't feel arrogant about it, mind you; it was just the least I could do because after all, I'm a human, and humans have been given dominion over horses, and rightly so. It was more that I felt a sense of obligation to aid and abet in the development of this fine animal. Standing by the barn in the open pasture thinking how glad I was we were not limited to the small-minded confines of a round pen - and besides what real cowboy ever used them anyway - I leisurely stepped up on him for the first time at his new home. He just stood there patiently waiting for instruction like the superior horse I knew he was, and I touched him gently with my spur in his right side. And Shine politely... *stepped out from under me!*

My feet hit the ground, and to my amazement, I realized that I was standing upright. A moment earlier I had not been standing, but sitting - on a horse. And now that same horse was no longer under me, but standing calmly staring from a short distance perhaps at most some two feet to my left.

"Hmmm..." I thought.

I looked around to make sure no one had seen this expert horse-training maneuver and slowly walked back over to him. After reaching for the reins and saddle horn, I once again pulled myself up in the saddle and on to the big gray. For a second time, as patient as Job, he stood there waiting for instruction. I made a tug on his right rein solely intended to produce a half-turn to the right. Shine executed an instantaneous violent 360-degree dustdevil whirlspin that came within a whisker of almost unseating me again. And he stood there patient as Job waiting for further instruction. Very slowly...I stepped off.

And I stood beside him for a time gently petting his neck, and right out there at the edges of my mind, this little thought peered over the rim of my consciousness. For the first time, I began to consider the possibility that maybe – just maybe – I might need to rethink things here. Then I heard his voice. It was the first time my spirit ever heard his. As I made small circling motions on the side of his neck, he turned, craning clearly visible muscle and sinew, and with his head finally fixed in the serpentine position he wanted it to be - so as to maximize the possibility he had my full attention - he fixed one big black eye on both of mine and said, ***"You have no idea what you're doing, do you?"***

That was the day I took my spurs off. That broke my heart 'cause I love my spurs. But on that day, I took a little baby step down a better path and toward a better place. I realized that two kinds of people wore spurs. Damn fools who think they know about horses, and true horsemen who really do know about horses. Certainly not wanting to be the first, and that little thought out there just forming in the mist on the horizon of my mind had just put the first chink in my armor that maybe I was further than I thought from the second. So I decided to start with something he could handle.

"Whoa there amigo, hold on right there for just a New York minute. Let's all go back up there and re-read that last paragraph. He's gonna' 'start' with something I can handle? That's really rich. How lucky I am the Lord gave me to such an idiot. If you've seen one two-leg with spurs on, you've seen 'em all. And by the way, if you ever see one jabbing a three-inch shank in the side of a horse deep enough to bring blood, you can bet he treats his wife, kids, and stock-dogs the same way. No wonder the Devil hates 'em."

--Shine

"Wait...wait – I'm not done. Don't cut me off like that. I may have what some would consider a tendency to go on and on, but I'm not through.

See? What he just did is what they all do. That's what they all do – they never think about what we need – just what they want. If I ever meet one, if I ever meet a single one who ever thinks about what I might need, I swear to the One who made me, I'll change my ways. But I'm not worried about that happening, I can be perfectly comfortable being what I am right now 'cause that ain't gonna happen.

Think about this…think about what I really am. I'm a horse. I'm a creature designed by the Spirit to help Man…that's what I'm for. That's the only reason I was made. And this patronizing, condescending… this what? You call them humans, I call them two-legs, and I hate'em worse than an Apache hates the White-Eyes, but this…this ' human' thinks he's doing me a favor 'cause he's gonna give me something I can 'handle'? Good grief! And some of you, I know about you. You think it's me. And he does too. That's why we don't do things for you. You're liars!

Just let me prove my case. I ask the Judge to instruct the jury to consider the testimony of… wait, wait, a thought just occurred to me…not my testimony, but the human's. Did he or did he not say just a few hundred words before to the other human, 'It takes as long as it takes?' Did he or did he not say that? This is someone who claimed to be 'parroting the words of great horsemen,' and when I did exactly what I thought he asked me to do – we find out later that wasn't what he meant for me to do - that's my fault? The defense rests. He's an idiot! And here's a *question you can't answer. Why did the Lord in all His goodness send me to him? Why did the Lord give me to him? The defense rests!"*

--Shine

While that initial session didn't go to my liking, I wasn't really too concerned. People who have experience with horses know that time is what it takes, and for a horse like this, I planned to take all the time necessary. So, we shifted focus. I decided since Shine was destined to be a great rope horse, we should begin at the beginning. My new goal was so simple a child could do it, and of course, such simplicity was necessary. Animals should not be expected to master a list of complex tasks. Because of my experience and background, I was aware that this is the exact location of the place people get into trouble when trying to teach any skill to another living creature – be they human or horse. Great animal trainers know the secret.

And that secret is that when trying to teach any living creature, we must begin with baby steps. The smallest tasks must be repeated many, many times and instilled repeatedly. As has been said, "repetition is the mother of skill." Once baseline desired behavior is achieved – that is, exhibited repeatedly by the student – then and only then can we move to the next task, and that next step also becomes of critical importance.

When we ask the student to progress, the next step should be so incrementally small, the student isn't really aware that new behavior is being asked for, nor is mastery of any increased difficulty required. All my background as a psychologist and countless hours in university classrooms listening to endless lectures regarding the esoteric science of the discipline called "learning theory" apparently were finally about to come in handy after all.

"What an idiot!"

--Shine

My next and newest task for Shine certainly conformed to and around the above principles in every respect. I planned to ask him to simply stand still. I knew he could do that.

The next day, after repeating a remarkably similar experience with previous saddling difficulties, we began. I took Shine to the same location in the pasture, but this time, we had company. And when Shine saw the company, he snorted, shied, and finally spooked at this strange new creature, the likes of which he had never seen. A monster called "The Roping Dummy."

My roping dummy is a fiberglass, fully shaped likeness of a roping steer minus the conventional four legs found on most cattle. Hardly threatening by any stretch of the imagination, "Jake" as he is known, bears a striking resemblance to a timid and chronically shy blind bovine lying quietly in the sun. I led Shine by his reins around the corner of the barn for his first lesson and immediately learned something about this particular horse's history. Even though James had neglected to tell me – and surely he should have known such an important detail - apparently Shine's mother had been frightened by just such a creature at the exact moment of his birth. And when he saw this vicious – even though sightless – predator, he wanted no part of this task - regardless of how simple I thought it was.

27

He whirled with a grace and speed that barely reached my awareness and athleticism I never thought possible for an animal his size, and in an instant we had a runaway stage with Gabby Hayes being dragged along behind, and this time, neither Roy nor Gene was there to save him. After being skinned, bruised, and scratched for some two hundred yards, I found my voice was completely gone - not that he had paid the slightest bit of attention to it anyway. And probably only because of the thing called Grace, or due to the fact he was suffering from exhaustion or had tired of me screaming at him, he stopped. I picked myself up, and tried to somehow comfort him and help him stop trembling so. He was terrified. We walked back to the barn.

My wife, who had seen none of this, picks this moment – naturally - to come from the house and yells out to me, "How's it going?"

"What?"

"I said how's it going?"

"How's it going? It's going fine."

And so would begin an experience so typical of Shine, one destined to repeat itself countless times. With just a handful of phrases, I could give anyone a true feel for Shine and all his complexities. One of those at the primary apex of the list would certainly be that to teach this horse anything, to get him to do the simplest thing, was precisely like sanding a massive marble stone with a too-tiny piece of four-ought steel wool. You could work for days on that marble sanding with all your strength, and after the longest time, the only fruit of your labor would be a pile of dust so small you could count each individual grain with ease. And

I didn't know then what I know now. I would learn
that trying to force him or out-pull him or "out man"
him, would be akin to a four-wheeler standing up to
a 100-horse John Deere tractor in a tug-of-war. But
Shine hadn't counted on one thing. He didn't know
something about me, and at the time, I didn't either.
He didn't know how determined I was. I knew this
horse had something in him, and I was determined for
it to come out. Trust me when I tell you I was, in fact,
determined for it to come out.

So day after day we approached the blind and
vicious predator, which after an almost interminable
time, at last came to be only a shy old harmless blind
dummy. Even though I spent a considerable amount of
money on fire-ant treatment – Shine would get "happy
feet" every time we practiced. I felt sorry for him until
I realized there were never any fire ants there in the
first place. One fine day while sitting on Shine's back,
I finally threw my loop and watched it settle around old
Jake's horns. To my amazement…Shine stood still.
When we began, I had estimated thirty minutes for the
exercise and would have been quite disappointed had
anyone told me the time required would be more like an
hour.

"Just a bit off on my estimate," I thought to myself,
as I counted the black row of X's on what had now
come to be called my "Shine Training Calendar." An
X for each day stared back at me. In the beginning, I
would have bet a $100 bill that even one X representing
an entire day would not have been required. But when
the task was accomplished, and my original goal of
having Shine simply stand stone still while I roped
lifeless old Jake - lying helplessly down on the ground

- just one time, the number of X's showed I had been off just a smidgin' off on my original estimate of time. What I thought would take no more than thirty minutes, had anyone told me the task might actually take a full hour...well, in my opinion, that would have been best described as pure "sloth," yet there they were...the X's all in a row, each one representing a full day. I counted them again, and for a second time, their number totaled... twenty-one days.

"What exactly is a calendar?"

--Shine

Yet there was no denying we had made progress. The horse had seen who was boss, and my patience could always outlast his. I had bent him to my will, and if necessary, I would do it again...and again. I knew that method worked and came by that knowledge honestly. I must give some credit for my accomplishments to my uncles of course. One thing my uncles always hammered home – one horse training commandment that surely must be somewhere in the Bible if we consider the force with which this iron rule is pounded into every male child on all farms south of the Mason-Dixon Line – and that commandment is... *"Thou shall not let the horse win."*

Chances are not only good but excellent that Moses must have tripped coming down the mountain, and while he was too embarrassed to tell anyone, the tablets fell from his arms. Hastily, he picked them up and found to his eternal relief, they were not too severely damaged... just one little chip containing only one sentence gone; just one little line. But thank the Lord for dads and uncles who owned horses on all farms...somehow they knew what had been written on that little chip. That vital piece of information had not been lost. On that broken-off little piece of stone was the Eleventh Commandment, and every kid in Texas, Oklahoma, and New Mexico can recite that one before the age of three. All across the South, families sit in living rooms when Grandma and Grandpa come over, and after supper when they are all gathered around, Momma says, "Tell 'em what you learned in Sunday School, Timmy. Can you recite the Eleventh Commandment for Mimi and Paw Paw?"

And little Timmy pushes his cowboy hat back on his head, puts his hands on his hips, and shouts, ***"Thou shall not let the horse win."*** And everyone claps and just beams with pride 'cause they know they are raisin' that boy right, and he's not only gonna' grow up to love Jesus and probably be meaner than hell, but that boy will know how to handle a horse. Because everyone in our parts knows that sometimes you have to be mean... especially when it comes to training horses.

"You wasted your money buying this book."

--Shine

Yes, as I said, we had made progress. There was no denying that. Shine had done what I wanted, and while it had taken far too long – and I was a bit disappointed in that - I knew this response meant we were on our way. And in my mind, the time had come to stretch and reach for just a bit more. Since my plan for him involved his being transformed from useless horseflesh into great roping pony, the time had almost come for him to go to his first roping. I knew how to start a roping horse because once again, I had seen it done and done it myself on more than one occasion. Yet I planned to deviate from conventional family customs this time.

The men in my family trained roping horses by the method they referred to as "wading in." Simply stated, this meant that the first thing you did was to rope something alive off the horse. Ideally, the first step in this procedure would be to break the horse to ride – not necessarily a hard and fast rule. Then, whether in the arena or pasture, the way to teach a horse to rope was to spur him a sufficient number of times to reach within striking distance of some living object and hurl your weapon. That weapon of course, being a manila rope bought at the local hardware store from one large oak barrel with a hole in it where the rope came out. After cutting to your desired length, tying your own honda, stretching the rope from fence post to truck bumper, then waxing said rope with a bread sack wrapper, you were ready. Once you threw it - whatever target you were locked onto at the moment was at your mercy and had no chance if you could really rope, be that target cow, bull, horse, mule, goat, or buffalo. Provided you could rope – and what real man can't - that ornery mammal would be within your snare in a heartbeat. What a useful, handy, sorely missed piece of equipment it is…ropes from the old days.

The highly trained expert roping horse trainer - after roping said object animal - would then either choose to stop or turn left as quickly as possible dragging the hapless target behind - provided his total body weight did not exceed the horses' weight multiplied by a factor of two. If the roper chose to stop or head east, either choice resulted in shock and awe on the part of not only the "catchee," but the "trainee" as well. That's the way my daddy and uncles trained a rope horse. And what I am about to say next speaks to the mystery and wonder of horses more than perhaps any other single thing. With that method, *every single horse we had roped his heart out for us.*

While humor is such a good thing, and hopefully some will be found in these pages, there is none in that line above. *Every single one we had always roped his heart out for us.* I write those words with such sadness. Can you imagine the trauma a prey animal must feel when subjected to such treatment? Humans are often frightened the first time they rope a steer in an arena, and we have the advantage of words, books, schools, and instruction. Yet so many horses are told, required, and demanded to perform complex tasks without the slightest instruction. When the horse fails to execute, he is often punished severely. Not by mean people in every case, but in far too many cases by ignorant people. And ours were often punished.

At the time, even though not a mean person, I thought nothing of it. Instead, I watched carefully so I could learn to do the exact same things so as to become a master of the rope horse. Paul would feel that way later when he realized what he had done as he stood calmly holding the cloaks of the men who stoned Stephen. Later, Paul couldn't get over that. He couldn't forgive himself for doing that. I know how Paul felt now. I'm still sad about what I did, and I can't forgive myself either. I literally held the coats of men who in a real sense threw stones at *our* horses, the same ones trying the best they knew how to help Man. The

33

same ones who roped their hearts out for us. And I watched and listened so I could learn to do the same. I'm sad about that now.

"It just never occurred to us."

--Morris McCarty - Cowboy

"Yeah, I know. You feel sorry for him now, all sad and teary-eyed, but re-read that part up there about 'ignorant people,' and don't you think for a minute he ain't still one of them. Just watch what he does later."

--Shine

Certainly the PETA people will be on my trail and on my tail for this, but I really don't think the horse suffers permanent damage from such treatment - what we might call a "non-caring" approach. Some do of course, and we can say those horses were "not good ones," but most bend, acquiesce, and conform to the wishes of the one spurring them. As noted trainer Craig Hamilton once said, "We should be so thankful the horse is not a predator." Craig's point being of course, if we consider the way they have been treated, if horses were predators, the first thing they would kill to eat would be…us.

"First intelligent thing he's said."

--Shine

Thankfully, I had mellowed a bit in my old age, and for that reason, I planned to take Shine down a different path. My intention was to introduce him to the world of roping by employing a more gentle approach. But I knew he would be ready soon – after all, I still had thirty days before my original target of sixty days to make him a finished roping horse was depleted - and I knew just what to do. I planned to ask a friend to help me, and his name was "Buford."

Buford, as he is known, is a mechanical device and another of my roping dummies - but because of his sophisticated electronics, that term "dummy" hardly does him justice. Buford is no dummy. He is quite some distance up the evolutionary scale and a far cry from such lowly creatures as Jake.

Like Jake, Buford bears a striking resemblance to the real thing, but unlike Jake, Buford came into the world with all four legs. A much more life-like and exact replica than his cousin, Buford is attached to a long tubular steel bar. That bar travels from Buford's side to a pivoting bracketed center-post, some thirty-three feet away. Because of his mechanical configuration – much like some human beings we've all known are prone to do - Buford spends his life going around in circles. But this circle is quite large, and measuring sixty-six feet in diameter, this circle is just wide enough to teach horses that we hope one day may rope, a different kind of mechanics – one being the mechanics of the correct "position." Buford is also qualified to teach a variety of other concepts necessary for the eventual finished rope horse we all hope to one day have, including the thing called rate – the ability of the horse to maintain a constant position in relation to a running steer, many of whom possess an annoying tendency to change speeds without a moment's notice. Buford, even though lacking in personality, can provide and help create a substantial list of the desired reactions and responses found in the competent rope horse.

Like all good teachers, Buford has the ability to help a wide variety of students – some skilled and some not so skilled. Provided the student listens of course, Buford can help them improve. And his greatest strength is that he can go *slow.* Teachers who can teach us to go *slowly* when necessary are often the ones that help us most. My buddy taught me that. My buddy's name is Darrell.

One of my best friends in life, Darrell once gave me perhaps the best tip I ever received to improve my roping. Some time ago, I found myself in one of those slumps that plague all hitters, golfers, and ropers, and I was at my wit's end as to how I might break out of the slump and improve. Seeking help, I called my friend, neighbor, and traveling partner, Darrell Buzan. Darrell lives just a few miles down the road from my farm, and in addition to being an old Oklahoma cowboy who raises fine quarter horses, he's a pretty fair hand with a rope. Not only could the man spin his twine, the man is well known as a gifted teacher. Just what I needed - a roper who could communicate – a rare creature indeed.

"I can't catch my butt, much less a steer," I said as the phone call began. "I can't even *hit* my butt much less catch it."

Darrell laughed and said, "Well, you're usually more consistent than that." (Obviously a gifted and talented man.) "What seems to be the problem?" he asked.

"That's just it," I sighed. "I'm in a fog. I can't even give you a good description of any mistake I continue to repeat. It's more like something wrong this time and something completely different the next. There's no consistency."

"I'll come down and watch you run a few," he said.

Darrell sat in his favorite position in my arena. He and his lawn chair rested just inside the scant shade offered by the roof covering my heading box, and he watched as I ran perhaps a dozen steers, maybe slopping my loop on three or four at the max – and I felt just like Mickey did when he had one of those 0 for 4 days at the plate. And had I had a water-cooler, I would have attacked it with a baseball bat and smashed it to pieces - just like Mickey did on one of his bad days. Darrell never said a word.

Darrell gained national recognition across the country as a music teacher, and his choral groups performed all over America and Canada to high acclaim. A man known for his ability to elicit high performance from students, Darrell was not only a gifted music teacher, but a really good teacher in other areas, including *life.* And how Darrell works his magic is of great interest to me because the magic he works has mystery.

When you ask Darrell for help, he doesn't make a list of what you are doing right, then make a list of what you are doing wrong, and then tell you what to work on. That's what most everyone else does. They tell you what you are doing right, then tell you what you are doing wrong. They observe whatever task you are trying to perform, look for mistakes, and after finding and identifying those mistakes, then offer suggestions on how to correct your errors. Everyone does it that way – what other method could one use to help another? Everyone I've ever known does it that way -

everyone except Darrell.

I've admired Darrell for years. I've also been thinking about exactly how it is he works the magic he does. After focusing my attention on him and this strange and different teaching technique he uses, I have found some answers. I've found at least some partial explanations for his effectiveness. When someone asks Darrell for help, he doesn't just observe their behavior, then make a list of mistakes to work on. He does something else. He does other things.

What he does do is…watch.

What he does do is…listen.

What he does do is…carefully think about what he can say to help.

An interesting thought has occurred to me after watching Darrell for so long a time - those behaviors are precisely the same characteristics of all teachers who move us down the path. The people who really help us in life do those same things. Instead of focusing on how we should correct our mistakes - rather than focusing on what we are doing wrong - real teachers watch and listen, and then carefully think about what they can do to help us become more.

"Hello…? HELLO?… "

--Shine

But on that day in my roping arena, I really didn't need a lesson about life, I needed one about roping. And as has often been the case in our times together, Darrell had more to offer than I realized at the moment. After missing steer after steer, and trying harder and harder to no avail, I finally rode my roping horse, Little

Blue, to a stop and dismounted.

"Well?" I said, somewhat red-faced. "Did you see anything that might help me?"

Not having spoken a word for the longest time, Darrell rose from his chair. He seemed to be in no hurry to speak one now. He turned to the west, and faced the setting sun with his back to me, and thought for a time. I knew he was carefully forming his words about his opinions and overall impressions of all the runs, not just one or two, but everything he had seen in the last hour. Without turning around, he said, "I always told my music students something."

"And what was that?" I asked hurriedly.

"You can't play a piece of music fast until you can play it slow."

"What?" I was quite sure what I heard, but definitely unsure of exactly what he meant.

"You can't play something fast until you can play it slow," he repeated. And he walked out of the arena, made his way to his truck, and he was gone.

I stood there thinking to myself. I stood there for some time. Try as I might, I couldn't get it. I thought we were talking about roping, and Darrell's off in left field spouting some Buddhist nonsense about music. While I really respected and admired the guy, obviously this time, he had missed the point.

"You said you didn't need his help about life, but about roping. And HE missed the point? Yeah, it couldn't be you. It couldn't be you that's missing the point. It had to be him. It's never us...it's always them. He's telling you you're in too big a hurry, you idiot! He's trying to tell you

that's why you're missing steers. You're in too big a hurry! Oh, and by the way, while you won't hear me any more than you heard him... that's why you're missing me."

--Shine

Over the next few days and weeks, I couldn't stop thinking about what Darrell had said that day. What did playing a piece of music too fast or too slow have to do with roping? I still didn't get it, but knowing Darrell, I knew that I should get it. So finally, I called him and admitted the truth.

"Do you remember a while back when you watched me rope and you talked about that line you said to your music students?"

"Sure I remember," he said.

"Okay, I'm a little embarrassed, but I didn't exactly get that. What did you mean by that?"

"I meant that you seemed to be in an awful hurry."

"And what's that got to do with roping?"

"Tempo," he said.

"Tempo?"

"Yep, tempo. I meant my music students would try to play a new piece too fast too soon, and they would lose all sense of tempo. As I watched you rope that day, I thought about them and how you were doing the same thing. Trying to be too quick. As I watched you rope that day, I thought, *That doesn't even look like Michael. The Michael I know ropes smooth, and without any jerkiness or appearance of being rushed."* The fellow in your arena that day – he was wearing your hat, but he wasn't you – that fellow was in a kick-ass hurry, and there was no timing. No tempo."

"Oh," I said, as the light finally started coming on. "Well, uh…hmmm…why didn't you say that in the first place?"

"I thought I did," he said. "Perhaps I should have chosen my words more carefully. I meant to say that timing is everything. We need to go slow first. Being in a rush never helps."

"You can't play a piece of music fast until you can play it slow."

Darrell Buzan - Cowboy

"I know this is really wacky, but is it just me, or might this thinking be applied to some other area of your life?"

--Shine

And that's where I got the idea to use old Buford. I realized Darrell was so right about my roping, and then I started to realize I had been doing the same thing to Shine. I had been in a rush with my roping and in a rush with him. Perhaps I had been a bit too impatient, and after all, I had only been working with him a few days. Even though I had planned on taking him to a roping soon, maybe waiting a little longer would be best. I felt a small sense of pride in that realization because for the first time in my life, it occurred to me that while I did possess a fairly extensive amount of knowledge about horses, there was a good chance I could learn a little more. Darrell had been right about the roping, and I expanded that concept of "rushing is counter-productive" to include horse training. Once I slowed down, my slump faded and my roping improved. Maybe there was something in that manner of approaching things that could help me with Shine. And I knew just what that something was…a slow and easy lesson with Buford.

"'Maybe something about that could help me with Shine?' Naaaahh! That's not the cowboy way. Sure, you can try to let us try to understand something a time or two, but if we don't come around – the first time you lose your patience - you really know inside that you need to take charge, don't you partner? A firm hand is what you need. After all, you feed us grain, you buy us hay, you take us to the vet…surely we should do something to repay you for all that! And I'm going to…I'm going to repay you. The first time I get a chance, I'm going to buck your John Wayne lookin' butt just as high and far off of me as I possibly can. And that's a promise!"

--Shine

Early next morning after the usual saddle tussle, we were ready to go. Well, actually my horse wasn't. Shine seemed in a bad mood and not quite as pumped about my newly found optimism as I was, but that was his problem. I had worked all night on exactly what I intended to do and had little doubt today's training would go well. My intentions were to let him see and inspect the Buford as much as he so desired to insure absence of any fear on his part. Because of my background in psychology, I was fairly certain that Shine would not be afraid of the other dummy, or at least not for long. Even though this one was mechanized, he was so physically similar to Jake, I had strong expectations that Shine would easily generalize from one to the other. It's called "conditioning" in the experimental laboratory world of psychology, and I was quite familiar with all aspects of that area of the science called "Learning Theory." Also, by setting the Buford on the lowest possible speed - old "Bufe" only clipped along at about one or two miles an hour – I felt quite certain this lesson really would take only thirty minutes.

We rode from the barn without any major problems, and that's the last good thing that happened. The day went downhill from there. Shine began with his most severe "fire-ant attack" dance routine to date. Surely someone must have buried hot coals just inches below the surface of the little path that led to the roping dummy. As he hopped from one foot to the other like some damn Spanish trick-horse in a big city parade, I began to lose my patience. I was just asking this horse to walk for goodness sake, and he responded by having a silly, and in my opinion, ridiculous anxiety attack. Yes, I know that patience is a virtue, but I feed this animal, I buy him hay, I take him to the vet, and surely, surely to God, he should be required to do something right once in a while. I decided right then and there to require him to do something. Being a true believer in all Eleven Commandments, Shine was just gonna' have to get with the program. We headed toward old Bufe. *And Shine bucked me off and broke my finger!*

At the emergency room, the doctor walked in and said, "How's it going?"

"How's it going?" I said.

"Yeah," he smiled. "I said, 'How's it going?'"

"How's it going? It's going fine."

At this point, I constructed a new plan. Soon as the doc fixed my finger, I planned to go home and kill Shine.

"OKAY, HOLD IT! Let's just everybody calm down and back off a minute! Easy now...take a deep breath, and let's just sit here for thirty seconds. Okay, are we under control? Good. Now... It was an unfortunate incident, and yes, it makes me look bad. That was the day humans – that were his friends, I might point out – started saying things about me.

That was the day all the other two-legs started saying I was...well, they called me 'crazy.' They started saying I was unstable, and things like that. That I couldn't be trusted, and that maybe I was an outlaw, and all sorts of things. People started saying maybe I should be sold, and one guy even said if I was his, he'd put me on a 'kill-truck' whatever that is. But would you even remotely consider the possibility there are two sides to every story? Probably not, 'cause I never met a two-legs that would, but there are two sides to every story, and I have mine. Just think about this....

First of all, I was in a new place and okay, I was nervous. It's just the way I am, and the reason I am that way is that it keeps me alive. When I'm in unfamiliar surroundings, I inspect things, I snort to scare things away, because let me tell you, there are things out there that will eat you, and I have a strong desire to stay alive.

He rode me to a place I had never been, and yes, I now know who Buford is – and I now know that Buford, bless his heart, wouldn't hurt a fly. But on that day I didn't. How could I? He never let me inspect Buford or even smell of him. Instead he got mad and kicked me right up next to this thing that to me was...well, okay, this will make me sound bad, but I'm unable to give testimony as to what I really thought Buford was. To me at that moment, I thought maybe he was a panther for god's sake, or a mountain lion. I know that makes me sound crazy, but I could clearly see he had horns, and he made an awful clanking noise that would scare anybody like me. As a matter of fact, I'm sure that at first, Buford would even scare a small human. But of course if a small human were scared, all of you would go running to comfort it, now wouldn't you? Anyway, I was terrified, and that's why I did what I did. And I must set one thing straight - and nobody will believe me, but it's the truth. I did not buck him off.

Yes, I know I threatened to just a bit earlier, but you have to believe me. I've never bucked in my life, and that's the God's honest truth. What really happened was he got mad, and I got mad, and when he turned the Buford on, I shied. I will admit to that, but is jumping sideways really 'bucking?' Believe me, if I had really bucked, he wouldn't have hit the ground yet.

I shied...that means I jumped sideways to get out of the way of what I thought was a panther or a lion, and he fell off. That's what happened. For doing something I'm hardwired to do, that's cause for bein' put on a kill-truck? I didn't buck him off, he fell off. And I don't say this to be mean, but the reason he fell off is...well, he's not that good a cowboy. And the last thing I can say about all this is that I'm sorry about his finger.

And to set the record straight, he didn't break his finger. He told everybody he did, even the doctor. But the doctor said he just sprained it. Till this day, he tells everybody I bucked him off and broke his finger. He fell off and he just sprained his finger. If you don't believe me, don't ask him...ask the doctor."

--Shine

Chapter Three

DOES JESUS KNOW WHERE IDABEL IS?

Okay, so I didn't kill him. Another plan revised
Seems like that's all I've been doing since my initial
beginnings with Shine – revising one plan after another.
But I did consider that – grudgingly, you understand
– even though for the life of me, I couldn't understand
this horse and why he did the things he did; maybe
something was wrong. Because something definitely
wasn't right. And I knew it wasn't me.

***"Oh, no! Couldn't be you. Couldna' been.
Not even the slightest chance."***

--Shine

Obviously, the problem was with the horse. I really
missed my dad and uncles on many occasions, but none
more so than now. How much it would help me if I
could sit at the kitchen table or in the barn with them
and talk about this horse. About how he didn't seem
to exactly fit my preconceived notions of what horses

47

were supposed to be, how they were supposed to act, and what they were all about. Then, it struck me that I knew all of them so well, I really didn't have to be in their presence to know what they would say. Whether I could actually talk to them or just pretend to talk with them, I knew precisely what they would say about my problems with Shine. So I created an imaginary barn in my mind just like the one where I spent countless days with my uncles long ago. I knew the conversation about Shine with the world's greatest horsemen would go something like this.

The Barn

As I walked in, my uncles would be sitting 'round an old weathered cedar barn coffee table made by their own hands, and only one would speak.

"Howdy, son. What brings you home? Sit a spell if you'va mind to, but 'fore you do, hand me a beer there, will you?"

"Sure, Unc. Uh…well, I have this horse that's giving me problems, and I wanted to talk to you about him."

"Well, what's the matter with him, son, what's he doing?" he would ask.

"Uh…well, that's just it," I would say. "It's hard to describe. It's just that…."

"Hmmm…he's crazy is he? Is that it? He's crazy?"

"No sir, he's not crazy, he's…well, he seems like he's…."

"What do you want him to do? Come on, boy, spit it out. Quit beatin' around the bush."

"Well, I want to rope on him, but…."

"Well, hell son, go over thar' and get you a rope off

'at wall right thar', get on your horse, and go lock onta something. There's your problem right there. If you want him to be a rope horse, you gotta rope on him, son. How else is he gonna learn? Now go over there and get me a beer, and next time, ask me something hard."

"No, wait, Unc. Wait. I think he's afraid. I don't think he's crazy, I think he's afra...."

"Hell boy, they're all afraid. They're "flight" animals. We taught you that. You know we taught you that. Just go rope on him."

"But...but something in me tells me he's not ready for that now. And it seems to me to make him rope right now would frighten him even more, and...."

"Listen to that 'something.' Please."

--Shine

"Ahh boy, there you go again with that dang softness of yours. That's always been your problem. Told you and told you all the time you were growing up; you're too damn soft. Don't worry 'bout the horse, son; the Lord made 'em to help us work cattle. Don't question the ways of the Lord. And let me tell you what to do 'bout your horse bein' afraid. Get you a long shank spur...."

And at this point, my uncle rises from his chair, and bends kneeling down beside the barn coffee table, and draws a line in the sand with a stick that somehow magically appeared at just the right moment, and says....

"Get you 'bout a three-inch shank on your spur, and when he goes to actin' up, drive that sucker as deep

as you can in his side. Drive it all the way to the hilt,
son."

"And doing this will…will…uh…do exactly
what?"

"Damn, son, do I have to explain ever' lil' ole'
single thing to you? You're a good boy, but you ain't
never – never a day in your life – have you ever had a
lick of common sense." And all my other uncles would
sit quietly slowly nodding their heads in sad-eyed
agreement.

"Well, I'm sorry, but I just don't see how…."

"There you go arguin' again. You asked us for our
help; then you argue with us. You're the same as you
always was, too soft and too concerned. Look, son, I
don't mean to be too hard on you. Don't you see what
I'm talking about here?"

"No sir, and I'm really trying to understand. I'm
just wondering how driving a shank in his side will help
him not be afraid?"

*"Driving that shank in there will make him be
more afraid of you than whatever he's afraid of, son!*
Anybody with common sense can see that, and I ought
not to be so hard on you, you bein' born handicapped
and all…that is bein' born without a lick of common
sense. It's a damn good thing you didn't drive the
tractor in the pond 'cause you'as born without the
common sense to know you'da drownded. I ain't tryin'
to make fun of you son; I'm tryin' to help you."

"I know you are, Unc, but it's just that…."

"But you always – always – was such a hard boy to
help. All them questions you'as always askin', 'bout
why the Lord did this, and why the Lord did that, and
we told you and told you, don't ask questions, son.

Don't question the ways of the Lord. 'Just do what we say,' we always told you, but you didn't listen, son, and you ain't listnin' now. You too busy wonderin' all the time."

"I'm sorry, Unc. I promise I'll listen. Try me one more time…."

"Okay, son, but my patience is wearin' mighty thin. Here's your whole deal in a nutshell. What I'm tryin' to say is you're my nephew, and I'm s'posed to try and help you, and I wanna' help you with your horse. Here it is…you got to show him who's boss! Now do you see what I'm talking about? Here's your answer - *Just go make him do it!"*

And then you can bet your bottom dollar something like this would happen….

My uncle would say, "Now, go over there and get me another beer, and like I said before, next time, gimme' somethin' hard to answer."

And I would get my uncle a beer and leaving this imaginary barn, I would hear him say to the others, "That boy…he ain't never been right. Got a damn doctor's degree and don't know how to start a rope horse. If he don't know how to do that, then itsa natural fact, them college people stole that boy's money."

And all my other uncles would sit in stone silence, with the only sound being the occasional soft explosion of a lone pop-top to break the stillness, and all would be slowly nodding their heads in agreement that the college had in fact… cheated me blind. And there would be great sadness in that imaginary barn because all of my uncles would be remembering the night of little Michael's birth - the night they learned that the poor child had been born handicapped - born without a lick of common sense.

*"The acorn doesn't fall far from the tree...
and some idiots do escape the asylum. I'm in
real trouble here."*

--Shine

While I enjoyed reminiscing about the men in my
family, none of that would have really happened – at
least I hope not.

*"It wouldn't? Really? If that's so, then where
did those memories come from?"*

--Shine

It is sad, but true however, that conversations like
this really do happen among certain horse people all
the time, and those involved truly do think such poorly
thought-out recommendations are the correct answer
to problem horses. While I don't think my uncles
really would have been so insensitive, recalling old
memories like those described caused me to begin
thinking in earnest about men like them. Such men's
typical behavior is much the same when the topic
turns to horses. I thought I was only having fun in my
imaginary barn, but now I was beginning to see some
truth in the tale. It bothers me to admit this, but that
barn conversation with my uncles might have been
more on target than I would like to believe. And for the
first time in my life - because of Shine - I felt myself
breaking away from that old thinking. I had to admit
I was really not like these men. They *knew* what to do
with a problem horse, and you could bet the answer

would always involve...force.

I had always believed that too. But now, somehow the method of simply increasing pressure on *this* horse seemed hollow and mean to me. And there was an even more important reason for my hesitation in using "the old way." I knew it wouldn't work. My spirit knew it wouldn't help, and simply using more force would only make things worse. Maybe I was being soft and weak - and they would have surely thought so - but the simple truth was I knew that this horse with all his issues would not respond to a heavy hand. In fact, I knew a heavy hand would only make things worse. I was beginning to see they were not the experts I once thought they were. I was beginning to see I was not like them. Such people, when dealing with horses, have all the answers. And if their "answer"doesn't work, then... it's the horse.

"Of course it is. How convenient for all of you."

--Shine

I began to see the shallowness of such an approach. I also remembered I never really did like those folks who have all the answers – few of us do. I'm not one of those people. If there was ever a man without the answers, it's me. I second-guess, I have doubts, I ask for guidance. While listening may not be my strong suit – I should do much better in that area - I do in fact seek and ask, and those are qualities for which we should all strive. I've always been much more of a "seeker" than a "joiner." And I was beginning to see something else.

If I really *had* been able to ask my uncles what to do about Shine, they would have had a ready response, and after assessing his behavior and implementing their solutions, those solutions would have resulted in their finding themselves puzzled, confused, and failing just like me. And if they had an honest bone in their bodies, they would have admitted they too had never encountered a horse like Shine and didn't know what to do with him either.

So I decided to take him to a roping.

"What? What did he just say? Oh, wait, I know. There's some typographical problem here. That's it. Surely, he's accidentally left out a paragraph – several in fact – that would explain such an unbelievably stupid statement."

--Shine

Like most bad decisions in life, it seemed such a good idea at the time. I don't know why I did it, and now of course, I know it was the wrong thing to do. I suppose I was just frustrated and wanted to "make him do it." The inaugural event was just a small jackpot, and my confidence that he could handle such an outing began to grow.

"Well, of course. I understand now. I'm terrified of a roping dummy, and he plans to take me to a place with live, blistering fast psychotic cows, honking horns, waving banners, crying kids, and beer-swillin' low-numbered heelers. There's no need to load me...hey, I'm so happy, I'll just get in the trailer all by myself...under

***one condition. I will not get in the trailer if
somebody this stupid is gonna drive!"***

--Shine

I had trouble loading Shine that day, but I finally
arrived at the arena some forty-five miles from my farm.
Shortly after unloading the big gray, people began to turn
and stare. Shine snorted and pranced, raising his head
high and tossing his mane in regal fashion. I felt like just
like I did in the eighth grade the first time I fell in love.

"Fine looking horse there, son," said Mr. Markham.

That made my day. Mr. "M" was seventy-five, and
it was said he could still rope a jack-rabbit, and he didn't
need to neck him either. He could catch ears only and
turn that rabbit sweet for his heeler. A compliment from
someone like him meant the world to me.

"Yeah, he's a Sugar Bars horse," I said, trying to
make my voice sound deep.

"I'm just startin' him."

"Don't want to go too fast," he said.

"No, we don't want to do that," I said. "My daddy
and uncles hammered me pretty hard on that."

"That's good," he said. "It's good you have that
experience. The old ways are best."

"My God...they're everywhere!"

--Shine

"Got you a new one, huh?"

I turned feeling all fuzzy that another admirer had
stopped by, and then I saw the visitor was... Bill. I
did not have the same feeling I had when Mr. "M"
stopped by. Bill was one of those fellows who's hard

to like. He walks around with a little sneer on his face, and everything he has is a lot better than yours, and everything you have is nothing. Bill's that kind of guy.

"Yeah, I plan to head on him," I said. "I think he has a lot of promise."

"Well, we know one thing for sure," Bill growled.

At that moment, I knew what Bill was going to do. And I decided that when Bill criticized my horse – which is what I knew he was about to do - I planned to hit Bill two separate times as hard as I could somewhere above his left eye. I know that sounds a little crazy, but if you knew Bill like I do, and you had heard him say and do all the things I have, you would bet ten dollars that nobody could hit Bill just once.

"And what's that?" I asked, secretly doubling my fist.

"We know he's a good-looking scamp."

Bill's not all that bad.

"Not that bad at all."

--Shine

I roped on my other horses that day, on Little Blue and Old Buddy, and really enjoyed the entire afternoon. I would rather spend a day roping, and then talking and cooking with friends – tailgaiting it's called – than any other single thing. And I'm a little bit proud of that, the fact that such a simple thing gives me joy. The down side is that such behavior does tend to cause divorces.

At any rate, I had such a good day, it seemed like the logical thing to do was to give the Shine-Man a whirl. Time for his turn in the barrel. Not to rope on him of course, just to ride him in the arena. I had told several people about him by now, and most everyone watched with interest as I rode him toward the ropers sitting astride their mounts. As I was about to enter the pen, Shine turned and did an instant about face, which obviously meant his sole intention was to head back to the trailer. Already having learned the futility of trying to out-muscle him, I shouted back over my shoulder, "Be right back. I forgot something."

"Look, you," I said to him when we reached the trailer. "Do not do this to me here today."

"I'm not going in that arena," he said.

"Yes, you are," I said.

"No, I'm not," he said.

"Yes, you are!" I said.

"No, I'm not, and you can't make me."

So we did that for about ten minutes until someone called out, "Hey, Michael! You're up. You want us to skip you, and have your run a little later?"

"Yeah," I yelled back. "This dang bridle…I'm having tack trouble. I'll be right there."

I turned back to Shine. "Come on now, really. Let's go," I said. And this time, he walked into the arena as if he had been doing it all his life. We sat for a time just talking with the men and women I love to be around, and I found myself feeling relieved this horse was finally calming down, and try as I might, I could not help but feel my expectations rising that I might even track one on him.

> ***"I won't go in the arena, and he's gonna' track one on me? Jeez Louise!"***
>
> ***--Shine***

Not rope, just take him in the box and follow a steer

to the other end. I saw a steer without a horn-wrap making his way toward the chute about three or four cows back. I knew the other ropers wouldn't rope that unwrapped cow; they would just turn him out – scoring him it's called – and I thought, "Here's my chance." I nudged Shine forward.

"You make me go in there, and I'll break your finger," he said.

For some reason at that moment, I thought about Shine shying from the Buford and how much my finger still hurt. I decided this particular trial might not be the best course of action, especially in front of all these people. I turned Shine away from the box and headed outside the pen.

My roping was done for the day 'cause all my heelers missed in the third round. Dang heelers. For years, I've planned to invent a new type of team roping where you do all the things you normally do in team roping, but without the added burden of heelers. I don't have all the details nailed down yet, but I'm working on it -'course all my heeling partners feel the same way about headers.

Since my other horses were unsaddled, and the roping had some time to go, it seemed a perfect opportunity to take Shine out in Johnny's pasture and give him something easy to do – you know, like lope in a circle or something non-stressful like that. John had a beautiful place with a nice roomy arena and ample acreage outside that provided a perfect spot. I was feeling good about this day, and Shine's progress – except for his "return to the trailer trip" – and my spirits were high.

I selected a grassy knoll....

"Uh oh. I've heard bad things about grassy knolls."

--Shine

It was a pretty spot, flat and with a thick cover of three-inch high Bermuda grass. I nudged Shine up into a little lope, and he hopped off nicely. I felt special and important at that moment. I just couldn't believe how lucky a man could be to have a horse like this, and then, I noticed Bill sitting on the fence with his back turned to the arena watching us. I felt even better. Shine loping along under me, and me up on him on this pretty day, and old Bill up there trying to act like he wasn't jealous as all get out. "Heh heh," I'm laughing to myself...*and Shine fell down!*

One instant we're on top of the world, and the next, the horse's feet go sideways out from under him, and his big wide dapple-gray butt hits the ground with a vulgar sounding "splat." He falls on my leg which almost kills me, but wounds me not nearly so deeply as the ear piercing shrill of Bill's screaming laughter.

"Hey everybody, Michael's horse fell! Michael's hurt! Michael's hurt!"

It's Bill, of course. "Mr. Paramedic" had no desire whatsoever to offer assistance of any kind. He just wanted to make sure everybody turned in time to see me on the ground with Shine on top of me. I'm furiously squirming like some mink caught in a trap, and unbelievably, Shine picks that moment to decide there's no real hurry to get up. Now all of a sudden, he's perfectly content to be completely still for the only time in his life.

"I'm ompfkay!" said a muffled sound from the

ground. "I'm okay. He just slipped."

Shine finally gets up and shakes himself off real good and just stands there - not a foot from me.

"The least you could have done was run off," I hissed at him.

"No need to," *he said.* **" I'm fine."** Then, he let out a big yawn.

"Are you hurt? Do we need to call an ambulance?" It's Trooper Bill of course, running up acting all concerned, leading a posse of laughing hyenas trying to act like they're ready to offer any assistance necessary, and who probably would take me to the hospital provided they didn't have another steer to rope. But if, any of them did...they would let their own mother die.

"I know you can't breathe mom, but we'll go to the emergency room just as soon as the short-go is over. If I had drawn a bad steer, we'd go now, but he's a good one, Mom. Mother, listen to me, this steer runs dead straight! Try to hang on."

"I'm okay," I said. "He just slipped. We're fine." I desperately needed to get out of there 'cause my leg was hurtin' so bad my britches were gonna' catch on fire any minute. "I'm okay," I repeated, and the crowd reluctantly headed back to important things like their next run, sorely disappointed there was no blood or even a serious injury. As Bill was walking away, he turned to someone and said, "That's how it is with them shiny horses. They look flashy, but you can't depend on them to do nothing. Now that bay horse I got...he ain't all neon lights, but he's one of the best I ever rode. I know he's mine - but he really *is* a good one."

At that moment, I decided to kill Bill. I planned to make a movie about it, and call it "Kill Bill, Volume

1," and then make a second volume called "Kill Bill, Volume II," 'cause Bill is the kinda' guy you can't kill just once. Quentin Tarentino would later steal this idea and make a fortune. Happens all the time. Famous people are always stealin' stuff I thought of a long time ago.

"What did you do that for?" I spit at Shine when we arrived at the trailer.

"Hey, I slipped. I didn't mean to. I just fell down. It could happen to anybody."

"Why did you have to fall down at that particular moment? In front of Bill, for God's sakes!"

"I thought you didn't like Bill."

"That's just it! I don't like Bill!"

"Well, if you don't like Bill, why do you care what Bill thinks?"

"I don't care what he thinks! Why did you have to fall down in front of him?"

"If you don't care what he thinks, why does it matter?"

"Just shut up and get in the trailer. We're going home!"

"Fine. I was going in there anyway. I didn't want to come down here in the first place."

And then something odd happened. One of those little moments in life that you don't think much about at the time, but later returns to haunt you.

"We think the significant moments in our lives are weddings, bar mitzvahs, graduations, and the like. They're more like old dogs that come sniffing around, and we hardly notice them at the time...not knowing we will remember them always."

--Eudora Welty

It was a moment like that.

"I like your horse, Michael." I turned to see Irv Pond.

Irv is one of my favorite characters in life. The world's oldest living teenager at fifty or so, he's known for being a bit wild and crazy, or maybe being a lot wild and crazy, but people who know Irv know something else about him. And that is, Irv has the gift of helping troubled horses. Those who don't know about that gift fail to take Irv as seriously as they should, and Irv – like Dad and my uncles – could care less. But when someone takes a troubled horse to Irv, he changes...and later, the horse does too. In the presence of a suffering equine spirit, Irv changes from a happy-go-lucky, good time Charley, into a special man who feels deep concern for a tortured soul. And Irv is one of those who has the magical ability to apply a healing salve to his equine brothers. Some say he "witches" them. I don't think that's what he does. I think Irv somehow knows how to tell them he loves them and will cause them no harm. Because of that, horses curry his favor.

And when Irv said, "I like your horse, Michael," I said, "Would you ride him for a minute, Irv?"

"Yes," he said. "I will."

And even though I gave Irv no indication – cowboys never show any sort of concern or emotion lest the world discover they're not real men – I was troubled. I was confused and discouraged about Shine. I thought so highly of this horse, but I was beginning to feel a nagging concern that the resources I possessed internally were inadequate to help him. My prideful conceit about my vast experience and extensive knowledge of horses seemed pitifully weak and small at that moment. Then something wonderful happened.

Irv stepped up on Shine and rode away. He headed to the arena, which I noticed had emptied as the roping had come to an end. Irv seemed to be doing nothing special on Shine, other than looking down at him as the big gray walked slowly along, and I felt something good inside when I realized Shine didn't seem to be afraid.

The two made their way in a slow circle around the arena once, and then Irv walked Shine into the head box. Surprisingly for his first time, the horse offered no resistance, and just dropped his head and walked in. Irv spun him gently, and Shine did an effortless about face, turning to the open arena and stood soft and still. Irv slowly dismounted and walked to the front of Shine, and standing there, Irv peered down into Shine's right eye, and stared for quite some time. Shine didn't move.

Irv then remounted and repeated his previous lap, slow and easy. Sitting on Shine's back, Irv rode along with the easy grace of men who sit a horse in that special way that tells you they know how to sit a horse. As Irv reached the far end of the arena, he walked Shine through the gate and headed toward my trailer. Dismounting from Shine, he looked at him for a moment and then turned to me.

"This horse is hard to understand," he said.

I was impressed. Irv couldn't have been on Shine for more than five minutes, and all of that spent in the slowest walk possible. Yet in such a short time, he had already sensed what had taken me weeks to feel. To say the least, Shine was hard to understand.

"Yes," I said. "He is."

Irv took a deep breath, and then he said, "You're discouraged."

I was stunned. First of all, I didn't have "mope" all over my face when I asked Irv to ride Shine. I had just asked him in a normal voice, "Would you ride him for a minute?" Yet Irv - happy-go-lucky Irv - a fellow I thought never had a care in the world much less a serious thought, in that five minutes had not only seen down into Shine, but into me as well. He didn't *ask* me if I was discouraged. There was no question in his tone, but rather a simple statement of fact. There was a "knowing" in his tone – a declarative statement. That Irv could understand something so complex about both Shine and me so quickly was something truly unexpected.

"Yes," I said to his statement about my being discouraged. "I am."

Reaching over in the back of my truck, Irv took a beer from the ice chest. Unscrewing the cap from the bottle, he turned it up and drank almost all of it before swallowing once. He wiped the back of his hand across his mouth and said, "I don't know what to do about your horse...but I do know one thing."

"And what's that?" I asked.

"Don't be discouraged," he said.

"I shouldn't be?" I asked.

"No, you shouldn't be. There were over a hundred horses here today, Michael, and not one is like him. You're right about him, Michael...he has *greatness* in him. "

I just thought I was stunned before. After hearing that, I was *really* stunned.

And Irv handed Shine's reins to me, and Shine and I both watched him walk away, another beer from my chest in his hand.

I stood there for the longest time. A feeling began to increase in me. Something good and sustaining – a feeling that it means so much in life to be *confirmed* by others whose opinion we value. At the same time, I knew some were already laughing at me for thinking this horse had promise, but that didn't matter. There was one somebody who agreed with me, and he was a man that real horsemen knew had the ability to discern a good one from a bad one. As I drove home, my mood became even more expansive, and my smile even brighter because of one other thing he said. Irv had used a phrase....

"Funny," I thought to myself driving along. *"The same words. I used the same ones."*

Irv not only agreed with me about Shine, he agreed in precisely the same manner. He didn't say Shine was "okay," or that he "would be a good one." He expressed the same thought I had the first time I ever saw Shine. I hadn't told Irv about that. I hadn't told anyone about that. But now I had the beginnings of an understanding about why I had done such an impulsive thing when I bought Shine. It was because of something that happened in me...something I *felt* when I saw him. Irv had felt it too. He had said the same words even though I hadn't told him the words or how I felt about the horse. But somehow, he knew what I felt. Irv had said, "You're right, Michael. *He has greatness in him."*

Well, this did change things indeed. I knew my world was different now. My suspicions about the uniqueness of this animal had been confirmed by another more experienced than me. This set off a cascade of potential choices and alternate paths, all which were to be carefully considered and analyzed in minute detail. I wasn't some silly schoolboy infatuated by false promise after all. This was real. Now I faced an entirely different set of challenges.

Driving home that night, the answer came to me, and this time, I knew I was right. This time I wouldn't depend on the "old ways," or on a foundation built on sand. I would admit the truth, and that truth was going to set not only me free, but my horse as well. I knew what to do with Shine.

"You just watch how many times he says that."

--Shine

"How on earth could I have not seen this before?" I thought to myself, as I turned into my farm. 'Course I had only had that thought hundreds of times about so many things – *why didn't I see that before?* And that's the way we are, isn't it? Whenever we have a particularly vexing "life" problem, and we finally see the *real* solution, we always have the feeling the answer was simple and obvious all along. That's the way I felt that night.

I planned to do what most everybody does with problem horses. Now that I think about it, this may well be the Twelfth Commandment in the horse world. And that is, whenever you are faced with a problem horse, *"Send thy problem horse to someone else!"*

Of course, that was it! This new awareness was growing in me that I didn't know everything I thought I knew about horses. All I had to do was simply find someone who knew more about them than I did and send Shine to that person. Once this real roping horse expert taught him a few things, my problems would be over. I could ride a finished roping star in the ring and take home not one, but all the blue ribbons from the county fair.

This idea was shaping up to be the best thing thought of to date, and after looking at it and thinking about it from all sorts of objective angles, I could not for the life of me see how such a fresh and honest plan of attack could possibly fail.

"You know what kills me about this guy? It's when he has one of these 'spiritual illuminations' about me, and thinks all his problems are solved. Like I'm some simple one cell organism, and just one or two little things are going to 'fix' me provided he can just figure out what those one or two things are. I hate to admit this, but I feel sorry for him. I hate to admit this too, but sometimes, in spite of my dislike for him, I actually think he means well. But I get over any feeling of trust or like for him pretty quickly because even a fungus grows on you. And when he keeps coming up with ideas like this, I realize he's just getting stupider as we go."

--Shine

"I don't like it." Those were my friend's first words. I couldn't believe what I was hearing.

"What on earth do you mean, 'You don't like it?'" I asked. "What is there not to like? I can just send him to someone, and all my problems are solved."

"I don't like it because it's like me saying if I can't reach a student, I can send him to another teacher."

"That's not the same thing at all," I protested.

"First of all, you don't have to send any kid anywhere. You are a much better teacher of kids than I am of horses. You know about kids and teaching school. And even though this is a crushing realization for me, the possibility may – I say may - exist I don't know quite as much as I once thought I did about horses. What you are failing to understand is there *are* people who can help him – people who know far more than I who can fix him."

"I do understand that. I'm sure there are people who know more than you about roping horses. That's not the problem."

"Then what's the problem?"

"When he gets home, you won't be fixed."

"Attention please! I have just had my first experience with a human who has some sense!"

--Shine

"You don't get it," I said. "They can teach him things, and he will be different."

"You don't get it. After he's been home thirty days, he will return to the same horse he was before because you won't be any different."

"Second experience! Second experience!"

--Shine

Some people just don't see things in the proper perspective. I knew this would work, and just because someone else couldn't see...well, because...well, because...okay, that made a lot of sense. I had to face

68

it. The words were true. As much as I wanted to send my horse to someone else, I wouldn't know what to do with him or for him when he came home.

I've always had this theory about "truth." I always thought when you heard the "truth," the words had a ring to them. Other words are not like that. Some words are pretty and some are ugly. Some are boring and some are unnecessary, but when words are spoken that have "truth" in them, those words have a "ring" to them. Whenever I've heard a truth I can't get away from, I've always heard this little ringing sound. On the night my friend spoke those words, that ringing sound was loud.

"Somebody else can't solve your problem. Especially when you think somebody else is causing the problem."

Dr. John Hall, Professor of Psychology
Texas Wesleyan University

Chapter Four

THE HORSEMAKER

Since my problem horse would have to come home to me, I didn't send him to someone else. Another plan requiring revision. Made me very sad in a way because one moment I had the "solution to Shine," a phrase I found myself repeating several times a day like one of those old fifties songs that gets stuck in your head...one that was quickly turning into an all too-consuming life goal. I was beginning to get a bit worried.

I knew I was thinking about him too much. The first clue was what came to be known as "the losing of friends" syndrome. I had one guy backed up against a tractor tire for almost an hour talking about Shine, and he finally said, "I have to go home."

"NO! NO!" I yelled grabbing him by the shirt. "We have to find a way to help this horse!" And probably the worst thing I can say about me is that I got mad when he left.

Another good friend came to help one day. Apparently, he was unaware that you cannot help people suffering from severe obsessive-compulsive disorders. He began his "doomed to failure" therapy session by saying, "I don't want to hurt your feelings, Michael, but you must rid yourself of this horse. He's crazy, and he's going to hurt you." (Actually, none of my friends would ever utter the words "you must rid yourself of this horse." The official transcript of the conversation reads more like, "You gotta giddaridda' issdamidit!")

We were sitting in lawn chairs in my drive-way on a day that had been blistering hot, but now the sun was mercifully easing down in the west, and we found ourselves in the "cool cool cool of the evening" as Bing crooned long ago.

I thought about my friend's observation for a moment, and as any psychotic would have said in a similar situation, and with the same dead-eyed certainty all loonies possess, I replied, "He's not crazy. He's afraid."

"Michael, I'm worried about you," he said in earnest. "I saw this horse flying down the arena running *sideways* trying to catch the steer. And you say he's not crazy?"

"He didn't do that," I replied, completely oblivious to reality as sane people knew that condition to be.

"There's your problem right there!" he exploded. "You're blind about him! You love this horse so much you can't see the truth!"

I listened carefully for the slightest bell tone. His words had no ring at all.

"I saw him with my own eyes running sideways down the arena trying to catch that steer!" he shouted.

"He didn't do that," I repeated with the typical glassy stare of all truly disturbed people.

My friend bolted upright from his chair and

slammed his baseball cap on the ground – said cap being standard attire of all mediocre horse people who wouldn't know a great horse if one walked up and kissed them on the lips - and then he sat down and heaved a long sigh of resignation.

He was mercifully silent for a time and said, "All right, Michael. If you don't think he was running sideways down the arena trying to catch the steer, what do you think he was doing?"

I tried to form my answer carefully because I knew my friend was one of those "normal" people unable to see what was is so clearly apparent to those "touched in the head" as my grandmother always referred to them. "He didn't *try* to catch that steer," I said. "He *was* running sideways, but he didn't *try* to catch the steer," I said, struggling as hard as I knew how to help this poor disturbed soul. "As a matter of fact, he caught that steer easily. I actually roped the steer even though Shine *was* running sideways. How many horses running sideways can keep up with a steer that's runnin' at full speed?" I asked him, somewhat smug in the knowledge that now even he had to know he had just been - shall we say, "nailed?" "Now let me ask you this, my misguided blind-as-a-bat friend," I continued with my dagger raised high for the kill. *"What would this horse be if we could get him to calm down and run straight?* Answer me that, Amigo!"

There! Trump card played! Checkmate. I know how heartless it was to run him through the brain with my brilliant "lance of words," - or whatever you call those stickin' deals - but it had to be done. Comes over to my house, drinks my beer, and tells me I need to "getaridda" my horse? And expects me to sit there and be reasonable - even objective - about it? Cite me a case in the last one hundred years in Oklahoma history, where someone spoke ill of another man's horse, and that someone was not killed instantly. Can't do it, can you? I didn't think so, 'cause there isn't a case like that. Most horse people in Oklahoma would have just cut him in half with their wife's Ouzi, and they would have been found "not guilty" by a jury of their peers – as long as the lawyer made sure only ropers were allowed to testify. Surely, even this blind fool could see the truth now.

"Michael," he said quietly. *"You desperately need to see a Christian counselor about that horse!"*

I felt sorry for old Frank at that moment because he didn't know that if I could have only found such a counselor who would actually listen to me about Shine, I would have gladly given him all my money. But it would have done no good to tell Frank that. He wouldn't have understood. But I was beginning to. I was beginning to see that Shine - the horse that in time, five ropers, all much better than me - would advise in no uncertain terms that I really should rid myself of this untrustworthy communist beast...because he was "crazy." But Frank was right.

I was beginning to understand the best possible thing I could do would be to talk to a Christian counselor and tell him that I was coming to know the Spirit had given me an "assignment." And that assignment was to help a troubled horse. If I could have found such a person, right then and there...I would have gladly given him all the money I had.

"Oh good grief! Say it ain't so! Just when I thought it couldn't get any worse. Now like most

humans, he's gonna hide behind some wacky religious crusade so he can justify everything he does to me.

Okay, that makes me sound a little cynical, but.... Hey! Don't get me wrong. I'm religious. All horses are. I don't tell everybody about it 'cause I always thought I didn't have to. I thought they would know it by the way I lived

It's just that if he's thinking I'm supposed to be here with him on this farm because of some Divine Plan, that can't be true! And I know what I'm talking about – I have proof! I'm not supposed to be here, 'cause while I don't know exactly what happened, I know something went wrong. I was shipped here by mistake. I don't know exactly what happened – but I think somewhere down the line, somebody must have loaded me in the wrong trailer. It'll take me a minute to explain.

Everything was really good in the beginning - when I lived in the first place I mean. Beautiful pasture, shade trees everywhere, cold clear water, and grass so thick and green you couldn't believe it, and always 'bout stirrup high. I didn't do much in those days except run around with the other horses, and we spent all our time just nickering and nipping each other a lot, and running. We ran all the time. I'm not bragging, but I could outrun every one of them. I could outrun 'em sideways. And I enjoyed every single minute. Best time of my life. 'Course

I'm thinkin' things are always gonna be like this – why wouldn't they –and then I hear Manuel whistlin' to me. I loved Manuel.

Gotta tell you a good story about Manuel before we go on. You'll like it. He's the one who made me...well, not exactly. It's complicated. Manuel is a Horsemaker, but he's not the one who made me come alive. He said only the Master could do that, but he does have the title 'Horsemaker' 'cause he helps arrange all the composite materials that make up a horse...and I was the first one he ever helped make.

How he came to be in the Horsemaking Section was 'cause when he's processing in, the Intake Angel – her name was Maxine - says, 'I see here you always wanted to be a Horsemaker.'

Manuel says, 'Well yes, but not to really make one. I meant I always wanted to develop one.' The Intake Angel says, 'Yes, I understand. Develop... make... same thing. You want to make horses.' Manuel, thinking the Angel means to help one learn to rein, stop, back up, and all that says, 'Yes.' The Angel stamps his papers, and says, 'Up here, your dreams come true. Welcome to the Horsemaking Section.'

And that's how Manuel got the job.

It all looked like a mistake of course, but later they explained it to us – up there, even though when what looks like a mistake happens, those mistakes are rearranged to make good things happen. *And that's what happened when Manuel was makin' me.*

He said he was sent in the lab to make his first horse, and he tried to tell the Angel in charge he couldn't do it, and that he didn't know how. The Angel says, '*Of course, you don't. No one will ever expect you to do something well when you've never done it before. Besides your part is just to try the best you know how. The Master will correct your mistakes.*' Then the Angel says, '*But don't tell me you can't do it. I know you can. Now...get after it!*' And the Angel slams the door.

So Manuel is shakin' all over thinkin' there's no possible way he can do this, and that's when he sees this little crocheted sign hangin' on the wall that says, 'When there is no way...God will make a way.' So that gives him strength, and he turns around to see all these beakers and vials, and living cells, all different colors of horsehair and manes and tails, and liquids and neurons. So he starts feelin' a little better and begins reading the instructions about all the necessary ingredients to make a good horse. He said he put all those in me, and he was feelin' pretty darn good about the whole thing...when he noticed there was a little problem.

The manual – not Manuel – the Horsemaker Instruction Manual showed a picture of where the level of material should be when the Angels came to take the horse to be born. Problem was Manuel was just a little short. Even though he *followed the instructions to the letter, the stuff of life in the beaker was just short of where it should be. That's when he saw the bottle. He noticed it 'cause it was shining.*

'So there I am,' *Manuel's telling me,* 'and there's no way I'm calling those Angels in there and admitting I've messed up on my first horse... that's when I noticed the bottle with the liquid in it. Noticed it 'cause it was shining. Some of the label was rubbed off, the part that told you what the stuff really was, but underneath that part you couldn't read, it said, 'No. 3 - Liquid Lightning....' Like an advertising slogan or something. And after that word 'Lightning,' a word was missing, but I couldn't see it.'

'So...' *Manuel tells me,* 'I figured, Hey, this can't hurt. Probably some kinda' speed booster stuff, so I just poured the whole dang thing in there. Beaker filled up perfect, and as a matter of fact, there was a whole lot extra in there. Man, I was happy. And that's when I saw what else was on the bottom of the bottle.' *Manuel always shook his head and laughed at this part....*

'On the very bottom of the bottle, in tiny print, were the words...Warning! You can't put too much of this in a horse.' *Manuel would just laugh and laugh at this point, and no matter how many times I heard the story, I did too.* 'Man, I thought my goose was cooked that day, Bandy.' *That's what he always called me...Bandy. Sometimes he called me by both my names, you know like southern people do- how they call you by your first and middle name?   But mostly, he called me Bandy.*

'I worried myself sick in the next few minutes,' *he said.* 'And with just seconds to go 'fore the Angels came to take you to be born, hey, I knew I had to tell'em. I couldn't let you be born with somethin' in you that had a warning label on it.' *And then, Manuel would tell my favorite part.*

'The Angel comes in, looks at the beaker and says, *'Good job!   Well done for your first time!'* And I say, 'No...no. It's not well done at all. I've probably killed the poor little guy.' *And then Manuel tells the Angel about the bottle, the one with the shiny stuff in it. And how the label was worn off and how sorry he was, and....*

'The label's worn off?   Oh, I can fix that,' says the Angel. *And next thing you know, a brand new label appears on the bottle staring back at Manuel. 'Don't worry about that,' says the Angel. 'My fault.   I didn't know the label was worn.'*

And Manuel yells, "No!   No!   You don't understand. I poured all this into him, and I've probably kil....' *And the Angel smiles and says,* 'Calm down, son.   Read the new label.'

'I picked it up, and my hands were shakin' to beat ole' Betsy 'cause I was terrified to see what I'd poured into you, and the new label said....'

THE ELIXIR

Made solely for, found only in, and distributed exclusively in Heaven.

THE STUFF OF GREAT HORSES

CONTENTS INCLUDE...

1. TALENT!

2. HEART!

3. LIQUID LIGHTNING SPEED!

WARNING! YOU CANNOT PUT TOO MUCH OF THIS IN A HORSE.

'But I thought...'

'You thought what? That you made a mistake, and you were afraid of that?' said the **Angel**. *'Course you did. We all do. Get over yourself.'*

'I thought I had killed him,' *said Manuel.* 'The label said....'

'The label said, "You cannot put too much of this in a horse" meaning it's impossible to put too much! See? It means the more the better! Hmm... now that I think about it, maybe that's what I should put on the label - to clear up the confusion. Thanks, Manuel. You've not only made a great

horse, you helped me out today," said the Angel. *'Good job for your first time. Come on, we have to hurry. It's about time for Bandy to be born.'*

And Manuel would always end the story with my really favorite part. 'We took you down to the Delivery Stable and put you in your horse momma. 340 days later, bingo...Baby Bandy hit the ground.'

'And my human momma was there too,' I said to Manuel, remembering her.

'Yes, a wonderful woman. What was her name?'

'Her name was Kyla,' I said.

'Yes, Kyla - a wonderful woman.'

And that's the story about Manuel, the Horsemaker. The story about how he made me and how up there, mistakes are turned into good things. And up there, everything happens for a reason. Manuel said that was true here too, but I think he's wrong. 'Cause that's when all the trouble started. That's what I was gonna tell you, but I got a little sidetracked.

All the trouble started on that day Manuel came to see me, not that I wasn't glad to see him. Manuel, the Horsemaker. He was my friend. But on this day, he seemed different. He was business-like.

'Bandy?' he said.

'Yessir?' I said. Manuel taught me a lot of things, and manners were at the top of the list.

'Are you doing okay in there?'

'Fine. It's dark, but warm and I have everything I need. I would like to get out and run around if I could.'

'Soon, son. You are about to be born, and you'll be able to run all you want.'

'Good. I'll look forward to that. Were you just checking on me?'

And Manuel was silent for a time. And then he said, 'Bandy, you have a lot of heart. I want you to remember that…when…well, when things don't go right, okay?'

'What do you mean when things don't go right?'

'I mean that no one's life is perfect. Well, actually it is, but that's hard to see when things are happening to you that you don't understand, but are really for your own…oh, never mind. You will have plenty of good times, and sometimes things won't seem so good. But at those times, remember you have heart, son! I put too much of it in you, and that's a good thing. Can you remember that?'

'I suppose I can,' I said. 'Horses have a good memory.'

'Good. Time to go soon. I'll always be watching you. I'll be helping all I can.'

I appreciated him coming to see me like that when he did. People who love you always come around just when you need them most. And I do wish he was here now.

'Cause at first, it was okay. My horse momma had me, and my human momma was there too. I was so happy then. But something must have happened to that rule about mistakes being turned into good. 'Cause one day they took me away from both my Mommas and since then, it's been rough. On a strange farm for a while, and I guess that wasn't so bad, but I didn't know anybody there. And now, I've ended up in the middle of God knows where – someplace in Oklahoma – with this Jerry Lee Lewis lookin' idiot who doesn't give me time to catch my breath, much less learn something from his endless list of 'goals.'

That's why I said he's full of it about this religion thing. Manuel said the One who really made me – put life in me I mean – was kind and good, and had our best interest at heart. How could that be true if I have to be here? Why is this happening to me?

Why didn't He send me to somebody that knew something about horses, not somebody who just 'thought' he did? Even I know the difference between those two people – all horses do. I'm discouraged and depressed. Manuel was wrong. I don't have the heart for this.

But there is something I'm confused about. While I have no doubt this Michael character means well, and I know he can't be serious about the Spiritual Assignment thing - yet there is one thing bothering me. It's about my middle name. You know, the one Manuel started calling me after he saw the liquid in the bottle with the light coming from it. That's when he gave me my middle name. How could Michael have known about that? How did he know after that Manuel almost always called me by both names like Southern people do? How did he know that Manuel stopped calling me just Bandy? From that time, on he called me by both names... Bandy 'Shine.' How did Michael know my name?

And I'm sorry I said he looked like Jerry Lee Lewis. That wasn't fair. He doesn't.

I meant to say he looks like Jerry Lewis. He does look like Jerry Lewis."

--Shine

Chapter Five

SPIRITUAL ASSIGNMENTS

Yes, a Christian counselor might have been just the thing. Because I was considering the possibility, there was more going on here than just a man with a stubborn horse. This experience seemed too out of the ordinary to be solely the province of everyday living. I'm not saying it was mind you; I'm just admitting the thought crossed my mind. There was a strangeness about it all. If I viewed each event on its own, individual items were just annoying little thorns in my side. But if I stepped back and looked at the entire picture, C. S. Lewis' words came to mind....

"Something was pursuing me."

--C.S. Lewis

I couldn't shake the feeling something was out of the ordinary. None of it made sense. I rarely, if ever, *buy* horses, preferring to raise them instead because a bond develops with that method like no other. True, it takes longer, but I enjoy the wait, and raising colts is such a rich experience. So why, then, do I suddenly see a *five-year-old* horse that has hardly been touched, owned by a man who advises in no uncertain terms, *"Don't buy him!"* and I buy him anyway? Such a rash purchase was truly unlike me - indeed I can't think of one I've made in my life, but well…let's just say something came over me.

Finally, there was this feeling about Shine. A feeling like few I've ever had. Even though this horse seemed hard-headed, difficult to understand, unable to do the simplest things, and uninterested in doing them even if he could, still…I *knew* he was something extraordinary. The most puzzling thing of all was that Shine had never given me the slightest objective evidence – had never displayed a single behavioral response – that would indicate there was anything special about him at all. That's why my friends (sorry, ex-friends) thought most of my oil had leaked out. The horse was fidgety, nervous, spooky, snorty, and with the worst case of jumpy "fire-ant feet" known to man. Yet I knew.

If I said it once, I said it a hundred times, and every person who knows me would say, "Amen to that, Brother," I *knew* there was something different about him. I knew that something was down inside him, and it wasn't *me* who knew it.

The intellectual, rational, modern, educated, normal part of me thought all my friends who considered Shine a very low performer and "special needs" horse were absolutely correct about him. On the other hand…the primitive, earthy, mother-wit, old brain, *Divine* part of me thought differently - Paul said *"It"* was in us, and if

Paul said it, that's good enough for me. Those "old soul" parts of me said, *"They're wrong, and you're right. Stay with him."* And I complained to that part of me on a daily basis.

"Okay," my self would say to me. *"Let's just assume for a moment something is here. Wouldn't it be nice if I could see just the tiniest smidgin' of that something... whatever it is?"*

Silence.

I looked down into the bottom depths of the thing called "self" and said, *"What is the matter with you? You really are losing friends. They really do think something is wrong with you. In your former B.S. life - that is, Before Shine – you were a reasonable man. You had some other hobbies. True, we can't recall what those things were now, but surely you went to the mall or a movie on occasion, didn't you? What's happening here?"* At one point, I seriously considered slashing words written in lipstick across my bathroom mirror... *"God help me before I rope on him more!"*

That's when this other explanation started tugging on my psychic sleeve. Maybe there was something more than me going on here. In recent years, I had become more sensitive to the meaning of events that seemed confusing in the rational world.

Before we pitch the revival tent here, it might help to explain a few things. In the past ten years or so, my life had taken some odd and quirky turns. Living through those experiences – some joyous and some rougher than I ever imagined - hadn't caused me to become a bit more religious, but had caused me to become decidedly more *spiritual.* And besides, like most people, I already considered myself to be religious. My little Momma raised me a Methodist, and everyone knows that Methodists are already religious... they're just careful not to let anyone know it.

Prior to these experiences, every day of my life had been a photocopy of the day before - for some twenty years. At twenty-five, I had left the world of rodeo and horses to pursue an education. Eventually, I obtained a doctorate in psychology – which you will be relieved to know I never took too seriously – and worked in the corporate world for some twenty years. Married, with two really good kids, we did what every other red-blooded 'Merican family does for so long a time, I knew those were the things we would always do until the day I died. Not that that made me particularly unhappy because I had a nice wife, nice kids, nice home, and a nice life. A little boring at times, but hey, that's the way life is.

I went to work every day, taught classes at the university at night, played golf, went to the Methodist Church on Sunday, attended endless little league games, and spent several million dollars on braces so my kids could have shiny teeth and grow up to be just like me, and do all those same things over again. Pretty good life. Then in the short space of about 120 days, my whole world *vanished!*

One day, I'm cruising along catching a few rays on life's balmy shores and didn't really know what year it was because they all seemed to be speeding by so quickly. And suddenly, I noticed my kids were packing up to go off to college. Happy days! No more dirty clothes, no more late night misery wondering where they were, nothing but free time to enjoy the things we had always worked for. I was one of those people who

said, "The empty nest syndrome will never bother me!"
And the day they left, I almost died.

No more little league games, no more conversations
with two people I loved, no more golf with my son, and
I was crushed. Just a few days later, my long-standing
rock-solid employment position starts teaching me a
new word I had never heard before… "downsizing." A
most troubling word. While I was desperately trying
to learn what industry heads meant by phrases like
"scaling back," and words like "trimming," in the midst
of all that, my wife of a number of years walks in and
says, "Since the kids are gone, and looks like you're
going to lose your job, and we can't keep our lifestyle
in the same place, maybe we should go ahead and get
the divorce now." Hmmmm….

So, 120 days before, I'm floatin' on a rubber raft in
the pool one minute, and the next – four months later
– my wife, kids, job, and house are gone, and I look
down to find the wind has blown a hole in my soul.
Like some character in a "Twilight Zone" episode, I'm
the very lucky and perfectly happy nitwit who wakes
up one morning to find himself walking through a town
where no one is home. Friends said, "Well, you must
have done something to deserve it." And I might have
agreed if I had only known what that something was.

Completely at a loss as to what successful move
life might approve of next, I retreated to a little cabin
in the woods. Beautiful place, and a river really did
run through it. Like some wounded deer crawling off
in the brush to lick his wounds, I went there to hide.
Not sure if I could live, and with not the slightest hope
of resurrecting, I hoped at least to somehow find the
answer to the question we all ask at such difficult times

in our lives, and the question was *"Why me?"*

Arriving there in the late summer, I found myself sitting and staring through my window at that silver little river as it rolled on by. I sat there a long time. I watched the leaves turn red and gold, and then wither to the rather boring brown color of death. I knew just how the leaves felt. I was boring and brown and dying too. On some occasions, while I didn't plan to end it all, I felt the internal resources I possessed were simply inadequate to continue in this process called life. On many of those days, I had no doubt that I could not go on. Then to make things worse like life does when we're down, the wind blew and the snow came, and the trees seemed cold inside, and their souls were bare. I knew how they felt. Mine was too in this dark time. Then something happened.

Spring came. Moving, creeping so slowly at first, but when I saw her heading my way, I said, "Come on, Girl! I had forgotten all about you!" And she came... tying all her bright little bows everywhere, and hanging each and every one with such grace and care in just the right places. And I began to notice something else. Life was coming back with her. Both She and Life brought red buds, and cardinals, robins and blue birds, and leaves and grass and bumblebees...and mosquitoes, hummingbirds, ticks, and flowers and most of all, She brought what Emily Dickinson called "that feathered thing" - the thing called "hope." Hope came with the spring, and far surpassing even my highest expectation that anyone or anything could have ever helped me, She brought me some too. To my surprise, spring helped me feel like living again. One little special gift She brought during that dark time was the answer to my question, *"Why me?"* And She said, *"The reason this happened to you is... 'because.'"*

George Bernard Shaw once said, "If you live long enough, *everything* happens to you." In those days I considered to be my "trial," spring taught me the most valuable lesson; that the question was not really, "Why me?" *"The question is..."* she whispered with her pretty flowers, birds, bees, and new leaves on trees was, *"...what will you do with all the things that have happened to you?"*

I felt like some primordial man somehow connected to the very earth I was watching change before my eyes. She was renewing all that earth around and under her, and She was renewing me. In those days, Spring taught me that life comes back, that new growth can occur, and that "feathered thing" can bring choices and options we never dreamed of before.

I saw more clearly than ever before that I could choose to mope and feel sorry for poor me, or I could also select another option. I could choose to realize that so many human beings were far worse off than me; that I could be grateful for the fact that I could walk, and that I could see. I could get down on my knees and thank the Divine that I had my health, and that at forty-five, my life was not over – particularly, if I decided to live it in the way it was always intended.

And because I lived through that time, I became more spiritual. I didn't say I became "better" or more "religious;" I became more spiritual. The possibility that there was more to life than worshipping the "Retirement God" really began to make itself known to me. That thinking caused a complete reassessment of how I had spent all of my previous days. Dramatic and powerfully different choices about this thing called "life" and how I planned to live from this day forward would result.

Heretofore, I had taken one breath after another every day just to climb the corporate ladder so I could retire. And because of my time in the woods, I could now see that all my efforts - enduring all those boring meetings, listening to silly egos trying so desperately to convince other equally silly egos they were all talking about something important – all that effort expended, just so I could retire. So I could do...*nothing.* After my experience in the woods, I saw the hollowness of what has become the most cherished and ultimate goal in our culture, and what we so desperately hope for our children to attain...*retirement.*

My time in the valley taught me many things. Among them, that life was for *living,* not so we could eventually retire and get away from it, but so we could *immerse* ourselves in it, and never stop doing what we loved. A new awareness came that loved ones, children, homes, good horses, old dogs, and sweet smellin' alfalfa hay should be seen for what they all really were... *"gifts!"*

I sensed a new opening and awareness growing in me - that everything hangs by a tenuous thread that can snap and be gone at any moment. What a far better way to live to be *appreciative* of the gifts we have been given and to seek the thing called *joy.* Joy really does have something to offer. As opposed to *retirement* which only offered...dead air time.

My time in the valley changed me. I had learned that nothing much important happens to us in life when things are going well. We only really learn things that

help us when we painfully make our way through some
black hole experience that pulls our guts into the void,
and if that ain't enough, then it kicks the living hell out
of us while we're in there. And only when we reach the
other side of that distant shore, can we see how better
we are for the experience. I really don't like that rule,
but that's the way it is. My time in the valley didn't
make me more religious. It did cause me to go to
church and listen far more intently to what was being
said than ever before. My time in the valley made me
more spiritual.

"That's a good thing."

--Shine

I suppose I was like those people who report a
"near death experience." After emerging from their
trial, those people rarely become evangelists. But so
many of them do return to the world changed. From
the moment the episode occurs, they are never quite the
same. The same was true of me.

I didn't return to the world shouting about how
everyone needs to "get right with JESUS!" Almost
the same as I was, but now just a little bit different.
One of those differences being, I now had a suspicion
that maybe - just maybe - there was a bit more going
on down here than my self-centered, catastrophic, all-
consuming, petty, small-minded, little *"Why me?"*
approach to life.

For the first time ever in all my years of living, I
stopped asking, "Why was this *done* to me?" and began
to consider that maybe this hadn't been *done* to me

at all. Maybe some things at least happened *for* me.
Maybe, as C. S. Lewis said, "We're being carved by
the Master's hands." Now I viewed events in my life
not so much as "punishment" or "trials," but something
else – "assignments" might be a good word perhaps, or
"lessons to be learned" might be a useful phrase. Of
course at the time, I didn't want the lesson - I wanted
life to stay the same.

Where I live, the Choctaw have a saying about that,
"You never step in the same river twice." Meaning
no matter how hard we try, we can't keep things the
same. For years that made no sense to me. And now?
The difference between me then and me now is that
I am at a loss to understand how anyone could be so
dense as to not get that little spiritual lesson. Because
now it is quite clear that so many events in my life I
once thought awful and unwanted were actually "small
seeds in disguise" of the greatest blessings anyone
could receive. Simply put, I began to "re-interpret my
struggle." And that was why I thought old Frank was
right that evening in my yard.

I really *did* need to talk to a Christian counselor.
Not because I was crazy or because my horse was - that
was Frank's reason for wanting to make his referral.
He thought I had been "touched." Frank was right in a
way. But not "in the head," where Frank thought. What
Frank didn't know was – and if he had, he really would
have thought I was crazier than my horse – I had been
touched, but not in the head. I had been touched all
right…by something else. 'Til this day, I'm not sure by
what. To debate "what" isn't my business. That debate
is why people kill each other all over the world. I don't

know what touched me. I just know that whatever it was...it was something awfully *big*. Like Helen Keller said, "I know about Him. I just don't know His name."

So with all that said, is it any wonder that I began to "reinterpret" my struggle with Shine? What possible explanation could there be for me ending up in this place, on this farm, and finding myself with a horse like him? My previous life experiences held perfect pat answers to such questions. In those days, I didn't need any more cards. I could play the ones I held. "Because," the cards said, "since you are an 'expert horseman,' and the men in your life taught you all there is to know about horses, then if you have a horse who doesn't respond, surely you must have been screwed on a horse deal. He's an idiot, and you should put him on the kill-truck, 'cause if you've done everything you know to do, and it still doesn't work, well then, hell son, it ain't you...it's him. It can't be you. *Gedda ridda that idit!*"

But I couldn't. I couldn't let him go.

"If he refers to me as an 'idit' on more time, I'm leaving anyway."

--Shine

I kept thinking about something my friend and superb novelist, Jim Ainsworth once said. "You know those times when something starts "pulling on you?" he asked. "Those times when something whispers to you, *'go this way and do this thing,'* even though the thing makes no sense. You know those times?" he said.

"Uh...hmmm...yes, as a matter of fact, I do," I had replied.

95

"Those times," he said, "those times so often turn out to be the best of times."

This was one of those times, and this time had something to do with a horse - and something to do with me learning a new thing. Something was trying to tell me to stay with this horse and also to look clearly at the complete absence of truth in that "old way" of thinking about people like Shine – horses like Shine, that is. I had enough sense to know that it was very unlikely we can make every horse great. The awareness pulling on me was more that anyone who has felt a "widening" in their lack of knowledge - and realized how deep and empty that crevasse really is inside them – anyone who has felt that inside about horses, would certainly agree that the old way of thinking, the old way of force, coercion, and punishment is pitifully weak. And when like spirits do some serious thinking, we all come to the same conclusion. We may not know a more excellent way, but our suspicion that there is one is too strong to ignore. Something in us knows…there is a higher path to horses. There is a more excellent way.

At one time I considered myself to be quite advanced in the "best way." I now knew that was the worst way, and that I didn't know much at all. What I didn't know about horses would require a book so thick, you might never finish it. But I've always had one very strong suit. *Being ignorant never stopped me from doing anything.* I was determined to learn how. I would begin a quest and a search for that more excellent way. I wasn't really sure if the Lord or any of his angels had anything to do with that, but it was certainly beginning to seem like they did. But even if they didn't, I knew they wouldn't be too disappointed in my new desire. That desire being...to become a *horseman*. In my previous life, while I didn't brag about it, I just knew I was one. I had learned that I was sadly mistaken. And now I also had a feeling just like C. S. did – that "something was pursuing me." I kept looking back over my shoulder because a certainty was growing in me that whatever it was, it was not only coming... *it was gaining ground.*

Chapter Six

HORSES AND HORSEMEN

"To understand the horse, you will find you are going to have to work on yourself."

--Ray Hunt

I read those words just a day or two after my growing awareness that I had plenty of work to do. The Universe could not have given me a better quote at a better time. Again, I thought of a line from Lewis.

"What? Has that happened to you too? I thought I was the only one."

--C. S. Lewis

And after reading Hunt's words, I knew what had happened to me had already happened to this man long ago. I read Hunt's story of his experiences with the horse called "Hondo," and how Bill Dorrance had come to help him. Dorrance had not only helped Hondo, but brought Hunt a new understanding that would change

99

Michael Johnson

his life. When Hunt later asked Dorrance where and
how he learned these things, Dorrance would give him
an answer Hunt had never heard. "Any other man
I ever asked that question always told me the name
of some other *man*. But when I asked Bill Dorrance
where he learned, he said, "I learned these things from
the horse. The horse taught me."

Anxious to begin my journey, I couldn't wait to read
more. To read and learn more so I really could help my
friend, and Hunt's next line about horses gave me the
most hope of all.

*"Once you start giving, you won't believe how much
you get back."*

--Ray Hunt

"Giving what?" I thought to myself. I didn't know,
but I was bound and determined to learn. I was open
now with a "gash" in me, and the gash hurt. That "tear"
inside was the wound that came from my awareness of
what a fool I had been. Later, the scar would heal...
some, and the healing salve would come from great
horsemen. Their stories would help me heal. To this
date, I've never met one who didn't have the same scar.
Every horseman I have learned from had precisely the
same story as mine. And the story went something like
this.

*"I thought I was an expert. Then a particular
horse came along and taught me I was a fool. I wasn't
necessarily a mean man, but my old ways now cause a
sense of deep shame in me that I didn't see things more
clearly...and most of all, that I didn't see them sooner. At*

100

least now, I'm trying to do better."

Every horseman I've ever heard who has helped me has that same story, but I didn't know that then. I didn't even know where to start or whom to ask about my ignorance. For a former expert, that admission was embarrassing – an emotion completely unknown to all red neck horse trainers. But I picked myself up and shook myself off and said, "Forgive me. I'll do better." I began to seek...and I began to find.

I wish the lessons had come in a nice neat package. I wish they had come in a logical, sequential order that would make a nice tidy list...sort of a one, two, three cookbook approach...but that's not the way they came.

They came on their own, driven by, sponsored by, funded by...what? Who or what was responsible for presenting the lessons to come? If I only knew. But they came - at odd times in odd places like the Ray Hunt quote that just fell fluttering out of the sky one day to land on my kitchen table. I found lessons lying on my floor in magazine articles that had been there waiting patiently for months, and now finally, since my eyes were opening, I could see them and learn what they had to offer. They came from a list of people, events, and moments of such beauty that even I couldn't help but notice.

One of the most beautiful came from a thirteen-year-old girl in Ada, Oklahoma. While just sitting on her horse in the head box, she somehow moved this animal from place to place and from side to side, with what were - at least to me - completely undetectable physical cues. As I watched him respond to her slightest whim, him with his silky grace, I wondered, *"How is she doing that?"* Because try as I might, I found myself unable to see her give him even the smallest cue with her body. I would later learn there was no mystery as to why I couldn't see the physical cues. There were none. This little girl – far more horseman than I – was asking her friend, her willing partner, to move with more than spurs. She was moving him with her mind.

The lessons came from old men, and some from women, some from ropers and most of all, the best lessons came from my horses. I'm not there yet, and now I know I never will be, but at least I was no longer a "thirty-day fool." My sense of shame about my former arrogance had caused a desire in me to do better, and when I started paying attention – when I started doing what great horsemen do, that is watching and listening – when I started doing that, finally, I began to do a little better. One of the first lessons came from my friend, "Bronc."

Little Blue

Seems I've known one horse all my life, at least he's been popping in and out of it since I was three - maybe four. That was the first time he came around. My favorite book at that age was a small black hardback called **The Pokey Little Puppy**. I had little interest in the protagonist named Pokey, but there was a picture on one of the pages, sort of a background character off to the side, that I stared at for hours - a pony the color of a pencil lead. The author of that children's book thought Pokey's friend not significant enough to be a major part of the story, or even to have a name. I did. I named him Little Blue.

The children's book went to that place that all our

kid's toys, trikes, and books go...those things we swear we will always keep to remember, but we don't. They're all somewhere in the same room I suppose, missing all the Martys, Terres, Jims, and Jans, all of whom are grown now, and all of whom have forgotten about such childish things. And my Pokey Puppy book and Blue must have gone there as well. But apparently Little Blue became bored with all the toys, tricycles, and model airplanes...because he came looking for me again.

He found me in 1966. I was around twenty years old at the time, and I had just been booted off the rodeo trail by superior calf ropers and much better saddle-bronc riders – which I thought was terribly unfair at the time, and I still do. Because the IRS wasn't exactly on my tail for unreported winnings, a desire came in me - for the first time in my life – to become serious about school. I attended a small community college some twenty miles from my hometown. On those days when my old truck failed me - like people did back then - I sometimes hitchhiked to school. One morning about dawn, I stood on that Texas highway waiting on some kind soul to hitch me the remaining two miles to the college. I saw a baby colt come running over the hill out of the sunrise. I remembered him instantly.
"You're the same color as Little Blue."

He seemed to accept our re-joining - what I thought to be an amazing coincidence - as something foregone and always meant to be. With a whinnying little nicker by way of greeting, he broke his dead run with a sliding stop, spun around on his back end, and ran as hard as he could to the far side of the pasture. I couldn't wait 'til the next morning.

For the next several months, I drove by – or depending on the mood of my truck, stood by - that pasture waiting for a ride. I was never in a hurry to be picked up. I enjoyed being in the place where the blue colt lived. I watched the baby learn to buck and run, to prance and snort, and to chase bugs, nip at flowers, and flee from bees. I watched him be weaned by his mother, one of the few periods when he would actually come over close to me. Even though I fell in love with the blue colt in the pasture, I never learned his name. A name given I assumed by his owner, a man I also never knew. That fellow who I'm sure asked his wife every morning, "Who is that damn kid out there staring into our pasture?"

Courses and classes completed, my dreams of one day having a horse farm and owning a horse like Little Blue changed to plans for making a living. The time had come for me to leave the place where the blue colt lived. As I stood on that highway for the last time, I thanked him for making all my days with him so pleasant. He was standing in his usual spot beside his mother that morning. I wished I had learned his name. And then I knew that it didn't matter what the owner named him. His real name was Little Blue. I waved good-bye, and he nipped at his momma and disappeared over the hill at a dead run. I felt sadness that I would never see him again. I shouldn't have. I was wrong.

"Did he hear me, Momma?" asked Little Blue.

"Well, I doubt it, with you running off like that," said his mother. *"And don't talk so fast."*

"I was just excited. Did he 'weave?"

His mother looked toward the road. *"Almost,"* she said. *"He's walking away."*

And Little Blue nickered as loud as he could...

"See ya', Dad!"

Thirty years later, he would be back.

The year was 2000. I was driving along on a black top road in Oklahoma – which now that I think about it, bore a striking resemblance to that one in Texas so long ago. I took no notice of that at the time as I was in a bit of a rush to make it to our little Methodist church on time on this shiny Sunday morning. And I saw him... standing off to my right in a little trap. There he stood. I coasted the Dooley to an easy stop.

"Do you know that baby?" asked my wife, looking at the small colt by his mother's side.

I didn't hear her. I didn't hear what she said because at that moment, I was thinking about how we think *we* find horses. We buy what we are looking for, we breed bloodlines to get what we want. We go to sales and look and fret, and barter, and buy and trade, and...I was thinking about how after all that effort, maybe we don't find *them* at all. Maybe they find us.

"Do you know that baby?" she repeated.

"I've known him a long time," I said.

I made inquiries about him at the local country store. Such establishments being by the way, one of the Lord's finest creations...and He surely must have had a personal hand in making the one where I live. Or maybe He had Moses build it considering how old this one is. Like all real country stores, this store has not a single piece of plastic or steel anywhere within. Like country stores in the days of Moses, this one is made exclusively of wood.

The proprietor at the time was a fellow named Steve – a man who cooked with a skill and flair that would put even Emeril to shame. Halfway through one of the

world's truly great cheeseburgers, which caused the
carrying capacity of my mouth to be at maximum level,
I asked, "Whoof ownds at boo' coke?"

"What?" asked Steve. "I couldn't understand you.
Chew all that up, and ask me again."

"Who owns that blue colt?" I said after clearing my
mouth of the first half.

Steve put his spatula down, and while wiping his
hands on his apron, turned and fixed a stare on me.
"Why?" he asked.

"I don't know," I said, staring with pure lust at the
remaining second half. "Just curious."

Steve wasn't buying it. He knew why I was asking.
All men in Oklahoma know when you're interested in a
horse. "Forget it," he said.

"Forget what?" I said with all innocence.

"He won't sell him. He'd sell one of his kids 'fore
he'd sell that colt," said Steve.

He came around the counter, sat down in the booth
with me, and began to spin the tale. "Earl and his wife
– Mary's her name - birthed that baby. He's an Otoe
colt, and he's a good one. His momma came off the
Pitchfork, and she's bred just as good as the colt's
daddy. But the big problem in the way of you bein' that
colt's new owner is Earl. I guarantee you he ain't lettin'
loose of that horse, and I can tell you why."

Since I had ingested the whole second half of that
cheeseburger in my mouth at once, I decided to just
listen.

"When that baby was just born," Steve continued,
"a big money man came by Earl's farm. He steps out of
the truck and hands Earl a blank check except for the
signature line. His name was written on that line. And

this guy says to Earl, 'Put whatever you want on that, and send me that baby when he's weaned.' And then guess what Earl did?"

"Mafe a lop' of 'mufny?" I chewed back at him.

"Nope. Earl's retired Air Force – good pension, you know? What the guy don't know is Earl ain't somebody you can buy. Earl don't need the guy's money. Earl looks at him, then tears the check up and throws it back in his face, and says, *'He ain't for sale!'* And that's why you ain't buying that horse," said Steve rising to head back behind the counter.

I sat there for a while feeling dejected and decided to head home. As I was leaving, Steve said, "Hey."

Turning with just the smallest hope that perhaps he had thought of a way, I said, "Yeah…?"

"You got mustard on your face."

Later, I sat at my desk in the study for a while looking out at the pasture. Discouraged and despondent, I tried to concentrate on the fact that many people had real problems far more serious than not having a particular horse, but such mentally healthy approaches to life never have worked for me and didn't this time. *"Why did I even have to see him?"* I thought. The screen saver crawled across the computer. *"When there seems to be no way…God will make a way."* I didn't notice it.

Two weeks later, I'm sitting in the same place, and Earl drives up.

"Come in, Earl," I said. "What brings you out on this cold morning?" I asked, handing him a cup of steaming coffee.

He took a sip and said, "I come to sell you that blue colt."

Stunned, I said, "Earl, I could never afford that colt."

"I think you can," he said, sitting down at the old harvest table in the kitchen. "I'm getting' on now," he sighed, then said, "and I'm on the list for a heart transplant. I'm too old to do much with him. Me and Mary been talking about it, and it's important to us where he goes. I like the way you handle your horses. Make me an offer," he said sipping at his coffee.

With a shaking hand, I reached for a piece of paper and wrote a number – far more than I ever planned to give for a horse – and folded the paper in half. I handed it to Earl.

He reached for the note, but before opening it, turned to stare out the window. With his face turned away from me, he said, "Two conditions...one, I come see him anytime I want. Two, you make a rope horse out of him." Earl still hadn't looked at the note.

"Agreed," I said. And without ever having turned to look back at me, Earl continued to stare out the window, and as he handed the note back to me said, "Agreed." He never opened the note. He had never looked inside.

Finally turning to look at me, Earl offered his hand. I placed mine in his, and the deal was done. I looked past Earl out the window to see my pasture and stood there staring. After so long a time, Little Blue was finally coming home.

His momma came with him for a time. Earl had suggested she and Blue come together to allow them to become more familiar with new surroundings until weaning time came. When Blue stepped from the trailer – one small step for a colt, but one giant leap for a great roping horse - on to the earth of his new farm, I don't think I've ever seen a happier human being. He looked around in awe for a moment, then hurtled off in all directions at once. With a response that could only be described as "love at first sight," he ran and played with such unbridled – bridling would come later – joy, until exhaustion overcame him, and then like all new puppies do without warning, he would fall suddenly on the ground into a deep, restful, and well-deserved nap. Had you asked the little blue roan colt in those times, "Will you ever have another bad day?" I'm sure his answer would have been, **"Not in this lifetime I won't."**

But while we would have so many good times, maybe I should have mentioned to Blue, we're never quite done with the bad times. Seems there's always a few bad ones to come. And the day we weaned him from his momma would be one of those for Blue. Let's just say he didn't take it well. Earl would later scold me for not checking to see if the "signs were right" for weaning. "Whether it really works or not," he said, using the same words my granny did when referring to her garden always planted by the signs, "what does it cost to look it up in the almanac?"

Blue had such a painful and violent reaction to his mother's leaving, I wished I *had* checked the signs, and 'til this day I have never weaned another colt at a time the signs said I shouldn't. I still don't know whether such things really work or not, but as Earl said, "it doesn't cost anything to go by them," and if that helps my horses, so be it. And how I wish I had "checked the signs" for Blue.

A cold spell came along about that time, and when

Blue realized his momma was gone, he began to run. And he ran…and he ran. He ran from one end of his small paddock to the other as hard as he could, straining and squealing with every step and every breath. Sweat poured off him, and for a little creature I loved so, hearing his high-pitched screams soon became an impossible burden to bear. On the second day, the temperature dropped to thirty-eight degrees. That was bad, but even worse, the colt was still running. If he stopped even for a second to rest in the forty-eight hours she had been gone, I hadn't seen him do so.

On the third day, after running and losing so much moisture from his body because of the furious sweating brought on by stress – and heartbreak - he began to fall. Struggling to his feet, he would cry for her and run some more. Then, stumbling and falling with whimpering cries, he would fall again like some too young warrior called into a battle he could not win. And I knew Blue was losing the battle. I knew if Blue kept running and sweating himself beyond exhaustion, my little partner would catch pneumonia and die. And I knew if that happened, I might too. I couldn't bear to see him like that anymore. So, I did what all horse people do when they are scared of losing one…I moved into the stall with him.

At first he didn't know what to make of me. "I know I'm a poor substitute for her," I said, "but right now, I'm all you have. I hope I'm enough."

He stared with his bright little eyes, angling his head first one way, then the other, and with a puzzled look on his face that said, **"Who are you and why is this nightmare happening?"** Eventually, probably because I was the only game in town, he cautiously sidled over to me, first smelling me all over - including private parts - and then with a tired sigh of resignation, rested his pretty little head on his daddy's shoulder. He closed his eyes for a time and seemed to be just trying to forget about everything that had happened and be still for a while. And I was so thankful for one thing - at least he had stopped running.

By the second day, he wouldn't leave my side. When I came out of his stall on the evening of the third day, I had a friend for life. Six years have come and gone since that time, and now? If Blue had a choice, he would live in the house with me. Perhaps because of what Konrad Lorenz called "imprinting," Little Blue must have believed I was some sort of biological relative, and a bond strong as an overgrown wisteria vine still exists between the little blue colt and me, the one who had always been popping in and out of my life. When I left that stall on the third day, Blue would never leave again. Little Blue was home.

'Til this day, when I rope the dummy in the barn at night, the other horses – being normal people – wander off out into the pasture looking for a midnight snack. Not the Blue Man. The Blue Man stays in his stall with his daddy, with his head and neck craned out of his stall stretching just as far as he can watching every single revolution of my rope. No matter how long I stay, he stays with me until I'm done. We spent hours talking about how someday, we would give them hell at a big roping, all the saddles we would win, and we talked about both our mommas, and how we missed them so.

'Til this day, I have never taken the first step to put his halter on him. When he sees me coming, he begins a slow amble in my direction, and after arriving at the perfect spot, he places his still pretty head down into his halter. We have that bond I mentioned earlier…the one that comes from raising your own horses. And the only thing that bothers me about Blue – aside from his nosy-bug curiosity that would make the Lord himself just a bit edgy after a while – is that the bond is too strong. When he dies, it won't be long before I do too. I just wouldn't be the same without the Blue Man. After all, he's been with me since I was four. He kept me company when I was twenty, and he came again when I was fifty. I'm tied to the Blue Man. Probably shouldn't feel that way about a horse, but it's like my daddy and uncles always said about me… *"That boy…he's a good boy, but he's too damn soft. Always has been."*

"I love you too, Poppa. Wanna wope?"

--Little Blue

"BRONC"

So, knowing all that, is it any wonder when Blue turned eighteen months, and the time came to develop his reining and handling skills, that I wanted him to attend only the best schools? And I knew just the teacher.

John Fanning, or "Bronc," as he is known, is a cowboy. He's a roper, and a he's a horseman. I asked him once where he learned, and unlike Ray Hunt's friends, who said they learned from other men, Bronc said he gained his awareness, "…because I ruined so many good ones," and when he said that, there was sadness in his eyes.

His proficiency with a rope came about primarily
from one of those "thorns" we all have in our sides
- you know, those unwanted problems that humiliate
us, but are really gifts in disguise? Like me, John was
a stutterer, and like me, he prayed the Lord to at least
remove this particular thorn - whose only possible
purpose, it seemed was to cause others to scoff and
laugh. But the Lord wouldn't because He had other
reasons for putting them there in the first place. And
like Paul, little John was left to deal with his personal
thorn.

Because of that severe speech impediment, he hid
from the world, finding refuge only in long hours of
solitary practice. Day after day, to avoid the cruelty of
other children, John stayed alone with his only friend
for company. A little boy just spinning his twine, a
child who in time would grow up to be a magician
- with a wand like no other. His was made of hemp,
and because the rope was his best and only friend, in
time the rope would repay his kindness. In time, his
friend would do anything he wanted. The thorn was the
very thing he needed to make the others stop laughing
because the day would come when Little John Fanning
would grow up to become known as Bronc ...and take
every dime they had.

I'm convinced that other human beings gain
something of real value from watching Bronc rope, and
that valuable thing is "hope." Not the hope we could
rope like him – I mean watching him rope just causes
one to feel "hopeful." That's what people with gifts do
for us. They make us feel hopeful. That's the way we
feel when we hear Beethoven's sonata, when Hogan

hit a long iron, when Clemente played right field, and when my little momma cooked, and when Bronc ropes.

Remember when we were kids and the carnival came to town? In addition to the sideshows, the clowns, and the trapeze artists, there was always a knife thrower – always some black-haired guy from Italy or Bulgaria, or some place like that. Whenever I watch Bronc rope, I always think about that knife thrower. That's the way Bronc ropes – like that Italian guy in the carnival threw his knife.

In addition to being an accomplished roper, Bronc is my friend. Some years ago now, he gave me my first writing job, agreeing to carry my column in his rodeo magazine. Even though I had asked countless editors and publishers to consider carrying the column, no one would give me the time of day until I came across Bronc Fanning. He not only agreed to include my column in his publication, but he was supportive and encouraging, something all writers –and all of us, now that I think about it - desperately need, but rarely receive. Because of that relationship, I came to also know this man had something to teach me about my horses.

Since the first day Little Blue had come home, I spent time with him at least some portion of every one. I rubbed, petted, and brushed that little scamp constantly. I picked up his feet, scratched his ears, pulled his tail, and I roped him. I helped him become accustomed to the rope by gently swinging a piggin' string around him from the time he was a baby. Soon, Blue paid no attention to the larger "real thing" version. I could rope his back feet, front feet, or any foot I chose. I could gently drop my loop on his butt, and he wouldn't flinch. Standing a few feet from his head, I warned, "Close your eyes, I'm gonna' rope your face, and my buddy would squinch his eyes tightly shut - opening them only when the loop settled around his neck. My little partner had become accustomed to the rope.

> **"Sure, he takes all the time in the world with him. 'Cause he's the teacher's pet."**
>
> **--Shine**

I put a big bath towel on Baby Blue's back every day. He paid no more attention to that than to the baby saddle – total weight eight pounds – which came later. Bridling was the same. Everything was done slowly and without fear, and the little horse loved the attention. He knew his daddy would never hurt him.

By the time he was twelve months, I had leaned over his back many times preparing him for the day when I stepped up and on him. At fifteen months, he stood by the fence still as a stone while I eased my leg over his back time after time. Having been driven in the round pen with lead lines since he was a pup, Blue knew how to stop, turn, back up, and even side-pass a little before any human ever held his reins from the saddle or sat on his back.

I couldn't sleep much the night before his eighteen -month birthday. The coffee was ready at 4:30 a.m., but this time, that was the only way I planned to be like my uncles. At dawn that morning, just as the soft sunlight was spilling across my round pen floor – which I had now learned that all real cowboys use, at least the ones with any sense do - after all those years of waiting, I stepped up on the back of the blue roan colt. A moment I had waited for almost forty-five years had finally come…just me and the baby, and that soft orange fresh sun. The moment was worth the wait. And over the next few days and weeks, the little roan and I rode 'round and 'round in the arena. Blue never seemed to tire of our daily excursions, and I didn't either.

And while he was doing well, and this training regimen was successful, before long – thirty days of riding or so - I knew I needed some help. There was a small but growing problem. Feeling good about that admission, and knowing in my previous "expert" years, I would have laid the blame on Blue, I was now aware that the problem was most likely not Blue's fault, but mine. That's when I called Bronc.

"He's 'dull' in the face," I began. "I've been on him thirty days, and he still just won't respond. It's like plowing an old mule around. I have to just yank on the bit to get him to do anything."

"Hmmm…" said Bronc, "sounds like you have a stupid horse. After all, he's almost two years old, you've been riding him for thirty days, and he's not ready to take to the world show?"

I ignored the sarcasm in his scolding knowing he was chiding me for being impatient – a trait Bronc despises in people when it comes to horses. "Will you come down here and show me some things?" I asked.

"Be there in a day or two," he said.

A short time later, I looked out my window to see Bronc driving up the lane. As he stepped from his truck and trailer, I noticed all the horses staring from the fence line, each one craning a neck over the fence to see who all but one thought to be a stranger.

"Whoos'at guy? Nice twuck! Wooo, lookit' dat trailer, iss nice. Whoos' dat guy, Unca' Buddy? My daddy gonna' wope wid'em? 'Cause if he does, I'm gonna getta wope widda my daddy."

"Shut up, Blue, nobody can understand you when you talk that fast, and besides you've never run a cow in your life," snapped Shine.

"I can too run a cow! My daddy says I'ma gwate wopin' horse, and my daddy, he says I gotta lotta heart and ever thang, and my daddy, he says...."

"Shhhh..." said Buddy.

"Who you tellin' to shhhh, old man?" said Shine backing his ears menacingly.

At twenty-five years of age, the old Leo horse wanted no tussle with the young and powerful Shine. **"It would do us all good to listen,"** Buddy said, trying to calm the waters. **"That's Bronc Fanning."**

"I'm not listening to any two-legs. They're all the same," sneered Shine.

"No," Buddy said. **"They're not."**

"Tell usa story, Unca Buddy. 'Cause I luv your stories, Unca Buddy. You tella bes' stories, and my daddy, he says...."

"When I was young..." Buddy interrupted knowing Blue rarely stopped talking. **"Bronc Fanning roped on me. He could really rope, but he was deaf then, and he couldn't speak...."**

"I know! I know! My daddy said Bonk Fannin' st-st-st-stut-stuttered. I can st-

st-st-stutter, Unca Buddy. My daddy st-st-st-stuttered too...."

"BLUE! Damn, son, you'd make the Lord himself nervous... I'm not talking about human deafness or what they call 'stuttering.' I meant that man up there – when he was young – I meant he was deaf to us - to what we were saying. And when I said he couldn't talk, I meant back then he didn't know our language. Now let me finish...."

Buddy took a long sip from the water trough, snorted, and continued, **"Years later, he roped on me again, but this time something was different. He could hear and he could speak to me then. Something had happened to him. He had learned...."**

"I know, Unca Buddy! I know! His ears got well! Maybe he hadda bug in his ear! I hadda bug in my ear one time - woo, dat bug hurt my ear - and my daddy, he hadda take me to da wetamanavarian - assa horse doctor, Unca Buddy - and da wetamavanarian killed dat bug and...."

"No, Blue. His ears didn't get well, and he didn't have a bug in his ear. Humans don't go to veterinarians. I meant that when I saw him later, he could hear us, and speak our language. He had changed into something more than just a roper and a cowboy. He had become a horseman. That's why I said we should listen to him because they are the only ones who listen

to us. They're the only chance we have."

"I'm done with this," snorted Shine, heading out
to his lonely spot on the hill.

**"Who's Bonk Fanin, Unca Buddy? Whosa
Bonk Fanin'? Does he wope, Unca Buddy?
'Cause if he wopes widda my daddy, my
daddy wope on me 'cause my daddy says...."**

"Blue, be quiet," said Buddy.

I knew polite small talk was required after Bronc's
arrival, but I couldn't wait to get to the round pen to
show him what Blue needed to do. Bronc seemed not
to be in the slightest hurry to hear anything about that.
He sauntered around to the covered back porch and sat
down.

"I thought we were going to work on the horse," I
said.

"We are," he said, "but first, we're gonna' work on
you."

We talked late into the night that evening, and to my
surprise, I wasn't the one asking the questions. Bronc did.

"Tell me about your work," he began.

"I thought I already had," I said.

"Try me again," he said, and settled back in his
chair indicating we planned to be there for a while.

I began by explaining how I was a terrible failure
as a youth, and how people helped me. My work was
to try and describe what those people did for me to help
me change my behavior and improve my performance,
and how we might do the same for countless others.

"What do you do during these stage performances;
what do you talk to people about?" he asked.

"I talk about how I was such an abysmal academic

failure in school, about all the F's I made, and how I was diagnosed with a below-average I.Q. About how when all hope seemed lost in my life, people came to help me. And mostly, I talk about exactly what those people did to help me learn and do better."

"And what did they do? To help you get better, I mean."

I talked on for some time about the characteristics of people who truly help us. How they reach out to us, how they communicate the remarkable fact that they believe in us and have more faith in us than we do in ourselves. "There's powerful magic in that," I said. "I talk to people about how developing trust and respect with other human beings causes them to feel that we have more ability than we realize..." and I talked on and on into the night about my other passion – how we elicit high productivity from others, and ourselves. Each time I stopped, Bronc would have another question for me on how we help others learn and grow. I suppose I was flattered he wanted to know so much about the subject, but I still wished we had worked with the horse at least some part of the first day of his visit. Around midnight, we made ready for bed, and I said, "I truly enjoyed our conversation as always. I just wish we had worked on helping my horse get better too."

As Bronc headed to the living quarters in his trailer – he refuses to stay in the house preferring more familiar surroundings – just before closing his door said, "Oh, we did. We did. See you at sun-up."

I fell into a restless, tossing and turning non-sleep. Around two-thirty in the morning, I sat up in bed with a start. "He wasn't asking me all those questions about how we help others so *he* could hear my answers. He was asking me those questions so *I* could." I felt like

I'd been had by an old lion. I knew he had a purpose, but I didn't get it. Was he trying to tell me the same things that help humans help horses?

"Nnnaaahhh!"

--Shine

The next morning after a big farm breakfast, I was relieved to see Bronc heading for the round pen. He put a halter on Little Blue – who was quite capable of dressing himself – and motioned for me to follow the two of them inside. At last, I knew he planned to finally let me mount the colt and show him the problem we were having.

After saddling Blue, Bronc smooched at him lightly and sent him off in a soft canter around the pen for about ten minutes, just long enough for a small bit of perspiration to show at the base of Blue's ears. I was disappointed to see him then remove the halter and let the horse wander off. He wasn't going to let me mount the colt yet after all.

"Can you ride Blue completely around the outer perimeter of your arena without touching his reins?" he asked.

"Well, no, of course not," I said. "He's just a colt, and besides even if he were ten years old, I couldn't do that. How can you ride a horse without using the reins? That's how you turn them." Even I knew that. After all, I had *some* expertise.

"Nope. Sorry. I just double checked. Still not a drop."

--Shine

I fully expected Bronc to concede my obvious point. Instead he said, "Let's go get us some lawn chairs."

"Ah, finally. Are you going to show me some drill I can use with the chairs to help Blue do better?"

"No," he said. "You and I are going to sit in them. And I'm going to talk to you until you see that when you get better, Little Blue will get better."

Sitting in that round pen in those lawn chairs - with Blue walking around free as a bird, occasionally stopping by to droop his head over my shoulder to listen - Bronc talked for two hours. But the conversation was so rich and so full of information, the two hours seemed like only twenty minutes.

"These are only to communicate a thought to the horse," he began, holding his hands at his eye level, and waggling all his fingers. "And that's *all* they are for," he added with emphasis. "We don't move the horse with these. We communicate a "thought" to the horse with them. Once that thought is communicated in absolutely the lightest manner possible, the work of the hands is done."

"I have no idea what you're talking about," I said. That didn't seem to faze him in the least. He continued, "Once that lightest of thoughts is communicated to the horse, if he even *thinks* about moving…release. The key is to reward the thought, not the action. Gentle pressure, wait…wait…you feel the horse's thought – release!" he said, illustrating with a pantomime motion of his hands.

And he talked on and on. As he did, an image formed in my mind of me standing on top of a huge vat labeled *"Michael's Knowledge of Horses,"* and when I looked down inside…the tank was bone dry.

"At's what I'm talkin' ABOUT!"

--Shine

Yet, I heard soft splashes at the bottom. Bronc's words were flowing through me, and now there was some – just a bit - but real and lasting pieces of information that would become a solid foundation to learn, grow, and improve from - and not one built on sand. The only problem was I could hardly hear for the loud ringing sound created by his words.

"Now," Bronc continued, well into the second hour. "That question I asked you about riding Blue around your arena without touching him - don't feel too bad about that. Most people couldn't even come close. When we actually see someone riding a horse and do that, we are amazed. How could a person ride and direct a horse without using the reins? We do that by using our body. And primarily the lower part of our body; we ride the horse from our waist down," he said, standing and touching his belt. "From here down," he repeated. "We use our butt – use the muscles in your butt to communicate – use your thighs, use the calves a lot. When a rider turns his ankles, the horse can feel that. They can feel your feet, toes, and heels really well." He stopped again pausing to pet Blue who was, at the moment, keenly interested in Bronc's shirt.

"Where you get dat shirt, Bonk Fanin'? Dassa pretty color. Can I haffa bite?"

"Don't nip him, Blue," I said pushing him away. With a hurt look on his face, he waddled off.

"So many other things," Bronc said almost to himself. "You can cue your horse by shifting your weight just slightly, by turning your shoulders, or by redirecting your gaze. You can turn a horse by just *looking* in a different direction."

"How on earth can a horse respond to that?"

"I don't really know how they do that," he laughed. "If you and I were walking along, and you looked off, I doubt that would change my direction, but the horse knows when we do it. Maybe it's because of what we were talking about earlier – because of their keen hypersensitivity to the world around them."

Standing and stretching his back, Bronc said, "The horse can feel a mosquito anywhere on his body. So, if he's made to be that sensitive, is it really necessary to put an iron bar in his mouth and yank on it? Think about it," Bronc said. "If somebody did that to you, wouldn't it make you "dull" in the face?"

"But I'm not heavy handed," I whined.

"No, I don't think you are, but, Michael, *what's light to us isn't light to them!"*

And Bronc talked on and on. Still, as I looked down into the vat, I could see no sign of any substance, either liquid or solid, but with each new topic, with each new revelation, I could hear the soft drips of something hitting the bottom far below, and I knew what it was. It was knowledge.

We had entered the round pen somewhere close to seven that morning. The sun was almost overhead when Bronc said, "Come here, Blue." Blue sidled over to him, and before bridling him, Bronc rubbed his forehead.

"Hmmmm, dat feels good, Bonk Fanin'."

"Now step up on him," said Bronc.

And for the next twenty minutes, the master directed a choir of one, and I tried my best to stay in tune. "Slight move of the rein hand forward, body inclines just a bit, wait...wait. No response – slight squeeze of your calves – wait...wait. NOW! No. No." Bronc moved to Blue's side. Looking up at me, he said, "You asked him to move forward, and because you gave him enough time to understand, he moved forward. But when he did, you kept your legs tight. He did what you wanted, and you didn't let him know it. You didn't release your legs. None of this requires large physical movement," he said. "Slightest subtle moves you can make – that's his language – that's the way he communicates with his own kind. With just an unnoticeable flick of an ear, or just a glance. These are creatures that respond to the slightest cues, so talk to them in their language. Ask, and when he responds - release. Now...again."

We repeated that simple forward move many times, then applied the same principles to backing up. "Gentle tug...gentle pull backwards...wait – wait. No response – so give him another chance, another cue. Bump him with your right heel in his midsection. No more pressure on the backward pull – light, light – wait, wait. Now! Release! Good. Good. He made a small move back, and before he even took a step, you released. That helps your horse understand. Well done."

And then, Bronc did a most surprising thing. He walked slowly to Blue's head and gently removed the bridle, pulling the reins from my hands as he did. That bothered me. "Uh...I don't know about this," I said nervously.

"Good," he said. "That's smart to be cautious, but I have a strong feeling it's okay, particularly with Blue. Certainly, I wouldn't do this with any horse, unless

certain conditions were present." And with that, he
turned and headed to his chair. Careful not to make any
sudden moves, he walked over and slowly sat down,
gently opening the ice chest to retrieve a bottle of water.
While he did all that, I noticed he was eyeing the colt
each second.

"He seems a little nervous," I said with a croaky
voice.

"I think he is too. Why do you think that is?"

"Because he's a colt?" I offered.

"I don't think that's it," he said, taking a sip of
water. "I think it's because you are. Instead of being
worried about your horse, why don't you relax? Why
don't you let your air out, and that way, he can let his
out 'cause I guarantee you that baby ain't gonna exhale
'til you do."

I let out a deep sigh, and after a moment or two,
perhaps thirty seconds, Blue let out a soft little snort
and gently swished his tail. I could feel the tension in
him draining, and realized that tension had drained from
me first.

"Those conditions I was talking about," Bronc said.
"First of all, that's your baby. He loves you. You raised
him so he trusts you. Second, he's been ridden thirty
days, and you said he's never offered to buck. Finally,
we're in a place familiar to him – your or maybe we
could say his – round pen. And of course, he's warmed
up. Since we're safe – him and us – I took the bridle
off his head so you can see something. Well, maybe
'feel' something – that would be a better way to say it."

"Feel something in him?" I asked.

"No, not in him. So you can feel something in
you," he said.

Bronc rose from his chair and assumed a position five to six feet in front of Blue. "I'm going to help you a little here," he said. "I would bet a hundred he won't run off – and by the way, if he does, be ready to ride," he laughed.

"Very funny," I said remembering to keep the tension out of my body.

"If I stand right here in front of him, I doubt he's going too far. Now I want you to do all those same things we worked on for a half-hour or so. The moving forward, moving backward, with slight pressure, reward the thought with release...all that. I want you to do all that just like you are - without a bridle."

With the tension winning just a bit more than I liked, I cautiously lifted my hands with the phantom reins that weren't there and waited. Little Blue did not respond. Since he hadn't moved, I began to apply the slightest pressure with the inside of my thighs. "I don't think this is gonna' wor..." I said, and Little Blue took two steps forward. "Release!" snapped Bronc in a low voice. I did and Blue stopped still as a dead armadillo on the side of the road. I was in a daze.

For the next fifteen or twenty minutes, we walked forward and backward depending on which direction I asked the colt to go. We "talked" in horse language - the language of subtle cues, of almost imperceptible touch, a quiet and wonderful language I had never spoken, and didn't know I could. And the language was beautiful and full of dignity. I had learned only a few words, and with just those few, been transported to another world.

"I think you can get off him now," Bronc said in a low voice. "We're done for the day," And then with a little smile, he added, "And we were both wrong about Blue." Walking up beside the colt to pet him, he said, "If he can do all that without a bridle, he's not 'dull' in the face, now is he?" I felt like a fool.

"And Blue…" he leaned down to whisper in the colt's ear, "I'm sorry I said you were a stupid horse. You're not a stupid horse. If you can do all that with no bridle, you're a good horse."

"I alweady know 'dat, Bonk Fanin'."

Listening to all that hurt worse than if he had punched me in the stomach. In a few hours, Bronc, with his knowledge and with his humor, had shown me my little partner wasn't dull in the face after all. I was…in the head.

"Okay, I'm an idiot," I said from atop Blue's back. "And I'm sorry that I'm so…so ignorant. It's this…this *ignorance* in me that makes me keep having to admit I don't know all there is to know about them."

"Finally! Finally, he admits it."

--Shine

"Don't ever lose that, Michael," he said.

"What?" I asked, and noticed he was not smiling.

"That ignorance," he said. Still rubbing Blue on the side of his neck, Bronc said,

"As long as you remain ignorant of everything there is to know about horses, you will always be welcome in the presence of great horsemen."

Bronc Fanning

Chapter Seven

FAITH CHANGES EVERYTHING

For the next two years, I rode Shine and Blue most every day, and those days have become in my memory like those Dickens spoke of..."the best of times and the worst of times." I had two missions – and those two passions would take three amigos - Shine, Blue and Miguel - on a journey from the mountaintop to valleys so deep I knew we would never find our way home. Along the way, some moments would cause me to fall to my knees and weep with joy, sometimes to wonder about the solidity of my connection to sanity. Still others resulted in so much anger, I would shake my fist at the sky, and yell, *"Why did you give me this horse?"*

When I look back on the road we traveled – so long a road, and one with so many false starts, blind turns, and dead ends, how we ever eventually arrived where we are now is beyond me. The horses knew very little, and I knew even less. Yet, in spite of all my mistakes, clumsy impatience, and poor instruction, I still dreamed of the day when I would have what all men and women born to this strangely addictive life of roping dream of

- that dream being "a good pair."

Two finished horses. That's what we all want. Two, so we can let one rest while we rope on the other. Two, so if one is sick or sore, we aren't afoot. Two, because if a partner wants to break in thirty new steers, that's too many to rope on one – but if you alternate, and let the other horse rest – then thirty is just right to rope on two. And because if something happens to one, if you have two, you can still rope. We all want two 'cause a roper is like a heroin junkie – neither of us can quit. Someone asked me why all ropers want a "good pair," and rather than list the infinite number of reasons, I just said, "Because of what it says in Ecclesiastes."

"Two are better than one."

Ecclesiastes 4:9

But the question was, "How?" What was the best way to communicate to Shine and Blue the end game? How do you really go about helping the horse understand all of the complexities involved in a task that even humans take years to learn? Indeed, all great ropers openly admit they are *still* learning. So, if we assume the horse can learn the required skills - and obviously he can, because great rope horses do exist - what's the best way to teach those skills to the horse?

For many years of my life, I knew that "best" way because in those days, there was only one way. I was exactly like everyone else in that regard. I was like every other roper, all of whom have some experience, that mostly coming from riding a horse someone else taught to rope. Once that "learning" occurs, we make an unconscious assumption even we know enough to start a rope horse. And perhaps most importantly, we would never ever admit to not knowing how to do so, because that would be an admission we were not real cowboys. So, in the beginning everybody knows how, and it should come as no surprise that we find almost all ropers begin the training of a roping horse in the same way.

The "expert" begins by taking his horse to a neighboring pen, with cows usually weighing a minimum of six hundred pounds, all of whom either duck, drag, hook, or fight - if and when you catch them. Catching them is nigh on to impossible because if they cannot explode from a standing start to sixty miles an hour in two seconds, the neighbor wouldn't have them anyway. Because all real expert, old-way, cowboy horse trainers know if you're gonna rope fast cattle at the rodeo, you sure better rope fast cattle in the practice pen. And they all begin "Advanced Rope Horse Training 101," in the same location. The "training" always begins at some place like....

Uncle Mack's Coliseum

"Put him in there and let's see what he does," is always the first line at such establishments and always spoken by a character much like "Uncle Mack," owner and operator of the beautiful 80' X 50' outdoor arena complex made of half fallen and all rusted panels, complete with a small catfish pond just yonder. And you can bet old Mack has trained his share of them by the "'y God, they'll do what I tell'em to" method his daddy and granddaddy taught him. And don't let his full-time position as a long haul trucker lull you into thinking this fellow couldn't have won the National Finals.

"That buckle was mine," he says, telling the story for the hundreth time. "But I just couldn't find a good horse," and his eyes reddened just a bit at the memory of the failed dream, as he wonders how anybody could be screwed on every horse deal he ever made.

Taking another sip of beer, he loads the first cow they call, "Lightnin' Billy," a bony brindle longhorn Uncle Mack who, during the last four months, has won over $150.00 dollars betting on to outrun any horse in the county. So far, Lightnin' Billy's record is 23 and 0. With clearly visible tears in his eyes now, he looks at his nephew, Junior, and says, "They didn't want me to have a good horse 'cause they knew if I did, I'd beat'em." And then, 'nother sip. Actually, no one has ever seen Uncle Mack rope a steer because according to Mack, he "doesn't have to prove himself" anymore to anybody. "I was the best at one time," he says, followed by a loud belch, "Damn, s'cuse me. But now days, I just fool with these old horses and try to help these kids. If I couldn't make it, maybe they can," says Mack, now wiping his tears with his handkerchief, thinking to himself, *"How could I be this good a man after what's happened to me?"*

Clearing his throat and realizing in a new way how the Lord felt when they persecuted Him, Mack says, "Put your horse in there, Junior, and let's see what he does."

His nephew, Junior, dutifully rides his newly acquired horse, Paint, into the head box for the first time. Surprisingly, Paint, having been ridden only eleven days by Les, the fellow who lives down in the bottoms, drops his head and walks in.

Junior finds himself wishing Lester had worked a bit more with the colt, but he understood that Les couldn't 'cause his third trip to the penitentiary had cut the training time short. Junior is now ready to rope his first steer on his new horse. And Uncle Mack opens the gate.

Lightnin' Billy ignites 'cause Uncle Mack always delivers the "hidden hot-shot" at the moment of lift-off to show these smart-ass kids they're not quite as smart as they think they are - including his nephew, Junior, whom he cannot stand.

Junior holds Paint with a death grip to insure that Paint doesn't break out, and after two full seconds, spurs Paint violently in the side, and he and Paint exit the head box with a thundering roar. The steer is already in the stripping chute at the other end of the arena, and has been there so long, he has already dozed off.

"Okay...," says Uncle Mack, reviewing all the details of the run from the opposite end of the arena. "You need to pop'im on the butt with that rope. He let you get outrun on that one, and that's the one thing we can't have. Swipe'im on the butt with that rope pretty hard when you first come out, and that'll teach him to *run!* Now, let's do it again." Uncle Mack and Junior do this each day for one year.

At the end of that time, Junior is so frustrated because at one time, he had such high hopes for old Paint, but sadly, Paint "lost his mind," somewhere along the way, and Junior realizes he should have named him "Crazy Horse." "Why's he like that, Uncle Mack?" the kid asks with a broken heart.

Mack takes another sip of beer and feels for the kid. He's been down that old road. He knows what's happening here but can't bring himself to tell the kid the truth. He looks down in his beer can to see it only half full. *"Gotta walk all the way to the truck and get me 'nuther one 'cause this one's 'bout empty,"* he thinks to himself. Then, it hits him. He should just tell the kid the truth. *"If only they had leveled with me when I was his age, woulda saved me a lotta heartbreak,"* he says through gritted teeth. Realizing the rest of his beer will probably get hot, but if his life experiences can keep the kid from going through all the pain he did, Mack figures the sacrifice is worth it. *"Hell,"* he thinks, *"I can do it...I've drunk hot beer before."*

"Junior, come here and sit down a minute, son."

Junior dismounts, and Paint sees his chance. It's a long shot, but the only one he has...and Paint bolts for his life. Junior lunges, and his uncle says, "No, son. Let him go. He ain't worth it." Paint clears the fence in a single bound. Some say he made it all the way to San Antone. All they know for sure is the last thing they heard Paint screaming as he disappeared over the hill was some sort of paraphrasing from Dr. King, *"Free at last, free at last. Praise God Almighty, free at last!"* No one knows for certain, however, because since that day, Paint has never called, never written, and never even come by.

"Air's your problem right tare," says Uncle Mack, knowing he's about to break the kid's heart.

"Why?" screams Junior. "Why, Uncle Mack?"

"'Cause son," Uncle Mack shouts, with tears streaming down his face hating himself for what he's about to do. *"'Em big boys ain't never gon' let the little people like me and you have a good horse!* They gon' see to it that all we ever get is 'em fools like 'at paint you been ridin' for five years. And look at him, son. *He's crazy!*

I hate to be the one to tell you boy, but it ain't you. It's that damn horse! Now come here and gimme a hug, and go get me 'nuther beer...iss one's done got hot."

There. The conspiracy uncovered and the truth revealed. The big boys will never let the little people have a good horse. And that's the reason Uncle Mack never found a good one.

"Guess how he knows most people train a roping horse that way?"

--Shine

Is it me, or might there be just a teensy bit better way to start a horse? Is it just me?

"Oh, it's you. It's you all right."

--Shine

Mr. "B's" Place

Actually, there are many other methods. One popular second rather gruesome favorite among still living Neanderthals found throughout backwoods America is an approach we might call the "Cowboy Concentration Camp" experience. True believers in this hideous style can always be spotted quickly and with ease because they also love the sport of dog fighting.

They can be found at such gatherings every Sunday morning with family and friends.

Rather simple in style – much like his mind – "Bluto" *knows* he can train a rope horse with his method because he's done it so many times before. It is impossible to convince him otherwise or that any other way is better because in all his years of "training," he has never had a "bad" one. Bluto has been able to train every horse he's ever rode, and besides, if he ever had one that didn't work out…he just killed him. *"Now some of 'em ain't gon' make it! But who wants a candy-ass rope horse anyway? Hell, ass' all ay is out tare' now days anyhow. Yeah, I'ma little tuff on'em, but hey, you gotta' be!"*

And Mr. "B" - as all the junior ropers know much better than their parents - has plenty of small caliber handguns, and marijuana in his truck. A surprising number of other Neanderthals have money to pay Bluto…because they are also true believers in Bluto's "system." *"Heesa' best 'ay is widda' hoss!"* While I hate books that show how to build bombs and sharing this system is tantamount to the same thing, here it is. And Bluto's system is easy as one, two, three.

(1.) Load the problem horse, spooky horse, outlaw horse, or normal horse in the trailer - since horses are all the same, one size and one method fits all. Then, do not let the horse out of the trailer for thirty days. *"Aw, I might throw a little water in'nare now and again…but not too much. I'ma aimin' to tuffen'im up."*

(2.) After about a month, log, lope, and rope old "Rufe," all day – eighty steers minimum. Hire some dope-crazed kid to do this. They're cheap and easy to control.

(3.) Do this for thirty days. And Bingo! The horse will lose two hundred pounds, be starved to near death, and do anything you want!

And there you have it, brothers and sisters. Brother Bluto's Travelin' Salvation Rope Horse Show! Shortly thereafter, some offspring from one of the Neanderthals – God, how they breed – will show up 'cause they always do, and ask, "Is he right for me, Mr. B?" And Mr. B throws his head back like a mad scientist in the movie, and with a maniacal laugh, screams, "Son, I ga-ron-tee you, iss horse will do anything you want him to!" And Mr. B is right…until that horse gets fit, fat, and fresh again. Then he blows sky-high. Mr. B knows that will happen. He knows that's coming…he planned on it all along.

Kid brings horse back to Mr. B, and says, "My horse doesn't know anything about roping." Mr. B is ready, 'cause he's been down that road so many times. That's how Mr. B makes his living.

"On Judgment Day, Jesus is gonna want to have a little conversation with Bluto."

--Shine

"Hell, son," he says, putting his arm around the kid's shoulders. "You took him home and coddled him. Air's your problem right tare! But 'cause I love you – me and yo' daddy been friends a looonggg time – I'moan fiss you up. I gotta little red roan colt over here 'ats just what you need, and here's a' good news."

"He's just $6,000 more, and don't you tell annnyyyboodddy I let you have'im for 'at. You hear me, boy? 'Cause if anybody finds out I let you have 'at horse 'at 'tat price – just cause me and 'yo daddy been friends such a lonnnnggg time, *I'm gonna be rurned inna horse bidness!"*

Later, Mr. B will receive a call from Jimmy Wayne's daddy. "Bluto? Little J. W. says you gotta roan over'air 'at he likes. 'At other sumbitch was crazy, whut wazza matter widat horse?"

"Harold, I toellllldd ya'll when ye' bought 'at horse, you waddn't gonna like'im. Heeza too much for 'at boy. Don't you 'member me tellin' ya'll 'at?"

"Well, uh...."

"Wait jissa minit. Lemme ax you just one question. In alla years you known me, have I ever – I'm talkin' 'bout ever now, even when I'ze down and needed da money – have I ever in all'at time, lied to ya'll *'bout a damn horse?"*

"Well, naw, Blute. Like I always said, 'You da bess 'ay is with a rope horse.'"

"Assa natural fact, Harold. And heerz tha' other thang. Harold, I love 'at boy as much as you do, and if you tell anyyyboddy I let ya'll have 'at roan colt for $6,000, *ass gone ruin me inna horse bidness!"*

Harold, crying now, says, "I'll send J. W. over'air inna mornin' with tha' money."

"And you know, if you or J. W. or even Miss Emma don' like'im, ya'll can bring him back...no questions axed."

Blubbering now, partially from the anger Harold was going to use to cuss Blute out on the first horse deal, but mostly from the whiskey, Harold says, "You're a good friend, Blute."

"I try to be, Harold. I try to be. I don't care if I make inny money inna damn horse bidness. I'm iss tryin' to hep' eez kids. Uh…by the way, what time will J. W. be comin' over here widda money?"

And the beat goes on.

"You know what's really sad? The fact that so many will read those two methods and fail to see any humor at all. And there's one other thing. I'm asking again, how does he know about those methods?"

--Shine

So while it is far too common a practice that many do "start" roping horses in a manner like those described, for once in my life, I wasn't planning on doing what everyone else did. I wanted to do this the right way - the best way. Shine was something special, and I wanted to insure he had every chance to show and give the world what I knew was in him. But there was one small problem…I was inadequate. I felt just like Moses when the Lord called on him.

"Oh no, not me Lord, I'm too old," he said. "I'm eighty for goodness sake," and the Lord said, *"No, Mose', you're not too old. If you were, I wouldn't have picked you. Now, get your helmet on and go in the game."*

"Wait, Lord," said Moses. "I've never been good with words. As a matter of fact, while I'm sure you know this, I'm a stutterer." (Always liked that part, I knew how he felt.) And the Lord said, *"I'll give you*

*the thoughts; we'll bring your brother Aaron in for the
stage show."*

I felt like Moses – simply incapable of handling
the assignment. My internal reflections, new plans,
and general "big picture" view of the entire event of
training Shine could be best described as a hopeless,
soggy, confused, and dirty mess – an admission truly
difficult for a former "expert" to confess. Now aware
that my skills and knowledge regarding horses were
virtually non-existent, I had no clue as to what the next
- and perhaps more importantly – what the proper first
step might be in Shine's development. To make matters
worse, the realization grew in me daily that the tired
old remedy of sending my problem horse to someone
else had become in my mind a completely futile and
hopeless choice. To make what's called in the psych
trade a "referral."

The practice of "referrals" in psychology had
always made my butt hurt. I always thought if any
psychologist said to a patient, "I'm going to send you to
someone else," that couldn't be good news. The patient
would know immediately either the psychologist was
inadequate – never a good sign – or the patient was too
crazy for the present shrink to help…not exactly the
stuff complete recoveries and psychic healing are made
of. Sending our problems to someone else is just like
being on a horse walker…we just go around in the same
circle. I knew that solution would result only in us both
being caught and trapped in the same loop. Send him
off, bring him home, then, when he went south again
– as he surely would – my only choice would be to
send him off again. And the reason I knew all that was
because of a cartoon I had seen long ago in Peanuts

Lucy, The Psychiatrist was in with her five-cent-per-hour fee sign in plain view. In the first panel, Charley Brown says, "I'm leaving. I'm gonna' get on a jet plane and go far away from here and start over."

Lucy says, "Won't work, Charley Brown."

"Why?" asks Charley.

"Because five minutes after you get there, everything will be the same as it is here."

"Why?" asks Charley.

"Because..." answers Lucy, "no matter where you go, you have to take your *self* with you."

And that's why I knew sending old Shine to the best rope horse shrink in the world would never work 'cause when he came home, I would still be here.

Just didn't know what to do. I prayed about it, cussed about it, got drunk about it, drove people crazy about it, and one day found myself in the barn talking to the dog about it.

"Where IS that Christian counselor's number?"

--Shine

Long solitary conversations in the barn were the norm for me in those days, sometimes with the dog - or any other available living creature - but mostly with my *self.* I considered options, weighed angles, and most of all, wrestled with that internal voice we find inside us all; the one when someone else asks about, we deny knowing. "What?" we say. "No, I don't talk to myself; that's what crazy people do." I admit to hearing mine, and also that not only did I hear it in that barn, but we argued constantly. Then, to my surprise, I found someone – or something else – in there. I talked to my self all right, but at some point, somebody else butted in. Something - something more than me - started talking too. And by the way, what is that "thing?" That internal voice we all share our innermost thoughts with, that sparring partner we tell things we tell no other. Who is that?

Is that our "self" or is it the Spirit? Is that Jesus, and does he know where Idabel is? Is that voice the "Comforter" He promised to send? Be it guardian angel or deceased ancestor looking down on us from above, I have no idea – not a clue. Some seem to know. They *know* whose voice that is. *"Why 'at's JESUS, son, and He's tellin' you to get right with Him! 'At's all you gotta' do. Just get right with JESUS and all your problems will be solved."*

I just know that everyone of us who ever thought a lick about anything meaningful in our lives, sit with a cold beer between our legs, and that's who we talk to about what we need in life at the time. And Bubba, I was wrestling with this thing - whatever it was - about a horse of mine who needed some help, and I was not the only one enjoying the conversation. Not only was the voice interested in Shine, it was the only one – considering the number of friends I had alienated – as interested in the topic as me. Indeed, it seemed to want to talk about Shine more than I did, and that was saying something. Not just idle chatter either - this thing had ideas, suggestions, and thoughts I simply could not have generated on my own. And the voice even claimed to have the answer. And the answer was…
"You do it!"

And this something kept giving me that same

answer. And while that thought kept coming to me, I didn't like it. The answer kept coming, and I kept arguing with it. My spirit, or maybe better said - something spiritual inside me, kept repeating this little phrase...and I didn't like it.

"You do it."

"Where did that come from?" I said looking up at the ceiling.

"Best way is... you do it."

"What? Are you nuts?" my self said to me. *"I can't! That's the problem. I've been trying for over two years, and he's no better than he was the first day. I thought I knew all about horses, and now, I think I'm hurting him more than I'm helping him. I just want to let it go."*

"NO! Don't do that. Don't let him go. Besides, you can't."

"Yeah," I sighed to the barn walls. *"I'm sick. I know that."*

"No, not sick. Right. And others wouldn't help him. They would become impatient. They wouldn't understand what he is. You know what he is."

"Look, SHUT UP!" I said, pulling at my hair, trying to quiet this...this...what? Not a voice, not that. Something else. It was me talking, but it wasn't me. I looked around to make sure no one had come within hearing distance of the barn. What a fool I was stomping around out here by myself in the freezing cold, in the blistering heat, on pretty spring days when I could have been catching catfish. I could make a movie I suppose, something like, "One Flew Over the Cuckoo's Nest, and He Can Be Found Just Outside Shine's Stall Talking to Himself."

"I like it! Title needs a little work, but I like it."

--Shine

I fretted, whined, paced, kicked things, stomped buckets, had fits, and took long walks. And the only thing all that accomplished was the maddening little phrase that kept coming.

"You do it."

"Let me alone! I don't want this assignment anymore. Whatever this is in me is wrong! I'm...."

"No. Not wrong. Right! You do it."

"Good gracious alive!" I screamed at me. *"Don't you get it? I can't find the answer!"*

"Answer found you."

"What?"

"Answer found you. Long ago."

"What do you mean the answer found...?"

"John Redwine. John Redwine told you long ago."

I hadn't thought about him in years. A man I loved so. An old roper. "John Redwine was his name, and roping was his game." I had forgotten that too - the line in the magazine article I had written about him. An article about how he taught me something when I was young.

John Redwine

I have a weakness for old fellows – particularly old cowboys. They have so many stories about the way things were. You have to search far and wide these days to find someone who is knowledgeable about bits, hackamores, and even horses. But so many of those older fellows talk about the tools of a

real and true horseman with ease. They know how
to elicit cooperation from horses in a manner that
evokes wonder from the rest of us, and when they
work their magic, you can hardly see their cues to the
horse. Horses sense the presence of these special men
immediately when they come around, and horses curry
their favor. I knew some of these men, and I miss them.
And I miss the best one I ever knew most of all.

His name was John Redwine. Built like a running
back, with leathery tanned skin, and steel dark eyes, at
5' 9", John must have been the model the Lord used to
make all old-time ropers, and brother, he was one. I
never remember seeing his hands without gauze and
bandages on his gnarled fingers. If anyone ever painted
a portrait of John Redwine, the focus of the picture
would have surely have been his hands complete with
twisted thumbs broken too many times.

He was a pleasure to watch in the branding pen.
Few "draggers" as they were called, could match Mr.
Red. If you needed horns only, John Redwine caught
horns only. But if you needed the front inside left foot,
the loop went there just as quickly and no place else.
His best feat with a rope, which I am still unable to
duplicate, involved placing a big loop under his arm,
and without swinging the rope, shoot the lariat across
the pen with unbelievable force. He often used that
loop to catch colts by the front leg.

Two special days of my childhood each year were
spent working cattle on the Redwine Farm. We always
arrived just as dawn was breaking to begin a day filled
with horses, hard work, and a sense of satisfaction
and accomplishment at dusk – and the best part was
lunch. John's true love, Miss Adrianna would spend all

morning preparing a feast for the men. Around 11:30
or so, she would ring the triangle hanging on her front
porch beckoning all the hands, and one famished twelve
year old, to come for dinner. Fried chicken and a pork
roast held center court on that old long wooden table,
surrounded by a supporting cast of perfectly prepared
squash, black-eyed peas, mashed potatoes, pickled
beets, cling peaches, and homemade bread. After
eating a plate piled so high, Miss "Aidy," as she was
known, would place a piece of one of the three pies she
had made before each guest. When we were done, a
moment of silence followed because everyone was just
too full to talk, and then someone would always say,
"What's for supper?"

And the men would laugh. The next line was
always, "Whew, I need a nap after all that," and there
would be murmurs of assent. But everyone knew
there would be no time for rest. A hundred head
remained, and the deadline loomed. Black leg shots,
de-horning, and de-worming must be completed before
dark – continuing tomorrow was simply not an option.
As a child, I was certain that rule was in the Bible
somewhere. I couldn't find it, but I knew it was in
there. The work had to be done before sundown...that
was the rule.

Just as we were leaving the table for the afternoon's
work, Mr. John and I observed our ritual. He would
take me down the hall and open a closet door. Therein
were shoeboxes stacked from floor to ceiling, resting
one on top of the other. The boxes were filled with a
lifetime of memories and a wasted fortune. Miss Aidy
would come alongside her man, and I would notice her
hand slip into his, and with wistful little smiles on their

faces, they would stand there staring at the boxes.

"Those were the days, Aidy," he would say softly. "Yes, they were, dear," she would agree, and they stood there remembering.

The boxes were filled with tickets. Losing tickets. The Redwines had a weakness, and their shared passion, their love, and their weakness was running horses. Every dollar the two made was saved as if they were old misers, and after a time of John driving heavy equipment, winning some here and there at jack-pot ropings, and Miss Aidy "taking in ironing" for people all day, they would generate a sizable sum. Then the Redwines would head to the track and always – every time - lose every dime on their beloved ponies. They saved the losing tickets, not for tokens of depression, but in some odd and wonderful way, they loved to show them to people and seemed proud indeed of their collection. As a young boy standing there with two people I loved and admired, I always sensed if they ever actually won any money pursuing their beloved passion, they would somehow be a bit disappointed.

Miss Aidy died in a fall. John would later say, "Planning a barbeque one minute, and a funeral the next." He was never quite the same, and even though everyone knew part of him died too, when the men would say they were sorry about Miss Aidy, John would say, "Thank you for remembering. I'll see her again."

I went to see him in his last days, and we had a time together. I was much older now, and so was he.

We spent the time remembering. Thoughts of that day come to me so often now; I wrote a song for him. I never sang it for humans, just for my horses in the barn on late afternoons.

I went to see him in the nursing home, just to talk one last time.

I took some good sharp cheese and slipped in a little bottle of cheap red wine.

He seemed glad to see me, and we talked about old times.

We spoke of good horses and a woman who was still on his mind.

Her name was Adrianna; she died in a fall in '69.

We talked about old saddles; he gave me his roping spurs.

He held a silver locket with a tiny picture of her.

I had a real good time the last time I saw my friend, John Redwine.

We played spades on the bedspread, and no one was keeping score.

We talked about old rodeos; he said he wished he could be in just one more.

His sister came by and brought him a piece of banana cream pie.

I fed him in small bites and gently wiped his face.

He said, "Son, I only have to spend one more

day in this place,

then everything is going to be all right –
Adrianna came in a dream last night.

She said the Lord loves cattle,and He needs
help rounding up his strays.

So tomorrow in heaven, two horses will be
saddled...
and we will ride in heaven for the rest of our
days.

So now I know they're in Heaven, and every
morning about seven,

they have coffee with the angels, and they plan
out their day.

And every sparkling morning, they hear an
angel wrangler say...

"You know, the Lord loves cattle, and He needs
help rounding up his strays.

So this morning in Heaven, we have two horses
saddled...

John, you'll be on the black, and Adrianna,
you'll be ridin' the soft silver gray."

And they lope softly off into Heaven, ridin' side
by side,

a handsome Cherokee cowboy, and his lovely
dark-haired bride.

And they spend all their sweet silver days,
tending cattle for the Lord,

roundin' up all His strays. "

And that's my song for John. Every time some
young person asks me for help with his horse or
roping, I think about John. I realize now how much
he must have enjoyed helping me. I'm grateful for his
suggestions, his patience, and his encouragement. And
I remember the best horse training tip he ever taught me
almost forty years ago, when I was seventeen.

I was having trouble with my roping mare, Susie.
Usually, she was the most cooperative and willing
partner you could find, but for some reason, she had
decided to become nervous in the box. I sought John's
help. As we sat in his barn, he listened intently to my
description of the problem, and at last, he said, "I think
I have a solution for you and Susie."

"Take your horse into the middle of the arena in
the late afternoon," he said. "Face her to the west into
the setting sun. You stand in front of her, about a foot
away facing the east, then...." John leaned forward
lowering his voice, "lower your head just a little and
wait 'til she drops hers. Wait 'til her head is level with
yours," he whispered. "Then, look down into her right
eye as deeply as you can, and there you will see what
she needs. There you will see the solution to your
problem." And he stopped.

The whole thing sounded a little strange to me. I
wondered if John was getting a little soft. What was I
supposed to do here? After looking down into Susie's
eye, would I see some sort of dream-like vision of a
horse in a box with some wise cowboy calming her

down? Once home, I led Susie to the arena, and just as John had instructed, faced her to the west into the late setting sun. Looking around to make sure my Dad and uncles weren't watching – it would have been just like them to be in on some elaborate scheme – I lowered my head just a bit, and sure enough just as John had predicted, Susie dropped hers as well. I stood on tiptoe, and peered down into her right eye.

I drove back to John's barn. As I entered, he was sitting in his favorite chair by the woodstove, deeply involved in a conversation with a big gray barn cat. He looked up.

"Did you try it?"

"Yes sir, I tried it," I said.

"And what did you see?" he asked.

"You know what I saw, John Redwine," I said smiling. "When I looked down into Susie's eye, the only thing I could see was a clear reflection of myself."

"There's hope for you yet, son," he said. "There's hope for you yet."

And on this day, so many years later, I sat in my barn now thinking about my old friend, John. About how so many times, I felt him in the barn with me. How he came to be in Oklahoma all the way from Heaven is beyond me, but I felt his presence. Even though it had been so long since I had seen him, on some soft days when things were going well, I would feel him standing off to the side, and knowing he was there and had perhaps caused those good things, I would turn and...he was not there.

And on this day, I sat alone wishing he was. Remembering how he taught me the best horse-training tip I ever had. As I began to rope better and entered bigger rodeos, the more nervous I became. And the bigger they were, the more anxious I became - and my little mare had picked up on that nervousness. When I calmed down, she calmed down. I hadn't thought about that in years, and that made me miss John all the more. But then I remembered while I missed him so…I would see him again.

And the little voice said, **"See? Long ago. John Redwine taught you answer was in you. Answer found you."**

And then that maddening phrase. Again and again, driving me crazy….

"You do it."

"JESUS!" I screamed again at the barn walls. This thing, whatever it was, just didn't get the point any better than Darrell did when he was mumblin' about some Zen crap about music being played too fast or too slow. Whatever had lit on the shoulder of my mind just didn't understand.

"I don't know about you, but at this point, I'm completely lost."

--Shine

…whatever had lit on the shoulder of my mind just didn't understand. The reason I was in this fix with this horse was due to my lack of knowledge. So why on earth did the answer keep coming to me that somehow the solution was in me? That was impossible.

"Stronger than you think…more than you know," said the voice.

"What? You just don't get it! I can't!"

"Not now you can't, but that doesn't mean you can't

154

learn! No one can the first time. Learn and fail, learn and fail. Try...learn. Don't be afraid. Don't be a wuss!"

"HOW? And don't you dare clam up on me now! Before I go off the deep end, surely you can tell me how..."

"Go off the deep end! That's it, that's it, go off into the deep!"

"What! Go crazy? No thanks, I'm already there."

"Not crazy. Right! Great horse!"

"What? What the hell are you talking about?" I yelled like a maniac at the barn walls. I was like some Oklahoma Captain Ahab being pulled down by my own great white whale, and the remarkable thing was, mine was the same color as Moby. And like Ahab, I was entangled in a rope, and like the good captain, I was beckoning everyone in sight to come and follow me. *"Help me with this horse,"* I begged them. *"NO!"* they shouted back, *"he's taking you to your doom!"* And I knew they were right! I knew they were right!

"No, they are not. Problem is you have your heart's desire...what you always desired, what you always dreamed of."

"What?"

"Great horse! You're just like all the others given the great horse. Now that you finally have him, like all the rest...you don't know what to do with him! They come with a price, and the price is high. Does the phrase 'No free lunches,' ring a bell?"

And that was when I got down on my knees and cried. Cried really hard. I was so grateful no one could see me because even I knew something was wrong. He was a flighty, spooky, uncontrollable idiot, and somehow because of some deep-seated compensatory behavior on my part, I was using this quest for some sort of substitute to fill some hole in me…and that made no sense at all either. I didn't know what was happening except for the most likely possibility…that I was losing my mind in my own barn.

"No! No! Great horse! You like all the rest. You pray for great horse. You say, 'Oh, please give me great horse.' You like all the rest. Get one, and what do you do? You say, 'Oh, he's crazy, I can't handle him, I need help, send him to someone else.' HEY! Are you listening? We didn't send him to someone else! We sent him to you!"

"WHY?"

"Teacher! Teacher! Teacher! John Redwine! Answer found you! See? Open up! Learn how to help him. See? He's the Teacher! Not you - he's the Teacher! Open up, get your head up. LEARN! Don't be a wuss…learn! Help us Lord!"

"I think you're doing fine! You don't want him to be a wuss. Don't you be one either. Like with horses, keep presenting it to him. He'll get it. Be patient."

"Wait! Wait! Who was that? I know him. He's the one who made me!"

--Shine

I walked away from the barn wet with perspiration, still angry and not trusting the thing inside. I had roped on him for months. No… more than that. *Two years!* I would never admit that to anyone. One secret I would take to my grave would be the one that said, *"I roped on this horse for two years, and he was worse when all that time was done.*" You can bet your bottom dollar that's one line I'll never put in a book or anywhere else, buddy. I would never admit that either of us was that stupid – the horse or me. I now knew that thirty days was silly and only the province of the great unwashed, but I was becoming a *horseman!* And surely even the greatest horseman in the world wouldn't spend *two years* on any horse!

"And this is the guy that said, "It takes as long as it takes."

--Shine

Actually, to be fair that's not quite true. Shine had progressed in many ways and for all his "issues," he did have number of pluses in his column. First of all, he ate anything put in front of him, he trailer-loaded well, and had impeccable manners. He never sat back on his halter rope, never bucked, bit or kicked any human, and was wonderful with children – all good qualities in any horse. None of the normal problems associated with difficult horses did I ever find in Shine. No anger, biting, kicking, bucking, or resistance, all common to so-called problem horses were ever present, and he was easy to catch. As a matter of fact, one of Shine's most remarkable characteristics was Shine would do anything you asked him to do. The problem was...*he did those things for the wrong reasons.*

This area caused a substantial amount of friction among fellow ropers. I discovered rather quickly as the problem began to make itself known, that if I tried to explain his behavior to others, they...well, they looked at me funny.

"What are you talking about?" they would say with just the beginning of a smirk on their face.

"Well, it's just that something is wrong. He's hard...his body I mean."

"So it's a problem that he's muscled up?"

"No, no...not that kind of hard. He's in a knot. He's bunched up, spring loaded, ready to explode."

"So has he ever bucked? You think he's gonna start bucking?"

"No," I would say, feeling my desire to ask for help begin to slip away because I knew what was coming.

"Well, hell, if he ain't gonna buck, and he's muscled up, whut'sa problem?"

"Nothing, I guess," I would say. "Nothing."

"Well then, why are we standing here talking? Just go rope on him, and quit over-analyzing everything, and just go rope on him!"

And I would fight the desire to let my *self* go and be honest with me and my horse. I hid my concern from not only others, but from my *self* for a time. He was just a horse, and I was making too much of this. And at the time, that seemed the only advice I heard in those days to confirm that belief.

"Wet saddle blankets are all he needs," they would say.

"Guarantee you a good ten-mile lope everyday for a week would solve most of your problems," was a familiar refrain.

"Hell, just rope on him. All that psychology stuff is messing up your brain. Just rope on him." While said with variations, that last thought turned out to be the most common theme.

So, because I assumed they knew more than I did about it all, I did what "they" said to do. And isn't that the way we all are? We rarely trust that thing inside called "self," but instead, follow the advice of others who seem to always know far more than we do.

"There's your problem right there!"

--Shine

And we forget the only people who ever do things of value always follow the beat of their own drum.

"How many famous lemmings can you name?"

--Shine

But to go along, to be accepted by the cowboys, to fit in with the ropers, I once again found myself pretending to be the same kind of men they were. The tough, hard, "bend the horse to my will man" I thought I had left behind. But good reasons were making themselves very apparent. That "Walt Disney" stuff wasn't working. Time to be firm.

"Fine with me, I can do that. Let's see, I weigh 'bout 1,150, and you...I'd guess you at about 165. Bring it on."

--Shine

I had roped on Shine for two years, and he still just wasn't progressing rapidly enough to suit me. If I could say anything positive about his "time in school," I would be forced to admit there was some progression, but pitifully little.

Shine would now go in the heading box, and believe me, that took some doing. For weeks, he had been very reluctant to go into the arena, much less the box. And for all those weeks when he did go in the box, you would have thought electric wire was in the ground burning his feet. He would shake so hard with what my granny called a "rigor," you could hardly stay astride him. And sweat? This horse would sweat so profusely, you could actually hear the droplets hitting the ground. The perspiration came with such suddenness and in such volume, I fully expected to see globules shooting sideways. *"Ridiculous!"* I fumed. Time to *force* him to move on down the line.

"There's the F-word again."

--Shine

The first steer I ever roped on Shine was a dark portent of things to come. The steer broke from the chute, and Shine did too. For just a moment, I was thrilled at the power and speed of this creature and elated that he was hurtling toward the intended target like some heat-seeking missile. I was to be severely disappointed in about 0.3 seconds.

Shine wasn't fighter-jettin' his way to the steer, he was just getting far enough out of the box to go around the corner and then ninety degrees left at one mile an hour for each degree…meaning he made a ninety-degree left turn at ninety miles an hour. The only part of my body touching the saddle was my right big toe, and it was just hanging by a thread.

"Well, well, I think we can all agree this

poor fellow is saddled – hey, made a pun - with a truly stupid horse. 'Course, he left out a few things. He neglected to mention that was the first steer I ever ran. And I had no idea what a 'steer' was in those days. In my mind – yes, surprise, surprise, I do have one – it could have just as well been a puma. After all, they had the thing in a cage. And I'm thinkin' 'What is that?' Whatever it is, it's black and fuzzy, and then it hits me...Thassa PUMA! How did that thing get in this arena? Then, if that wasn't enough - they released it! What was I supposed to do, let the thing eat me? And besides, when that gate or whatever it was banged and ranged, scared the bejeez out of me, at that moment, he kicks me! He kicked me! I never kicked him in my life. Manuel said, 'Never kick anyone,' and I never have. And I'm just standing there looking for a way not to be a 'puma sandwich,' and he kicks me!"

"At that moment, I'm thinking, 'Considering this guy's intellect, and the fact that he has no regard for my safety or his' – I mean the puma could have eaten him too...now there's an idea – I made an instant decision, and that was, 'I'm outa' here!'"

"So, now he writes all that making me look like I'm an idiot. That's not it. My way of thinking about that incident is that I did what I did on that day because I wasn't suicidal. No puma's gonna' eat me unless he runs his butt off for several miles. And this guy thinks he's saddled

with something stupid? He's not - I am!"

--Shine

After countless runs, more wrecks, and too many
scary moments to remember, Shine simply refused to
accept the process. He just wouldn't do it. When I
asked people for help, their answers were divided into
two camps, the "more force" group, and the "give up"
group. The first group held conventions with all sorts
of different banners that said, "Wet saddle blankets for
Shine," "Bit the Fool Up," "Run Him 20 Miles," 'Drag-
A-Big-Crosstie," "Reduced Rations for Shine," and
"Show Him a Picture of a Kill Truck."

The second - more PETA people in this one I
suppose - offered such thoughtful advice as, "Weellllll,
you can't make somebody do something," or "If one
don' wanna, he ain'ta gonna." And the most common,
"Maybe he's not cut out for this. Why don't you find
a horse that has some sense and will just let you rope
and enjoy yourself?" My goodness, mentally healthy
people do get on my nerves.

Of course I should find a horse that enjoyed the
sport, and that would be a simple thing provided I
wasn't caught up in some whirlpool obsession that
would make Ahab look like some small-time crappie
fisherman. Besides, they were wrong about Shine.

The strangest thing about those days is that in
all that time, and in all those trials, my faith never
wavered. If only I could be that strong and have that
much certainty and optimism during other trying times
in life. But this time I did. No matter what he wouldn't
do, I still knew. Down deep inside I still knew, _"He
has greatness in him!"_ And I'll never put this in a book

either, but the reason I felt that way was because of
that little voice. Every single time some well-meaning
soul tried to counsel me about the futility of continuing
with Moby, the little voice would say, *"They're wrong.
You're right. Keep on."* And then I would remember
my graduate school days, and how the first signs of true
insanity were always found in people who believed
they had privileged information and in those who heard
voices.

"Nope, that's not it. They're wrong, you're right,"
said the barn walls.

And the walls were right. I sat in my barn then
thinking about the thing that changes everything. You
know what changes things? What changes everything?
Faith. Faith changes everything. Not the kind of
faith motivational speakers talk about – the "stomp
your feet, and say you're great" kind of faith - but the
real kind. When the thing called *"faith"* comes into
you. Those moments when you somehow know an
idea will work. The times when you know a particular
person has a special destiny, or when you know about a
horse. You don't "talk" yourself into that kind of faith.
Those events bring their own faith with them when
they come. Real faith is a living thing that comes from
somewhere else, somewhere on the outer rim of the
galaxy or beyond, and with liquid lighting speed, real
faith invades us with that "feathered thing" as Emily
Dickinson described it, that thing called "hope," and a
certainty grows that the deal has already been done…
the cards have been dealt, and we have a pat hand, and
we cannot lose…we just have to wait 'til the required
time passes. We have nothing to do with generating
that kind of real faith. It's already alive. And it had

come into me about Shine. And regardless of what anyone else thought, I thought I had some pretty smart barn walls.

"The thing always happens that you really believe in. It's the belief in a thing that makes it happen."

--Frank Lloyd Wright

.

Chapter Eight

CRACKING THE CRUST

The big gray would do anything you wanted. He would do it quickly, and almost always too quickly. He never offered resistance; indeed, he offered too much of the opposite - if such a thing is possible. Gentle tugs intended to produce slow turns produced full – and fast - circles. Touches in the side that would cause any other horse to slow lope, created the "Runaway Shine Train." And when you recovered your wits from the startling rapidity of lift-off and realized how healthy it would be for you to get him stopped before the sudden meeting with the fence occurred, a barely audible "whoa" on my part would result in an instant silky slide. But there was something wrong.

I no longer talked to my cowboy buddies about it. They would do the same thing so many headers do - just wave me off. But in the way I knew about his greatness, I knew about something else. I knew about his *fear.*

Among his good qualities, the Shine Man had

the softest nose of any horse I had ever been on. The
special quality of this animal – such a ridiculous word
to describe him - really began to come through when
I learned not to pull on Shine's reins because such
harsh behavior on my part was not only unwelcome
but completely unnecessary. As was the gentle tug -
tugging wasn't really required either. Only leaning to
the side, or moving my reins so slightly that I was sure
he couldn't possibly notice, or better yet, just moving
my eyes in yonder direction, or better yet...*just thinking*.
Those cues and behaviors on my part created the
responses I was looking for in Shine. On his calm days,
I could move him with my mind. At first, I thought that
was due to my improved horsemanship, but...

"No."

--Shine

later I would learn that wasn't the reason. When I tried
such telepathy on Buddy and Little Blue, there was no
response. It wasn't me; it was Shine.

"Thank you. Thank you very much."

--Shine

As the certainty of his greatness grew in me daily,
the awareness that something was wrong grew just as
well and just as much. While the gray's quickness was
magnificent, his too-eager startle response made me
mindful of something I had seen in the dark hospitals
where I had interned long ago...the severely abused
child. Shine was like a little fourth-grader I had known
back then. When I met him, he was ten, and I was

twenty-seven. I walked into the children's ward whe.
he was living at the time and said, "Jeremy?" Jeremy
jumped when I called his name. I didn't know why, but
I would later learn. Jeremy was afraid. After a time
with Jeremy, I could feel his fear, and after a time with
Shine, I could feel his. Shine jumped just like Jeremy.
*"Could he be telling me the same things that help
humans help horses?"*

Because of that fear in Shine, I once again devised
another plan. And because of a Ray Hunt line that
fell out of the sky, this one actually helped a little. A
plan that actually worked to help ease the fear in old
Shine. Finally, I found something that helped him. A
completely new experience for us both.

The article wandered in one day like that old dog
of Eudora's come sniffing around, and I took no notice
of it for days until it finally caught my eye. The writer
spun the tale of his journey as a horse trainer citing
examples of the many things he had learned along
the way, including a time spent with Ray Hunt. And
how on a particular day, Hunt had given him one vital
key. He had asked Hunt what to do about a particular
problem horse, and the old horseman had been a bit
sharp in his rebuke. "Son," he snapped. "How many
times do I have to tell you? The answer is always the
same. When the horse is afraid or won't respond, go
back to a place where he isn't."

I didn't realize it at the time, but Hunt's words had
that "sticky" quality of all good lines that help us. And
his words, like those in good lines do, grew stronger in
my memory as days passed until one day I could think
of nothing else. *"If the horse is afraid, take him back
to a place where he is not."* A logical conclusion came

to me. Reasoning if Shine couldn't handle real cattle,
I decided we would begin at a place where he couldn't
possibly be afraid. We would rope "phantom cows."
And that's what we did.

I saddled Shine and started directly for the roping
pen. He turned to head out into the pasture to gather the
steers, but with the slightest of corrections, I changed
our direction toward the arena. "No need, son," I said
to him. "The steers we're going to rope today are
already loaded in the chute and already have the horn
wraps on."

I backed him in the box, dismounted, and loaded
the first ghost, making sure to include every single step,
every bang, creak, and slam. Mounting Shine, I built
my loop, and with three coils in my left hand, and with
a little piece of the tail of the rope at my side, pulled the
old cotton rope. The gate banged and we set sail. And
Shine was terrified.

He bolted and lunged, drifted in frenzy from
side to side, and shied from the imaginary beast he
was pursuing. I threw my rope, and oddly, he was
unaffected. Apparently my conditioning with the lariat
had some positive effect – at least, he was no longer
afraid of the loop. But when I wrapped my dally and
turned left across the pen pulling the weightless steer,
Shine fled in terror from the ghost who wasn't there…
and I knew I was on to something.

This time I remembered something from my
graduate school days and the science of learning theory
that *did* have value. This was no puffed up academic
tripe. What I remembered was simple, practical, and
real - the treatment for abnormal fear responses.

The process involved the treatment modality

employed with patients suffering from "phobias," or irrational fears of some object, place, or event. Symptoms included startle response, excessive perspiration, increased respiration and heart rate, and fear – irrational fear. Shine was a textbook case exhibiting all those behaviors and more. When psychologists encountered a person suffering from such a disorder, the treatment involved "desensitization," a term I had heard used in the horse world many times. The underlying foundation of the method - and the cause of its success - is "gradual exposure to the feared object or event." Behavioral psychologists show arachnophobics - those suffering from an irrational fear of spiders - small pictures of harmless insects in the beginning stages of therapy. In a similar fashion, I planned to show Shine the objects and events he feared in the most gentle and non-threatening manner possible. No longer would I have Shine pursue living creatures – and once again, I felt shame that I didn't see it sooner – but Shine and I would only rope what he could handle inside. If that meant banging the head gate a thousand times, I would do a thousand - one bang at a time for my friend. Now I truly understood "It takes as long as it takes."

"No, he doesn't. I know he almost had you there, but he still doesn't really believe that. But even I must admit, he's doing a little better. Not much, but a little."

--Shine

The days turned into weeks, and first, it didn't work, but I knew it would in time. With this new approach

– a more excellent way – Shine soon began to accept the banging and clanging of gates on steel without his normal startle response. He stood quietly in the box and left with an easy grace when I squeezed him gently. During this period, a more valuable time for me than him in terms of learning, I learned not to "kick" Shine. He didn't like to be kicked, and when I did, the results were hardly desirable. When I kicked Shine, he rose four feet straight up in the air like one of those standing lift-off Navy Hover Jets, and his jarring landing was never as soft as theirs. I learned to initiate a smooth "flowing water" exit from the box by *asking* Shine to impel. I learned to ask him in the language of horses, a subtle tongue, and one spoken with a soft dignity. And the part of my body I used was not my mouth or tongue, but a part of me I didn't know could communicate so effectively...small muscles on the inside of my thighs.

When at last, my partner and I could make a smooth run roping old "Ghosty," as we began to call him, I knew we were ready to move on, and this time, I didn't require him to move any farther down the path than he could handle. We started with a living real world version of Ghosty, and not much more energized or animated than the imaginary one.

"Speedy" was about the same color as Ghosty might have been, and his name was a joke. Speed was a steer who had been roped hundreds of times, and he had seen it all. He had been dragged down, run over, and stepped on more than a small guard in a 5-A high school, but in spite of having lived a hard life, the Speed Man was still an excellent teacher. When the gate opened, this old fellow was in no hurry to do anything. The bang didn't bother him; he just stood there for a half-a-minute or so chewing whatever was left over from his morning meal. Moving slowly with a "hitch-in-his-giddyup," like Walter Brennan, he would ooze out for a few steps, then rev his motor all the way up to a jerky little trot. Took him 'bout half the arena to reach his top speed of seven to eight miles per hour, but Speed always was a worker - and the perfect professor for Shine.

Shine was frightened at first, but I no longer interpreted such anxious behavior on his part as being difficult or "ornery." I now understood his language and marveled at how I could have ever been so deaf. *Note to self: see audiologist. Ear check urgent!* But I knew my ears were not the body part being used to understand him at this moment. On some occasions they might have been, but not now. Now, I was hearing him with my spirit.

"Wh..what..iss that? I'm leaving! No matter how I try to consider other options, I can't. Fleeing is the only thing in my memory bank, and please, for God's sake, don't get mad at me. That just makes it worse. You think I want to be this way? That's the last thing in the world I want. I don't want to be this way at all. Can't help it. When I'm afraid, I'm hard-wired to run, especially right now when I'm not sure it's good for my health to hang around."

--Shine

"Whoa, Bubba, it's okay. It's okay," I said with my spirit, petting him on the neck, holding a loose rein and insuring my legs and butt were just as loose. *"If you don't like that real cow - even though everybody loves*

Speedy - we don't have to stay in this box. If you're afraid, let's walk out of here real slow. We can head out to that open arena. We'll be safe there."

Shine pranced and danced, snorting at Speed on the way out. We rode around the arena a half-dozen times, and my spirit said, *"Let's go try that again, and we'll go easy. Let's just slow dance as opposed to jitterbugging. No rush here. Easy now.*

Here we go...."

"Michael, don't make me go in there," said Shine in a shaky voice.

"But Shine, we've already started. Do you realize what you're asking me to do?"

"What?" he croaked, as he stared with wide rapidly blinking eyes at old half-asleep Speedy.

"To violate the Eleventh Commandment" "Thou shalt not let the horse win!" We've already started, and now if I..."

"That's not the Eleventh Commandment. No. 11 says, 'Take Care Of Your Horse!' It means feed him, groom him, keep him fit, and take care of his mind, too!"

"Are you sure about that?" I asked him suspiciously.

Silence. Still staring with eyes blinking a mile a minute, in a low voice, Shine said,

"Uh, Well...I mean...I'm pretty sure."

"I think you're just stalling for time," I said sounding and feeling like an "expert."

It was the tone of his response that reached me. For the first time, there was no harshness or sarcasm in it. In a plain, honest, and simple voice, Shine said, **"Yes. Yes, that's exactly what I'm doing."** And then he hung his head. That got me.

"Ahem...well, uh, if that's the case, you can have all the time you need."

Back out into the arena we went, and rode 'round and 'round until his heart stopped pounding. *"Ready now?"* I asked him.

"M-m-maybe..." he said.

And old Shine walked in the box, made a silky turn, and stared old Speedy down. Apparently, all the fire ants had left.

And the little voice said, **"You're doin' it!"**

I was surprised the voice spoke at that moment, but more surprised at my reaction. I always thought if I somehow pleased the voice, I would swell with pride and know I had done something important. But I didn't feel that way at all. My spirit didn't feel like an expert, but rather different from anything I felt before in regard to horses. I felt humility, gratitude, and appreciation that something I did helped him. And most of all, I thought, *"Lord, after all this time, I still don't know anything."* And the little voice said, **"Now! There you go! Now you're doing it!"**

"Ever notice how two-legs get cocky over one small success?"

--Shine

I could hardly contain my excitement. At last, Shine seemed to be moving along the path to become the great roping horse I knew he could be. We added steers each day with a speed index equivalent to that of Speedy...almost none. All the steers we worked with could have been outrun by me and some other old person. They just barely loped. And each day,

Shine became calmer and calmer. He no longer lunged and reared out of the box - he no longer pranced and snorted. I was truly elated when he finally exhibited a particular behavior I had been waiting for after a little more than a month of roping molasses-fast cows. I had been waiting so long, and he finally did it. Standing in the box one day, Shine *yawned!*

"I'm bored."

--Shine

Funny the things that make us happy in life. We think it's trips to Hawaii, cars, boats, airplanes, and fancy watches. But on that day when Shine yawned, I was ecstatic! I'm sure I had been just as filled with joy on some other occasion, but for the life of me, I couldn't remember a time when my spirit soared as high as it did on that day. I slowly stepped off him, and right there in the box, uncinched his saddle, removed his bridle and took his boots off. I carried them all to the barn for him and returned with a bucket of oats.

"If he keeps treating me like this, I'm gonna' yawn more."

--Shine

I knew we were ready for fast cows.

"And then again, maybe I won't."

--Shine

Nervous Breakdowns

I'm a planner. I make lists, write goals, set
timetables, and keep yellow sticky notes on my
bathroom mirror. I plan my work and work my plan.
Everything was finally coming together. My horse had
calmed down, and I knew the time was nearing when
he would be "a finished rope horse." And I had just the
place to put those finishing touches on him.

When I built my arena, I thought of it in terms of
the "five-year plan," which so far had worked about as
well as the "five-year plan" the Soviets used up until
the time the Berlin Wall fell. But the failures I had
experienced were all behind me now, my horse was
almost ready – just days away - and my pen did have all
the requirements necessary to help transform him to the
big time.

The head and heel boxes were overly large – very
wide and very deep. No confined spaces here. The
boxes were 16' X 16' and big enough for a whole
herd to roam around in. No need for a horse to feel
threatened in here. Just too much room.

I deliberately made the boxes deep to require the
horse to really hustle to catch up to the cow. Also, the
slope of the land gradually rose from the head box to
the far end, creating an uphill climb throughout the
entire run. This was to insure the horse would build
strength and muscle by running against the grain so
to speak, on every steer. Everything about my pen
had been designed to be a place more difficult to rope
than in rodeo arenas. Best to practice in strenuous
conditions and win under easier ones. And now, I had
finally arrived at the place where Shine could begin

to show his speed. We were about to begin the Great
Races. Yessir, if you were gonna have to rope runners
in the rodeo, you sure better practice on fast cows
at home. My uncles always said that. I purchased
ten steers asking the buyer to look for only one
requirement. "If they can win the Kentucky Derby," I
said, "buy'em at any cost." Boy, did he do a good job.

I gave them names. The spotted one was "Bullet
Bob Hayes," the jet black was "Bobby Morrow," the
brindle was "Michael Johnson." Not me, the track star.
(Everybody gets us confused, but we're easy to tell
apart. I'm taller than he is.) Just trust me when I say
these steers were fast. Gold medal relay caliber steers.
And Shine really didn't like them.

Actually, he did pretty well for the first two or three
days. But the more fast steers we ran, the more he
returned to his old ways. My irritation grew when he
resisted going in the box, and when he did, he danced
and shied, and that just fried my egg. The more he
acted out, the more I made him run. Just a few days
before, he was behaving perfectly, and now after
only three or four days of being steady-dosed on blue
darters, he was having one of his prissy fits. I had had
it with him.

"Get in there!" I shouted at him.

*"D-d-don' m-m-ake m-me do this. I'm
afraid. We've been running them and running
them. My rubber band is about to b-br-br...."*

"You shut up, and get in that box and calm down!"

*"P-p-lease! I've had enough! Why aren't
you listening like you were before? Please...."*

"Shine! I mean it! I'm sick of your mental
problems. Just track the steer!"

"NO! No, I won't. This is like the other place. That horrible place where they tied me in the sun for hours. I thought you were different. I should have known. I'm afraid, I can't...don't...please, I just can't go on...I can't see...."

Then Shine lost his mind. He had a "nervous breakdown." The term was used in the fifties to explain the condition of anyone with severe mental problems - and did he have some. His mind just squiggled out and fell on the ground. He went crazy. Rearing and lunging, he stormed out of the box completely out of control.

Trying to hold all his crazed twelve hundred pounds was impossible, but at that moment, I was just as far out of my mind as he was his. I was just as ready for a fight as he was. Without any thought for my safety, I kicked him in the sides as hard as I could. He went straight up. Already running before he landed, we shot across the arena at lethal speed. We slammed into the fence, then wheeling and bolting again, he began to run. I let him go. "Run as long and hard as you want, you crazy fool. I'll still be right here when you're done!" And he ran...and he ran. The horse had lost his mind, but not his muscle. It seemed he ran for hours, perhaps a more accurate assessment in real time would be forty minutes, but all that time was spent exerting maximum insanity-driven effort. Almost an hour later, I was still sitting on his back waiting when he began to stumble from exhaustion. "I told you I'd be here," I said through gritted teeth.

Wringing with sweat, he almost fell when the demon run broke, and still stumbling and trembling, he began to pace and shake making one psychotic driven turn after another. He was like some caged beast now, trotting and walking from side to side in his prison. He shook his head like some wild and tortured thing, and I screamed at him with no intelligible words, just screaming with anger. Knowing he had no energy left, I dropped the reins on his neck and just let him be free to act the fool he was. He paced for another forty minutes. Soft nose gone now, he paid no mind when I touched his reins. I knew he hated me, and I hated him.

"I'll kill you! When you get off my back, I'll tear you to pieces with my teeth!" he said turning his neck to stare at me like some evil serpent. And there was no mistaking the message coming from his glistening, hate-filled eyes. *"I'll kill you, you two-legged bas...."*

I jumped off him in a fury. He wheeled, and I knew he was preparing to kick me as hard as he could. I kicked him first. Kicked him so hard I strained muscles in my leg, and almost broke my toe. It felt so good. I wished I could kick him again, and maybe this time, really break my toe. He grunted in pain, and that felt good too. Some autonomic impulse made him run twenty steps to escape someone just as infuriated, insane, and crazy as he was.

"I hate you!" I screamed at him.

"I hate you!" he screamed back silently.

"I'm done with you, you damn fool."

"There is a God! There is a God!"

"You shut up!"

"You shut up!"

"If I had a pistol, I'd kill you!"

"Go get it. Anybody that ropes as sorry as

178

you couldn't hit me!"

I left that insane, crazy, worthless fool standing out there in my arena – with all my perfect plans he had ruined. Without a single thought about clothes, toothbrush, or whether I had any money in my pocket, I hooked up my trailer, loaded him up, and set sail for Rosie's in South Georgia – 1,010 miles away. When I reached Jackson, Mississippi, 366 miles from my farm, I was still shaking with anger. Stopping for gas, I checked on the mental patient in the rear ward, not caring if he was dead or alive. Hoping he *had* died during the six hours we had traveled so far, I opened the trailer window. I knew the demon had taken complete control when I saw his face. Shine hissed at me like some old evil barn cat and bared his teeth, and said, *"Open this trailer door, and I'll kill you!"*

Rosie

I was taking him to Rosie's. I threw all that stupid talk about "not sending your problem horse to someone else" out the window just about ten miles east of Meridian and never looked back...just kept the cruise on seventy-five. I was done with making a fool of myself, and done with the fool behind me as well. I was mad and just wasn't gonna take it any more.

Rosie's one of those people who are just a little bit bigger than life. She lives in South Georgia, in the little town of Ludowici, and Rosie is a Trooper. I mean a "trooper" in life, but also a real trooper. Rosie is a highway patrolman.

I suppose Bronc introduced us somewhere back there down the road, but I didn't need to be introduced

179

to Rosie. Seems like Rosie and I had always known
each other. Like Herman Hesse said once, *"The best
thing in life is to meet old friends for the first time."*
That's the way I felt about Rosie. First time I ever met
her, I knew we had known each other before. I knew
we had been friends a long time. And it's easy to recall
one of the first things she ever said.

"How you doin', Little Blue?" she said, rubbing
Blue's neck the first time they met.

**"I'm doin' good, Miss Wosie. My daddy
tole me all 'bout you, Miss Wosie. My daddy
says, 'Miss Wosie wopes lika Chinese woman
spinnin' silk.' I wope too, Miss Wosie. Why
don' you wope on me?"**

"Well, I might Blue," she said to the little roan.
"Do you head or heel?"

**"I do it all, Miss Wosie. My daddy says,
I gotta bes' attitude inna whole world. When
da angels in Heaven making me, dey say,
'Boo, we gonna put talent and heart in you.'
And I tole dem angels, Miss Wosie, I said,
'I don' need dat. I got ever thang I need
and den some. I gotts da bes' attitude inna
whole world.' I tole'em, 'Put all 'at stuff you
got dere in one'dem ugly ass bay colts over
dere. Dey need it bad. I don' need nuttin'
else.' I'ma Boo Man, Miss Wosie. I do it
all!"**

"Cocky little scamp, isn't he?" she said laughing,
turning to look at me.

"He is that," I agreed. Then she saw Shine. And
after staring for moment, she said, "I see what you
mean."

"What?" I asked.

First time Rosie ever saw old Shine, her opening comment was, "He has greatness in him." Obviously, such a gifted and talented woman.

And she is that. Rosie was all-state in every high school athletic event she participated in, she's close to scratch as a golfer, and once she won the long-drive championship in the Georgia State Troopers Annual Golf Tournament. Not the Women's Division...the Men's. In addition to all that, she has a heart of gold, sweet spirit, and even sweeter hands with a horse. Rosie's good with them. She talks to them, "finds their spot," calms them down, and elicits high cooperation from every single horse she loves. And she always loved old Shine. I didn't plan to sell him to her, but she could certainly have him for a while because I had all of him I wanted.

"Hello?" she said, after I dialed.

"Rosie, it's Michael. I need to talk to you."

"Hey partner! How ya' doin'? What's up?"

"What's up is Shine's blown himself up," I said. "I need some help."

"Amen to that, brother. First chance I get, I'm gonna' blow him up."

--Shine

"What happened, Michael?" she asked with concern in her voice.

"I was just roping on him, and he went nuts. I guess he thought the cows were too fast."

"Why were you roping fast cows on him? 'Cause maybe he wasn't ready for...."

"Because not every cow at a roping is slow, Rosie," I snapped. "And in some *decade* or other – hopefully this one – I need this horse to figure that out."

"But I just meant...."

"Look," I said all patience gone. "You said once that I could bring him to you and leave him for a couple of months. I'm driving through Birmingham at the moment, and I should make Pell City, Alabama, by dark. I plan to stay over at the Vet Hospital there and get up at dawn. I'll be at your place three hours after that. Can you handle that? Can I bring him?"

"Of course you can bring him - if you'll calm down. I can tell you're mad, just calm down. You've blown up your first horse. We've all done it. Just calm down."

"Me blown him up?" I yelled in the phone. "What do you mean I did it?" I said in a loud voice.

"God, I love this woman."

--Shine

I made Pell City on schedule. Trembling a little less – not much – some eleven hours later, I turned into the driveway of the remarkable facility. The Veterinarian's Hospital in the small town of Pell City, a little more than one hundred miles west of Atlanta, Georgia, is a place we should all pray we never have to go. But if you ever have a horse with severe trauma, pray that you get there on time, because if your horse is hurt that hospital is the place to be. The staff there treats horses who have been severely injured and those who almost always have no hope of surviving. The most courageous and best people in the world work there.

Always faced with impossible odds of saving the creatures they love, they still walk the horse for hours if he is sick, spend all night sewing him up if he's been torn apart, and even learn how to build an artificial jaw if the horse's face has been ripped off. I just don't know how they do what they do because I could not. I can't even watch.

The staff has just as much kindness as skill, evidenced by the fact they always let me board my horses at their facility when traveling through. The grounds and stalls are impeccably clean, and on all other occasions, I had known such happiness when I stayed there. On every previous visit, I had been full of anticipation about the rodeo we were headed to or excited about going to some friend's house where we would spend hours talking, cooking, and roping. But not on this night. With a broken heart, I unloaded Shine.

He wouldn't look at me, and said nothing. His anger seemed spent though, and with his head hanging low, he gave me no trouble walking to his stall. I gave him grain and filled his water bucket. Even though he hadn't eaten in hours, he refused them both, and after turning his butt to me in silence, stood with his head almost touching the sawdust on the floor. I unhooked the trailer and headed to town just a mile or two away for the four basic food groups – hamburger meat, buns, cheese, and beer.

I made my way back to the hospital as the sun was going down. Camped just outside Shine's stall, I took the small charcoal grill from the side compartment of the trailer, built a fire in the pit, made the patties, sliced the cheese, and found the paper plates in the cabinet.

Stuffing a jalapeno in my shirt pocket for the evening meal, I took my lawn chair outside. As I sat there on that oil painting perfect, soft afternoon, sadness came over me in waves.

The stall was about six feet from me, and just inside was the horse I had spent two and a half years trying to reach, and no matter how I had tried, I had failed.

I had lost friends, admitted to stupidity, read books, watched videos, and gone to clinics...all for what? All just so a flighty, spooky, special needs, mentally challenged, idiot savant who could do anything in the world could refuse to do anything at all. He didn't even want to do the thing he had done hundreds of times... just track a steer. Just follow a steer so I could break-a-way rope him. Just follow a steer long enough for me to throw my loop and let the plastic honda pop off. After all I had done, he wouldn't even do that. *"If he don' wanna,' he aint'a gonna!"* kept slogging through my mind. I was heartsick. My heart actually hurt, not from some clogged artery, but something else...heart *ache*. I was done. The battle was over, and I had lost. It was over.

"Not over. Not done."

I jumped as if I had seen a scorpion on my boot. The first thing I looked at was the beer chest. *"Impossible, I can't be drunk on two beers."*

The sun had dropped and dusk had come into my camp. There was an eerie silence in the twilight, and I found myself feeling more than a little afraid. Not of any external threat, but an internal one. How on earth, after what just happened, could that...that *thing* show up *now*? If there was ever living proof of what a fool I had been, if ever anyone had picked the wrong pony to bet on....

***"No, not wrong pony. Right pony. You're right,
they're wrong."***

With deliberate slowness, I rose from my chair and
backed away from a stranger with a loaded gun, but I
was the stranger and the gun was in my head.

The voice couldn't be here now. It just couldn't.

Taking one step at a time, I walked a few feet away
from the glowing embers in the little pit I had cooked
on so many times. "What's going on here?" I asked
aloud to the fire.

***"They're wrong. You're right. Don't quit. Begin
again. Start over."***

Then the anger came. On one of the worst days of
my life, my horse had fallen out from under me; I had
admitted failure; I had driven 750 miles; and now I find
the 'Son of Sam' is still in me. "You're crazy," I said in
a low growl.

***"No. You're not. You were right. Not over...start
over."***

That's when I got out of there.

Even though I was afraid, after two beers I didn't
want to get in the truck and drive around because I was
more afraid of John Law than old Sam. So I started
walking. I made my way to the front of the hospital
and then remembered, *"They don't lock this place."*
Naturally, they lock up the medicine, but because the
vets and staff have office hours 24/7 and might be
called at any moment, the front doors to the waiting
room are always open. I made my way inside because
I saw a light on in the waiting room. Demons hate the
light.

I sat down on the leather waiting room sofa with

a tired and defeated sigh. I poured the last quarter of the now-hot beer into a big thirsty looking potted plant hoping the vets didn't have a keen sense of smell. Too scared to go back to the truck for another one, I just sat there. And then, Eudora's old dog came sniffing around.

Lying on the table right in front of me was a copy of *America's Horse*, the monthly publication from the American Quarter Horse Association. The magazine was opened to the last page, the page always containing memorable quotes about horses and the life we live together. Then the strangeness of the entire day's events made itself present.

At dawn, I was in Oklahoma planning a good day; next thing you know, I'm in Alabama - me and my zany sidekick, Chief Crazy Horse. Then I get scared 'cause some insane idiot inside is telling me to not only keep on being insane, but encouraging me to go even crazier. All that to find myself sitting in the waiting room of a vet hospital at 10 p.m. on a Tuesday night. Then I come up with another plan - I'm going to go find the guy who told me to start roping again, and after I shoot Shine, I'll kill that guy too. Trying desperately to remember where my pistol was, I looked at the magazine, and on that last page - the one with the horse quotes - one grabs me right by the eyes.

On my way back to the trailer, and Shine's stall, I noticed my fire had gone out. *"No supper tonight."* Then I saw Shine's head sticking out from his stall. *"How I love him,"* was my first thought. That seemed strange considering how mad I had been a short time earlier. Then I realized it wasn't all that strange. We all get mad at loved ones from time to time, but if you *really* love them, your core condition never changes. And mine hadn't changed for the most magnificent horse I had ever known. Seeing his head sticking out of the stall, I knew he was looking for me.

Finding his grain and water bucket empty made me happier still. I gave him a small late night snack and replenished his water. I stirred up the fire enough to cook a rare burger, and when I looked up to see the stars were out, my spirits lifted even more. And Shine and I just looked at them for a while, and at each other.

"I'm sorry," I said with my spirit.

"Me too," he said.

"I can't believe you would forgive me," I said surprised.

"Aw, I don't want to, but I can't help it. I'm hardwired that way too."

We talked most of the night.

At dawn, I called Rosie. "I'm not coming."

"What are you going to do?" she asked.

"I'm going home."

I thought about the quote all the way home - what the Dean of The Spanish Riding School, a man named Alois Podhaisky, had said in 1939. He said something all those years ago at his retirement ceremony to the faculty and the students - students who had accomplished the impossible task of being accepted in the Spanish Riding School. A place where if you were admitted, you must commit for *eight years* of instruction. And if you make it to graduation day, you are granted the title of...*apprentice.* The title of apprentice is given because the teachers at the school know even after eight years, we still have so much to learn.

"I must not forget to thank the difficult horses, who made my life miserable, but who were better teachers than the well-behaved school horses who raised no problems."

Alois Podhaisky, Director –
Spanish Riding School 1939

And right above that, I then saw an even more remarkable example of the thing Jung called "synchronicity," a word he used to describe events "so connected they cannot be explained by coincidence or chance." All the events of that day had brought me here to read these words.

"It is the very difficult horses that have the most to give you."

Olympic Rider Lendon Gray

I knew something had caused a connected chain of events that resulted in my driving all day to find an open magazine lying on a table in a hospital for horses in Alabama, and somebody or something had left that magazine open to just the right page. When I read those words, something inside me changed. Something had brought that horse to this hospital.

I found myself laughing out loud in my truck on the way home. *"If that's true fellows, I have a real crackerjack right back there behind me!"* And me and old Shine, both of us in a better frame of mind now, headed home. Just a little 1,500 mile ride to teach me a lesson I needed to learn. To find a couple of quotes in just the right place at the right time. After reading them, an understanding came. After two and a half years of working with the most difficult but special horse I had ever known, I still had yet to even attain the lowly rank of…"apprentice."

Once home, first thing I did was sell those demon cows. I had learned one of life's most valuable lessons, one all those who seek to be horsemen learn. And here it is brothers and sisters, and you don't have to put a dime in the collection plate.

"Fast cows ain't good for nothing 'cept to make you mad!"

--Michael Johnson

Take that and do what you will with it.

All the way home, I reviewed the "black time" as I came to call the experience of Shine's "nervous breakdown" and actually found some explanations for his behavior along the way.

"But sadly, probably won't think to look for any to explain his own."

--Shine

Shine had indeed showed definite signs of improvement in the last few months. He had calmed down in the box, he didn't bolt when leaving, and he seemed to have no desire to be what ropers call a "chargey" horse, meaning when he reached the desired "spot" – that is, his position in relation to the running steer's position – Shine did not "charge" past. Instead, he seemed perfectly willing to lope along beside the intended target allowing me to rope from my preferred "spot."

When ropers talk about the "spot," they mean the place you would rope from if someone held a gun to your head and said, "If you miss, I'm gonna' shoot you. If you don't, I won't. Good news is you can rope from wherever you want." Whatever position you would choose to insure a catch if someone was holding a gun to your head...that's your "spot." Shine didn't seem to mind staying at that spot. With all those positives occurring, why did he go "psycho" on me? Once again, the answer was the same.

While the big gray was just learning to handle the box with all its pressures and was content to lope along beside turtle-speed steers, he was not ready to run after fast ones. Even though no one could be stupid enough to fail to see that, I had been that stupid. I had been blind as an insensitive bat. I lost my patience and kept the horse in a place he could not handle. At least now, because of the experience, my thinking was changing from "Thou shalt not let the horse win," to "If you force the horse to do something he cannot, you *can't* win."

Should we then let them be "barn sour?" No. Should we let them bite and kick us? No. "Aw come on, honey, please do this for daddy," doesn't work.

But forcing a terrified horse is the opposite extreme of the syrupy sweet toleration of undesirable behavior. Neither works. Being too nice and being brutal are the same things in a way. Surely, if given a choice the horse would prefer our being too nice, but like the child with overly protective and doting parents, he learns nothing. If the horse is not disciplined – and that doesn't mean beaten – if his energy, talent, and ability are not channeled, he violates his purpose...to help man. The Creator made the horse to help man. He just assumed we would figure out the best way to ask the horse to help us. And that was my mistake. That is what I hadn't done.

I pushed him too hard. I *made* him do something he wouldn't do because he *couldn't* do it mentally. I didn't even ask him in his language, but rather in the language of Bluto and all those like him. Like some deranged Little League dad screaming at his son....

"Guess how he knows about those?"

--Shine

and the dad cannot see his screaming is the primary contributor to his son's poor performance, my horse training skills on that dark day when Shine lost his mind consisted solely of only two things...screams and anger. Such poor methods. Especially when you consider the two emotions horseman John Lyons recommends we have when dealing with horses, and only two...one being "patience" and the other..."a sense of humor."

What a difference it would have made had a real horseman been in the arena that day when Shine had his severe stress attack – brought on by me. "Stop, Michael. Stop!" he would have said. "You're not doing anybody any good here, you or your horse. You're not helping him," he would have said. "And from the looks of things you cannot because obviously you are not ready to help him." That's an excellent reason for us all to find help during our initial time with horses.

"And even if you've spent years with them and think you're an expert. Experience ain't all

191

it's cracked up to be."

--Shine

But not all of us know a horseman – they are rare – and if we do, we may not be able to afford them. So how do we learn? When I asked Bronc how he learned his skill, his softness, his knowledge, and acute awareness, he gave me the answer.

"Because I ruined so many good ones."

Bronc Fanning

And when he said that, I saw the sadness in his eyes. I understood that in a new and different way now. Now because of what I had done, there was sadness in mine. But that's how we learn. We learn by failing, by making mistakes, and from doing things we later regret. But we are so lucky because horses are such forgiving

"I'm hard-wired that way too."

--Shine

And so with at least some new knowledge, I began again. I sold the Kentucky Derby Cows and replaced them with a dozen perfectly matched little jerseys that blistered along at perhaps eight miles an hour, or on a good day, maybe ten. One by one, I was learning the steps – painful though the lessons might be – the real and lasting things you can do to help your horse. One of those lessons will stay with me always - *don't rope fast cows!*

I let Shine rest a day after our long journey, and the

next day, introduced him to our new family members, all jersey brown, dairy cow male equivalents of Elsie, the Contented Cow. And even though they were Olympic class slow, we didn't run them.

"I don't believe it. I just don't believe it."

--Shine

We just milled around among them all afternoon in the arena. At first, Mr. "Antsy Pants" couldn't handle it. Terrified of 250-pound baby wood duck-looking puppies - all of whom were exactly the same size as T-Ball little leaguers – Shine danced, pranced, and snorted with fear. But this time, I refused to become impatient or angry. Even though I knew the worst thing the new baby steers could do was lick him to death, Shine didn't know that. Each time he exhibited any fear response, I let him win. We turned immediately away from the evil imps – all of whom desperately wanted nothing but to be petted and loved – and I allowed him to move to a place Shine considered safe - the opposite end of the pen. After perhaps an hour or so, he began to breathe normally and finally came to believe his reaction to such grave danger might have been a bit overstated. By the end of the second hour - on his own - he moved close enough to actually sniff one's butt.

"Hmm...smells like chicken."

--Shine

During the next few days, we trained the babies to run – piddle along would be a better phrase - as straight as possible to the other end, and Shine warmed to the task. With no fear of being outrun and soft little lopers to follow, the big horse became calmer and calmer. And I knew I was on to something when the little voice said, *"You're doin' it."*

Eventually, I would introduce Shine to a faster cow. Not ten, but just one. One fast one mixed in with ten slow ones. *"You're doin' it."* I was certain this gradual insertion of one speedy steer among so many slow ones would allow him a painless method to progress. But as always, "Mr. Marble Mind" was much more hard headed than any other horse would ever be…and was he smart about that one fast steer.

When any jersey made his way into the steer chute, Shine behaved like an old man in church who hadn't slept much the night before - he nodded off. Sometimes when loping alongside the slower steers, he seemed about to yawn and sometimes did. But when that one fast cow began to make his way down the line, Shine knew he was coming, and even though he might be four cows back in the line, Shine would begin to quiver and shake knowing his duel with the real speed demon was close at hand. When Speedy broke, Shine went right back to his old ways of fear, shying and acting out with jerky nervousness and trembling. I didn't get mad. I just kept loping after the slow cows, and with every tenth one, I asked him to try and deal with the stress and pressure as best he could. And eventually – much longer than I expected naturally - he became a bit more able to do just that. There would come a time after almost four months of the "one-to-ten ratio method" when Shine would actually stand in the box and chase old Speedy down the pen under barely enough control to let me rope the steer. He looked like Don Knotts on his worst day, but he could do it.

"And you're doin' it. You both are. See? You do it, and he does it. You do it together."

When I began, my plan was to not only rope on Shine in thirty days but to actually win money on him at a rodeo within sixty. Now we were entering our thirtieth *month*, and we hadn't been to a jackpot roping yet. At least I was right about the number thirty, my timing was just a little off. I thought in terms of thirty days - I should have said thirty months. ***"You're doin' it."***

Yet there was no denying he was close. No one would describe him as a finished horse, but Shine was doing a substantial number of things right - really right. After running so many practice cows, I knew the horse was blessed with tremendous speed. Even though I had never asked him for it – indeed, had prevented him from using it – I knew he had tons. And he moved like Fred Astaire and George Raft; he seemed to float on air just like them when he moved. He had the feet of a dancer. And that was the good news.

The problem still remained. Shine's condition made me mindful of what psychologists call "inappropriate affect." That disorder in humans can be defined as someone who exhibits a response to a given situation that doesn't fit. While it's true we are all different and react in different ways to a particular happening, it's also true we generally react in similar fashions, perhaps at least in terms of what we don't do in those situations.

"I can see why people didn't understand when he tried to describe me."

--Shine

For example, when we hear about a child experiencing a tragic event, we don't laugh. We might all think or do something differently from others, but few of us would laugh. If someone did, that response might be described as "inappropriate affect," a surprising emotional response that most people would not emit. When anyone reacts in this fashion, psychologist or not, we all suspect that something is amiss. Something is not right in their emotional make-up. And that suspicion grew in me daily about Shine. Shine was just *too* afraid. So many times, when I asked him to do a simple thing, his fear was far more than the situation warranted. My imagination wasn't inventing the feeling, and for the first time, my lack of experience was not the problem. I was right, and this time, I had no desire to be.

As I mentioned before, I no longer talked about that aspect of his behavior with others because if I did, I knew what was coming… "Just rope on him. Quit analyzing and just rope on him!" Now however, I was being honest with my spirit and my horse. There was something becoming more important than roping. I began to care deeply about healing Shine…more than roping.

"I cannot believe he just said that."

--Shine

"Forcing" Shine to overcome his fear was no longer an option. I knew that wouldn't help. *"You're doing it."* There was mountain in front of me, and I couldn't move it. If Shine were ever to become the horse I knew he was meant to be, we needed help. This was no longer a matter of sending my problem horse to someone else but rather a matter of my knowing my reservoir of experience and knowledge was empty in this particular compartment. I needed someone with more *deep knowledge* than I. I thought about what an old mentor of mine said once.

"Any question you send out to the Universe will be answered. If you don't press, the answer will come."

--*Joe Charbonneau*

"Mr. Joe," I said to the sky just above the hill at the top of my arena, *"if you have any pull up there, I need some help. My horse is sick, and we need help. And I'm not gonna do too good on that 'not pressing' part, but I'll try."*

He must have been listening because just a couple of days later, the magazine article came - right on schedule.

Chapter Nine

THE HORSEMAN

Even in the early days with Shine, the feeling crept slowly around the corners of my mind. There was something I couldn't quite put my finger on. He was afraid, and while I had done little in my time with him to diminish his fear – even added to it on occasion, Lord forgive me – together, we had lessened it some. Still, even though he handled like a dream, I somehow knew he was responding for the wrong reasons. Instead of a relaxed smoothness in his body like my baby Bubba, Little Blue, there was a hard glass-like feel filled with fear inside Shine, as if he were so very worried he might do something wrong. This was not some excessively picky demand for unattainable perfection on my part – a sin I might have been guilty of before. But I was not guilty of that now. The horse was suffering. And no matter how hard I tried to be a cowboy and be like my uncles and the others who said, "Just rope on him," I could not.

The horse was suffering, and for once in my life, I

would have stood up to my uncles and told them, "He's
sick, and I can't stand it." Every move he made seemed
designed to prevent punishment and avoid getting into
trouble. While I had made mistakes, and even sinned
terribly on one occasion, I never hit him, and I never
punished him. Yet still, he tried too hard to please.

I handled this puzzling predicament initially like
we do most thorny problems in life. I ignored it...
pretended it wasn't happening. Like we do with some
old relative who grows a little more batty everyday,
we don't mention to anyone in the community that we
do know in fact what is happening. Early on, I told
myself the horse was fine and that I was just being silly.
After all, he was just a horse. As the days wore on, we
progressed to the point of roping slower cattle without
much difficulty. But on faster stock, he became so
tortured and nervous, and far more frightened than the
situation warranted. Everything I tried just didn't help.

I loped him ten miles many times to help him be
"warmed up," to "get the juice out of him," to "tire
him out," and no matter what I did, he was always the
same. All my efforts produced the same result - to
return to the arena and watch a familiar scene repeat
itself and play again and again. The same painful
stage play tragedy was acted out over and over. A
brilliant performer on slow cows and a nervous failure
who couldn't remember his lines on fast ones. He
was Laurence Olivier on the slow ones, and an old,
shaky, crying, alcoholic has-been on the fast ones. And
anyone with any sense would have said, "Why are you
doing this?" And I had an answer to that question. The
same answer Van Cliburn's mother would have used if
the young prodigy had said, "Mom, I just don't want

to play the piano anymore." Mrs. Cliburn would have said, "Van...we need to talk."

And the magazine article came right on schedule. The piece was written by Craig Hamilton. Hamilton was a man who had qualified for the National Finals in Team Roping in 1987 and 1989, and at one time was said to have "the fastest hands in the PRCA." At the top of his game, Hamilton walked away from professional rodeo, and when people asked him why, he said, "I just need to help horses." Wondering for a time if the strange calling he felt would be kind enough to allow him to make a living, he found that it would indeed provide sufficient income for him to make the work he loved his full time profession.

His article written for the rodeo magazine concerned chargey horses and how to help them improve. His words were sharp and crisp, and I enjoyed the piece, and while his subject wasn't exactly about the specific problems Shine and I were living through, something about the man's spirit came through in his words. And I did something I have never done. I decided to call this famous stranger on the phone.

I knew chances were excellent someone of his caliber wouldn't talk to me. I wouldn't be surprised to hear, "Well, son, I make a thousand dollars a day telling people what to do with troubled horses. You think I'm gonna' talk to you on the phone for free?" Or perhaps he might say as one author did to me when I asked for help, "You think I got where I am talking to rookies like you?" I was ready for that, and my plan was to talk fast and hope he would tell me one thing to help Shine before he hung up.

Michael Johnson

"Some plan."

--Shine

With shaky hands, I dialed the number at the end
of the article. He answered his own phone. I found
out something about famous people that day. The ones
who are really sent to help us have all the time in the
world for us. Doesn't mean we can abuse their time,
but the fact is, the really good ones remember the days
when they were scared, struggling, and desperate, and
thought someone else could tell them the secrets of life.
The good ones know they can't, but they also know it
would be unkind to tell us that and burst our bubble at
that moment, so they just play along and try to help us
the best they can. And that's what Craig Hamilton did
for me on that day. He talked to me for an hour and a
half…and it felt so good.

I just let it out, and for once, I wasn't talking to
someone who thought I was crazy. Rambling on and
on, the whole story came roaring out. The frustration,
the anger, shame, mistakes, knowledge and feeling of
the horse's greatness, and how I didn't know why, but I
knew, and on and on I went for an hour. And the doctor
listened to the patient. And when I was spent, he said,
"You've helped him." That almost tore my guts out.

"No. No, I haven't," was all I could get out of my
cracked voice.

"You have," he repeated, and he was silent for a
time, knowing I was in no shape to listen and certainly
not to talk.

"Let me think about it for a while," he said. "Let
me think about you and Shine, and I'll call you."

"Have you ever noticed when you ask an 'expert' a question, they tell you the answer immediately? But when you ask a horseman the same question, he always says, 'Let me think about that for a while.'"

--Shine

A short time later, Craig called and said, "I'm having a roping school in Chattanooga, Oklahoma - a short drive from Lawton – this weekend. Why don't you bring a horse to rope on and also bring Shine? You can work on your roping, and we'll both work with Shine." Best deal I had been offered in years.

"I'll be there," I said. A few days later, we arrived at the Crow Ranch on Friday afternoon. Hosts Rob and Penny Crow, and their sons, Cacy and Clancy, charmed each and every guest and kept a steady supply of "stick to your ribs" delicious meal-time fare available all weekend. Twenty men and women, ranging from physicians and college professors, to teachers, counselors, and skilled trades and crafts artisans threw loops, worked on horsemanship skills, and hung on every word spoken by the master, Craig Hamilton. Late on Friday afternoon while the others were practicing, I was surprised to hear Craig say, "Why don't you rope a few on old Shine, Michael? I want to see him work."

Whew! I felt like a nervous parent at a recital. I so badly wanted my partner to do well and look good in front of all these people, and to my great relief, the Shine Man didn't do too badly. He was a bit nervous, but he managed to get to the cattle, and we roped perhaps a half-dozen without him falling down or me falling off a single time. Craig nodded approvingly,

"Not bad, not too bad." I felt like a dad looking at my son's report card filled with straight A's.

Early Saturday morning, Craig had me saddle my warhorse, old Buddy. "I'll ride Shine," he said. At first, Shine performed as he had the day before, but as the roping runs increased, and the master asked for more and more from the big gray, the house of cards I had built began to fall. Shine became highly agitated and shook with fear. And his anger spiked, and finally, Craig rode him to a prancing skittish halt. He looked at me.

"Something's wrong," he said quietly. His words hurt me. Because I knew in just a matter of minutes, this great horseman had found and felt the fear down inside my Shine Man.

I looked away. "Yes," I said, my voice betraying my emotion. "Something's wrong." At that moment, the horseman knew he had two patients: a scared child inside the body of a warrior, and an old cowboy who didn't have the knowledge and skill to help the child not be afraid. Craig smiled down at me.

"Don't be discouraged," he said. *The words Irv had used.* "You have helped him a great deal." And then he said, "I know what he needs. We can help him." I never heard sweeter words.

Craig called all the ropers around him in a circle. "I need your help," he said. "I know you came to rope at this school, and you paid good money - and any of you can have your money back if you want - but if you will help me, what we're about to do may help you more than roping. I want all of you to form a line across the middle of the arena. Each rider will be on his or her horse about ten feet apart. I'm going to track a lead

steer on Shine. Keep the steer from running past you.
That way we will cut the arena in half and keep the
steer down here with us. I'm not going to hurt Shine or
be angry with him. I'm going to show him a better way
to live."

And I guess what all those people did next – all
those people who had paid three hundred dollars to rope
on *their* horse – says more about why I rope than any
other thing. Everyone turned without hesitation to take
up their position – every one. I didn't know what was
going to happen. All I knew was emotion was rising in
me.

Rob Crow released the lead steer. An old black
longhorn who had been around. Having taught many
horses, the old steer knew what to do and began his
leisurely trot. Craig, holding his rope with a break-
a-way honda, began to coax Shine to track the steer.
Sitting on old Buddy, I was struck by the beauty of
the moment. White arena sand, blue Oklahoma sky,
and riders all in a row giving of themselves to help a
troubled soul, to help in any way they could. But there
was one thing not beautiful; there was one thing sad and
wrenching. The big gray wanted no part of it.

Each trotting step seemed to raise his anxiety to
even higher levels. It was apparent that what he was
being asked to do should not have caused such terror,
but the task wasn't causing Shine to be afraid. More
like some old episodic memory, some night terror too
painful to be remembered. His condition worsened, and
then he looked at me.

"Help me!" he said. *"Don't make me do this.
I don't know these people. Help me."*

I looked away. Couldn't stand to look in his eyes.

And like people who help us in the worst of times do, Craig insisted that he continue. The master played the big horse like a violin. Pushing and pulling gently one moment, then firmly the next. All the while steady tracking the black steer and talking, always talking to the frightened animal. For over an hour, he whispered, listened, and encouraged Shine not to be afraid, to trot behind the steer, and over and over, I heard him say in a low voice, *"Don't be afraid, you can do this, you are more than this, you have no idea what you are...no, no...yes, yes! Yes!"* He talked to Shine, the warrior, and to the frightened child inside. And suddenly....

Shine stopped and stood stone still. He looked around at all the riders and then directly at me. He seemed to be waking from a dream. I didn't know if he was puzzled or lost or...Shine dropped his head almost to the ground, and then... *something came out of him.* Something we might call a *sound*, but that word falls so far and away from what it really was. This thing – this noise – came from him and crawled across the arena floor and into and up and out of me. It was an awful thing...this *moan*, and it was no ordinary moan. There was *pain* in it. A deep groan came from the inside bottom part of him, and I thought of those "deep moans from the soul" Paul talked about. Shine was letting something go, and whatever it was, it cost the big gray plenty to let it out. Emotion ripped through me, and I almost slid off Buddy. Tears came down my face 'cause I just felt so damn sorry for him. And then there was such a hard and lonely silence.

And in a voice you could barely hear, from Shine's back, the master spoke....

"There! You see? Surrender! *He's considering*

trusting Man again!"

Joy shot through me, and the tears came hard now. Naturally, I didn't want the others to see me, so I hid my face. Peeking over my sunglasses to see if I had been found out, I saw my tears were not the only ones in the line. All the riders had been deeply affected by what was happening. We were witnessing something moving and profound, and something *healing*.

"He's thinking, can you see it?" whispered Craig. "He's thinking about coming back to our world. Something happened to this horse long ago. Maybe something bad, or not so bad, but the horse thought it was bad. He has fear in him, but the fear is less now. Now we will see the 'softening.'"

And on his own, Shine looked at the steer as if seeing him for the first time. He began to amble toward him, trotting loose and easy with his head down in an athletic – almost predatory – position. Craig was right. Suddenly, this horse was soft from head to toe. He loped easily in tight circles, so sure of himself now, and gave Craig the perfect shot time after time with his rope.

A few minutes earlier, the horse wouldn't get within twenty feet of the steer, and now, he rated alongside with perfect precision, giving Craig perfect shot after perfect shot. He roped the steer once, twice, three times, and each time, Craig snapped his slack, and the little honda cracked like a .22 when he popped the loop, and then, again and again. And smiles began to show up on each face down the line, and soft laughter came as well. And Allan's son, the ten-year-old third grader at the end, the youngest in the school began to clap softly, and in just a moment, everyone in the line joined in muted applause for the master and old Shine. The big gray flipped his head happily and breathed a huge sigh, releasing all that tension that had made him so sick. So clearly now, the horse was doing what the Lord had made him to do in the first place…to help man catch an old cow, and you could see in his face the thing called *joy*. The child inside was laughing.

Then that gentle Oklahoma wind blew through me and took every desire I ever had to rope on Shine and carried them all to the far blue mountains visible in the north. "I don't need to rope on him, Lord," I said to the wind. "I'll trade all my tomorrows with this horse if You will just keep him like this. I just don't want him to be afraid anymore."

Craig pulled him to an easy stop, and Shine exhaled again. "We're done for the day," he said smiling. "Shine thanks you, and I thank you." Shine fell into an easy stride with the other horses as the riders filed out of the arena, and everyone headed for the supper table. I felt like a father who didn't care how his child did at the recital or what kind of grades were made. I felt love.

Later at dinner, Craig had a question for me. "How long do you think it would take me to develop Shine into a finished horse, Michael?" he asked.

"I don't know," I said stammering a little, unsure of myself. "M-m-maybe thirty days, or ninety?" I answered, knowing it wouldn't really take someone like him that long.

"I knew you were going to say that," he said laughing. "Michael, it would take me *years*. It takes years. It takes all the time we have to help them… Michael, it takes a *lifetime*," he said. "They're never finished any more than we are." He took a sip of beer, and then said, "Old Shine is lucky."

"Yeah," I laughed. "He found you."

"No," he said. "He found a horseman. He found you."

"Craig, I'm no horseman, I'm the one who hurt...."

"You have some things to learn like we all do," he said. "But I know you are becoming one."

"How do you know that?" I asked.

"Because," he said, "you knew what old Shine was the first time you ever saw him. You knew in your spirit. Only a horseman could do that."

"But I'm not...."

"Don't degrade my roping partner," he snapped, and he was not kidding. "We can never grow and improve if we deny our ability. When I tell you something good about you, just look me square in the eye, and say, 'Thank you. I work hard on that, and it means a lot coming from you.' Got it?"

"Yessir, I got it," I said trying to remember something anyone ever said that made me feel that good. Then I gave up. Couldn't remember.

"There's one more thing," Craig continued. "Michael, something happened here today. Something good. The incident we witnessed today somehow helped 'crack the crust' around Shine's mind. I think he had just as much to do with it as we did."

"What do you mean 'cracked the crust'?"

"Horses are like people. They develop coping strategies to deal with life, particularly to deal with painful events. Some people interpret that as misbehavior on their part, but it's not. Horses don't like confrontation. They want to cooperate; horses are looking for the 'answer' to what we want. At any rate, I want you to be aware of something."

"And what is that?"

"After what happened today, it would be easy for you to think all Shine's bad days are behind him, and so are yours. Something good did happen, but your work is not done. We saw a 'softening' in Shine's mind today, but that one step forward – that gain – can be swept away and erased if you assume he's 'arrived.' He has not. You've helped this horse a great deal. If you continue to do what you are doing –that is, taking your time - he will become softer and softer…more cooperative, more willing. But remember the things you've learned that helped him. There is no place for rushing and no place for force. No timetable, no certain date by which he must be ready. The horse will be ready when he's ready."

"I understand," I said, realizing had he not cautioned me about pushing Shine too fast; most likely I would have done exactly that.

"And I need to tell you," he said smiling, "I think your wait will be worthwhile. After riding him and feeling him, I think if you continue what you're doing, in time, he will be the best one you ever swung a leg over. And not just you…he might become the best one a lot of people ever swung a leg over." And then Craig added a line I didn't know I would remember, "Remember, Michael, the horse is never finished, and neither are we. The work is never done."

And once again, Shine and I made our way home. On the way, I realized I could never repay Craig Hamilton for cracking the crust on Shine and on me. He could have brushed me away. Instead he gave both Shine and me all he had. Of course that's what great horseman do. After that day, Shine was never the same. He began to change - and so did I.

Late that night, I went to the barn and stood in the stall to keep him company while he had his dinner. *"How you doin'?"* I asked. He looked at me for time, chewing. Then he took a deep breath and sighed, **"I'm better. That man helped me."**

"Me too," I said, burying my nose in his neck, smelling his clean smell.

"Me too."

"Your horse can't be any better than you are as a person."

Craig Hamilton - Horseman

Craig Hamilton

Chapter Ten

LET IT SHINE, SHINE

Every day would not be perfect in the coming months, but some were close. Seems now thinking back, we spent an endless time in my arena on the hill. And my only objective during that period was to make each session as soft as possible for my partner. I still wanted him to rope, but now I had another concern of even more importance - I wanted to help him be rid of his fear. Roping took a back seat to the condition of his mind.

"You're doing it."

Shine could still be nervous and flighty at times, but gradually, I learned more and more to execute what seemed small behaviors on my part to "decompress" him just a bit. I searched daily for some invisible valve on his body or in his mind to relieve the intense pressure he generated inside. And I found a few.

As he became more accustomed to pressure in the box – at least somewhat more accustomed – we continued to track and rope slower steers, mixing in an occasional faster one from time to time. Shine's mind held together and so did mine. While we had an occasional disagreement, not one was as severe or damaging to us both as the "black time." The growing trust was real and holding. After a longer period than I anticipated of course – a special day came.

My original thirty days had now stretched past thirty months. On Christmas Eve morning - almost the end of the third year - I saddled the horses and began our routine. We all warmed up, and Blue ran and scored his customary ten head. Old Buddy completed his practice as usual with not a single misstep, and then I mounted Shine.

Somewhere during the middle of his practice segment, I became aware of his calmness. The big horse hadn't fought me once, had tracked every steer with restrained perfection, and exhaled loudly after each one. And more importantly, when each run was done, he ambled back to the head box in no hurry, and with no tension for the entire length of the arena.

"We'd all be Clever Hans if given the chance."

--Shine

I realized this was not the first day he had done so. I quit the practice session and rode Shine to the top of the hill at the north end of my pen.

Standing just outside was a fellow who works on our farm. He's a massive blackjack oak, shaped with such a perfect symmetry only the Divine could have painted him. Wallace – that's his name, Wallace - has three duties here, one being to hold up an old wooden swing, another to provide shade in the summer for the horses, and finally, to just look beautiful. Does all

three really well. Every time I look at him now, he
reminds me of that Christmas Eve day. Standing up
on that hill with Shine, the one we could see for miles
from, I said, *"Shine...?"*

He was staring at something to the far north. I
noticed my neighbor, Harold McBrayer on his tractor in
the far pasture. Shine liked Harold.

"Shine? Are you ready?" I asked him. *"Shine, I
think you might be ready?"*

"Maybe," he said. **"If it's not too bad."**
Best Christmas Eve I ever had.

Wallace & The Dairy Queens

Michael Johnson

The Jackpot

Shine had been hauled many miles. I knew that because I actually kept a running total in my head. Shine, Buddy, and Blue all showed over 15,000 miles on their trailer-time horse odometer and had seen and smelled just about every sight and sound possible to experience. Semis, street sweepers, kids on scooters, banners, trash sacks, loud speakers, and bad drunk cowboys had all scared the bejeebers out of the three of them at one time or another, and all of them had helped the boys learn the rules of the rodeo world. In the process, they were becoming experienced road warriors.

Shine had actually already been to a number of jackpots, team ropings, and rodeos, and even competed in a few. But I had never asked him to be my Number One at any of them. I had only roped one or two steers on him now and then, just to see how he might handle his surroundings, and on most of those occasions, he was just too nervous to function, and on some, did surprisingly well. Now at this point in his progression, and with my nervous indecision just as shaky as his, I planned to enter a jackpot in the mountains and ask Shine to carry his load. The roping was certainly not the big time by any means, but if you live where my three amigos and I do – in Oklahoma – you learn pretty quickly that winning money roping in this state is not the easiest thing in the world to do. Okies can do two things well...raise hell, and rope like it.

I had no intention of running Shine ragged, but I did plan for the first time to ask him to rope in a regular rotation with my other two horses. At such events known as 'jackpots,' the roper is allowed to enter a good number of times as long as each entry is with a different heeler. By being able to head for several different partners – and if my entry fee money held out, always a concern – I planned on riding all three of the boys, and entering perhaps a dozen to fifteen times.

That would mean a minimum of twelve to fifteen runs divided equally among the three horses and that Shine would be asked to rope perhaps four to five steers - maybe more. More because if Shine and my partner were successful on the first steer, then we would be allowed to rope in the "second go." And if successful at that – if we caught the steer – we would make the "third go-round," eventually hoping to make it to the fourth round or "Short Go"…where the money is. Unlike most such events which are run consecutively - that is, different numbered ropings are usually run at the same time - this venue's format called for the 9 roping to be run first – Buddy would be my horse. The 7 would be next – ride Baby Blue – and finally, the easier, slower cattle filled No. 5 roping – and that's where the Shine Man came in.

I found partners easily for Little Blue and Buddy in the 9 and 7 ropings, 'cause while my associates are not too crazy about the way I rope, they do like those two horses. But after asking several heelers about roping with Shine….

"Uh…Shine? The big gray of yours? Well…uh, oh, would you look at that! Sorry, Michael, I can handle runs with Buddy and Blue, but after that…uh… hey, I'm full! It's not the horse; it's that my money is gone. You know, nothing against your horse."

Some were just a wee bit more forthright. "I ain't

heeling behind Shine! No way, Jose! I seen him drag steers through the fence. I'll heel for you if you head on Blue, but that's it!" Eight turn downs, I think. Asking these heelers to rope behind Shine made me feel like Truman Capote walking up to a big cowboy roper, and asking, *"Would you like to slthow dance just one time?"*

Being a man who writes and sells books for a living - none of which unfortunately are **Gone With The Wind** - and being a cowboy never deterred by such small matters as "Hell no! I ain't doin' it. Forget it!" I know something about rejection. So I simply returned to the front of the line and asked them all again. And this time, proving that perseverance truly does pay…three of eight who initially declined said yes, provided I would pay their entry fee as well as my own, and indicating they were committing to only one dance with Truman. And if I'm honest, what really swung the tide in Shine's favor probably included some vague promises about beer. Much like Blanche Dubois, I sold my very soul – like any roper worth his or her salt will do for just one more run - and paid for three heelers who roped at a level just below Martha Stewart. And then this kid comes up.

"Uh…Mr. Mike?" (I hate it when they call me that.) "They said you were looking for one more run on Shine. I'd be honored to heel for you if you would have me."

"Well, Billy Joe," I said, stalling for time because he was just a kid, and besides that, a kid who didn't rope all that well, and….

"If you're full or don't want to, it's fine," he said quietly, and then he looked away. "I know I don't rope as well as these guys," he said. "It's just that I'm havin' a little trouble finding a partner." And his voice trailed off.

"Can you count the times you have been that kid?" the voice said. **"When you were starting, how many times did you stand on the first tee hoping someone would let you join their group? How many people have turned you down in life, and how did you feel every single time? How many ropings have you...."** *"Okay, Okay!"*

"Billy Joe," I said as he was walking away. "I was just going to say I'm the one who would be honored to rope with you, and if you'll heel for me, I'll even pay your side."

"No you won't, Mr. Mike!" he almost shouted grinning from ear to ear. "I have my own money. I'll go get my horse!" Minutes later I heard him yelling to his nineteen-year old sweetheart, "I'm entered! I gotta' run with Mr. Mike!"

I hate it when they call me that.

The roping was underway, and I began with Buddy because when you rope on Buddy, you can forget about him. The mark of the good one is you don't have to think about the horse at all. All your focus, energy, and concentration can be directed the same place a ten-year-old with a magnifying glass focuses his on a hot summer day - when his only goal in life is to set an ant's butt on fire with the sun's rays. If you're thinking right, you can focus that heat on a spot about the size of a dime found at the base of the steer's left horn. It's a Zen thing. The world stops revolving, comes to a stop, fades away, and ceases to exist. The only thing in the Universe is that dime embedded at the base of the steer's left horn.

Sometimes I can keep my mental crosshairs focused on that dime pretty well, as long as my horse doesn't slow down, speed up, go right, go left, fall down, stumble, or think about when he wasn't a gelding. When he doesn't think about any other single thing except that steer ...and if he doesn't buck. See how many things can take your mind off that dime? Buddy's great strength was that he would let you think about that dime. Because you could be sure Buddy would take care of business, and everything else. The old Leo horse had thundered after thousands, and nothing fazed him.

Heeler missed in the second round. Seen one heeler, you've seen'em all.

When the 7 Roping started, The Blue Man was ready. The Blue Man was born ready. This colt came ready when his momma laid him on the earth. If Baby Blue had arms, he'd saddle himself. I tracked steers on Shine for eight months before he ever saw one. The third steer I ever chased on Blue, he ran over and bit him on the butt. This boy has the best attitude of any horse ever made in Heaven. And so many times, I had the thought, *"If only I could put Shine's ability in the blue colt's mind."*

"Whad you say, Daddy? You wanna put dat messed up, cwanky ass, pooty pants in my mind? I know! I know! You makin' a joke, Daddy! My Daddy tella bes' jokes and dassa good one! He gon' put old Bony Butt's mind inna Boo Man. Dassa good one, Daddy.

I got one! I got one! Shine's butt's so bony, you could dip it inna inkwell and wite somebody a letter widdit! Dassa good one

too, ain't it Daddy?

Now les'us go wope dem cows. Ain't no cow here out run da Boo Man, cause my daddy says I'ma bad motascoota. I'm...."

"Blue! Calm down, son," I scolded him for being all prancy, but I knew what his problem was. If there was ever a living creature that loved his work, The Blue Man was that living thing. He lived for two things...to rope, and to be with me. Since he had the two things in life that gave him joy, he was just happy. Riding into the box, I thought, *"You know, I never get on him much about anything no matter what he does, 'cause I know him. I know he's just excited and rearing to go. Maybe I'm a little too hard on Shine."*

"Maybe? Ya' think maybe?"

--Shine

With a flawless Blue under me, we made the third round in good shape. We were 18.0 on two, a long way from the lead, but we had caught two with two more still to come. If we could just be what ropers call "clean," – catch head and heels – on two more, four caught steers in most all ropings is akin to having four tens in a poker game. You may not win every time, but your odds are really sweet. Still on Blue in the third round, I "soft-balled" the best steer at the roping. My loop hit him in the back of the head – not that the steer noticed. My rope slithered down his side with the force of a deviled egg. *"Either throw your rope with authority, or don't rope,"* Darrell growled from his customary coach's box position in my mind. *"Either*

*commit to rope the steer, or don't go to the roping.
Give it your best effort every time or stay home."* I
had heard him say that so many times, I didn't need his
physical presence to remind me…he was always with
me. Darrell was with me at every roping whether his
body made the trip or not. *"So why do I keep making
the same mistake?"* I asked him. And Darrell answered
from inside.

*"Human being. We all make mistakes. Use them.
Channel the anger. Stay off your 'self.' For the rest
of the day if you miss, at least knock the steer's horn
completely off with pure force. Use the mistake to
win!"* Got it, coach. I unsaddled Blue, and headed for
Shine.

With four steers left, my chances were slim. I
began to focus less on my performance and potential
winnings, instead shifting my concentration to what
might help my horse. **"You're doing it."** As I loped
Shine around the pen to warm him up while the arena
was being dragged between rounds, I assessed his
mental state. He seemed "neutral." I had seen him
calmer, and I had certainly seen him more agitated.
Loping along, he turned his head left and right,
looking at the pretty girls and old men in lawn chairs
just outside the arena, snorted a bit here and there,
but "basket-case" would have been an inappropriate
diagnosis. If Blue had done the same, I would have
paid no attention.

**"Oh yeah, but Blue can do no wrong. The
horse you admit is at best 'mediocre,' and his
only real strength is he doesn't believe that… is
Mr. Perfect. He's the 'teacher's pet,' …and I use**

that word 'teacher' loosely."

--Shine

When they called my name for our first steer in
the final roping of the day, like Jeremy and Shine
were prone to do, I jumped. Not with fear, but with
excitement. I truly wondered if all my time with the
superb horse I thought him to be was worth ...well, I
just wondered. Trying to relax my butt, legs, hands,
and mind, I rode the big gray into the box, and of
course, like all temperamental artists...he didn't like it.

Earlier, I had paid no attention to the back "butt
bar" in the box on Buddy and Blue – because being
normal people who aren't impossible to please - they
didn't either. But because Shine curled his neck and
stared at it, I saw this particular butt bar was much
lower than any he had seen before. And I heard Shine
say, **"I don't like that. That bar will hit me on
the hocks when I leave. I don't think so."** I knew
we were in trouble when he refused to take his eyes off
it. I tried reasoning with him.

"Well," I said. *"I think the man who built this
arena years ago did this to you deliberately. It's a
personal thing directed at you. And while I'm pretty
sure about that, I know the 200 plus ropers here have
nothing on their mind but how you feel."*

"Be that as it may," he said, **"I'm not leaving
here. I'm not turning around."**

"Then we will just turn the steer out."

"Fine. Turn him out," said Shine.

Shine refused to turn and face the steer, and after
three calls from the announcer... "Michael Johnson,
first call...Michael Johnson, second call..., Michael

223

Johnson, third call…" the chute man smiled and shrugged his shoulders.

Offering me an unspoken apology with a look that said, *"Sorry, I'm just doin' my job,"* he opened the gate as he was supposed to do, and the second best steer at the gathering loped off down the arena - running dead straight - without a care in the world. That's when I looked over at my heeler and realized it was "Mr. Christian Counselor"…old Frank himself.

I rode Shine out of the box, (who now of course, had decided to handle like a Mercedes) looking for some area of the arena with enough room for only one horse so Frank couldn't make a counseling call. Couldn't find it. He rode up beside me.

"Michael…son…" he began. *"Michael, what is the matter with you?"*

"He's just nervous, Frank," I said. "It's no big loss to you. You said you didn't want to rope with me, and the only reason you did was because I paid your side. Didn't cost you a penny."

"It's not about the money, Michael," he said, with words devoid of any ring a'tall. And with this "John Wayney" gravel in his voice, says, "Why are you doing this?"

About to reply, I heard, **"He's wrong. You're right."** Not mentioning that auditory hallucination, I said, "That's a good question, Frank. I'm not sure about that. It's just that…."

"Michael, listen to me. You rope good…well, sometimes you rope good. Why in the world – especially when you have two good horses – do you continue with this *crazy* horse?"

And I said what had become my mantra. I said it so many times even *I* was tired of hearing it. And I said the words again, the same words I had said so many times, "He's not crazy, Frank. He's afraid."

"How many cows you run on him now, Michael?" he snapped. "Five hunnert? A thousand? And after all that time, you take him to a dinky little jackpot, and he won't even come out of the box? Or can't come out of the box 'cause he's a mental case? Crazy, afraid? What's the difference? We both know you won't have him six months from now. *Why are you doing this?*"

I looked down at Shine. His head was hanging low and relaxed. I thought about killing him again for making us both look like fools in front of five hundred people, and then I thought about how much I loved him. And then I thought about Esther.

"...And who knows but that you have come to royal position for such a time as this?"

--Esther 4:14

Which translates to cowboys as "Who knows? Maybe this is what He sent me for."

Instead of all that, I just said, "It's a long story, Frank."

Frank stared hard for a long time and finally said, "I'm done with you," and rode away. My first thought was we still had three more steers.

Some time later, I heard my name called again. I rode Shine into the box without much hope and very little in the way of expectations. He was "sticky" and didn't want to turn and face the steer. I didn't get mad. I stayed relaxed remembering the horseman's words, *"...your work is not done,"* and to Shine, I said, *"If you*

225

don't want to, you don't have to. We'll just turn this one out too. But you will be required to take your turn. We all have to sooner or later."

And Shine didn't turn. With a resigned sigh, and knowing I had yet another disappointment to deal with, one more failure in so long a line, and even though no horseman in the world would have told me I should, I nodded for the steer facing west with Shine facing south. The gate clanged, and the steer bolted...*and the Shine Man came alive!*

The big jet lifted off baby smooth, and with his head down low and stretched out like some Memphis greyhound shot to the steer. He didn't "catch up" to the steer, but rather violated the laws of physics. He didn't "catch up" to the steer, but seemed to make the distance between him and the steer fall into a black hole. At one moment in time, he's hopelessly outrun and the next, I look like Marlin Perkins in a jeep running alongside a giraffe, and all I have to do is snare "Mr. Longneck" with my rope on a stick. Without the slightest conscious thought on my part, the "no-mind" threw my loop, and I was just as surprised as the onlookers to see it settle peacefully around the horns of the third best steer at the roping. When I wrapped my dally – also done without any Miguel awareness - the "big gray train" – God, how I love him - lowered his jet flaps dropping into a smooth long, buttery slow motion slide. He toddled off pulling the steer with effortless power, and the heeler snapped up two feet. Shine pirouetted to face the steer with an easy style and grace, and before I realized what had happened, the announcer said,

"Michael and Billy Joe take the lead with a 7.7 on that one!"

And people say Jesus ain't real.

And on the next three, he pranced, he snorted, he was afraid, he was sticky, and he was out of position each time I called for the steer, and when they came from the chute, he just ate them alive, and we caught them all - and Billy Joe caught them all. When the dust was settled, the announcer's voice crackled, "Here are the results of the Number 5 Roping. Stevens and Phillips win first with 32.0 on four, Mackey and Jenkins second with 32.3 on four, Stoner and Hackney will win third with 39.8 on four, and let's see...*okay, Michael and Billy Joe were 40.0 on four, and that will be good enough for fourth place.*" In Shine's first roping, the first time I asked him to carry an equal share of the load, we had won *$600 dollars!*

"$572.00 actually."

--Shine

227

Let me see here…how to describe that moment.
Hmmm…would "happy" be the word? No, happy
wouldn't quite be the word. What would be a word that
meant….

"Get in my truck, roll all the windows up, lie
down in the back seat, and scream with joy for ten full
minutes, kicking the ceiling so hard the dents would
still be there on judgment day?" Is there one word for
that feeling? If there is, that's the word I would have
used that day at that moment. But I didn't do that.

I just unsaddled the horses, tied them to the trailer,
and stood by the bed of my pick-up looking real cool,
and waited for all – and I'm talking about *all* of them
– to come by and say, "Wow, congratulations," or
"Well, you were right about Old Shine all the time," or
"Good job, Miguel, you really roped good…and your
horse worked good too." Yep, there I was just standing
by my truck with my hat pushed back on my head like
Audie used to do. I was working really hard on trying
to strike a pose that looked like I had something else
on my mind. Maybe like I was thinking about buying
two hundred head of steers or putting some big land
deal together, and when they came up to talk, I had all
my answers prepared… *"Uh? Oh, the roping…yeah,
thanks. I think we did place."* Or maybe, *"What? Did
we win fourth? Well, I'll be darned, I didn't realize
that. Thanks, Jim. You roped well too."*

And I had lots of other answers too, and every one
of them was worded just perfectly to communicate that
we had been in this end zone so many times we didn't
need to spike the ball. We just handed it to the referee
real cool like.

So I just stood there until a little past dark. That

was when I began to realize that no one had come by in the last two hours, and since the pasture was completely empty of all trailers, horses, and ropers, and no one had said a word to me, and none even waved good-bye, I decided it was time to load up and head on home. They would probably call later - yeah, that was it. Bet I would have like ten messages on my phone – maybe even twenty.

The fact that not a single person said one word didn't faze me in the least because all the way home, I just pretended they did, and that was much more fun. As a matter of fact since they said nicer things in my imagination than they ever would have in real life, and my answers were just so cool, it was even better.

"Yeah, I've been working with him, and we've both come along a little."

"Hey, you're being too modest, Miguel. You roped great, and that horse...well, I tell you, son, that horse is something."

"Darn, Fred, you're gonna' make me get the big head here."

"No, no, really...just magnificent. Just a pleasure to watch...."

"Well, thanks. We did draw some good steers, and that was part of...."

"Fourth? Fourth at your first rodeo on Sbine? Anybody would be so proud."

All the way home, people just kept popping up over there in passenger seat. So many in fact, when I finally made it home, I had to sit in the truck for about thirty minutes by myself 'cause I couldn't leave. People just kept coming by. Women were crying, little kids were asking, *"Can I pet the great Shine, Mr. Mike?"*

What was I gonna do? Get out of the truck and just leave them in there talking?

Hey…Champions don't act like that!

After the adrenaline subsided – there were tubs of it – I pondered Shine's next move. We returned to our home field where stress was at its lowest, loping after the dairy queens for days. I could tell it did him a world of good. But I still didn't know where to physically go next. *"Where is the place that would help him the most?"* I asked myself and thought about how different that concern was from when he first came into my life. In those days, I would have never considered his needs. Because I was evil? Not exactly. I was never guilty of being mean to him, but I was guilty. Guilty of not asking him how he felt about the whole thing, and the reason I was is because of what Morris taught me.

> *"It just never occurred to us."*
>
> *--Morris McCarty*

Now I thought about what he needed and wanted – what would lessen his fear – more than my own desires. ***"Now you're doing it."***

I just forgot for a moment I had also already been taught what to do when I didn't know what to do next in life. The answer had found me. Joe Charbonneau had told me long ago, *"There's no need to worry about what to do next,"* he had said. *"Whatever question you pose to the Universe, the answer will come…if you don't press."*

Riding Old Shine around our arena real slow day after day during that period of waiting, I found my first

experience of what "not pressing" meant. Before, I had
always been really good at that "pressing" thing. Such
an ineffective method. When something important
is happening in your life, and you don't know what
to do, "waiting" is so much better than "pressing." It
wasn't wisdom on my part that caused the change in my
behavior - it was love.

Love for this horse caused me to know at some deep
level that waiting was actually a pro-active state. So,
I waited, and because I was quiet and didn't press...
because I waited, I remembered something else Mr. Joe
had said. *"When we don't know where to go or what
to do in life, there's no need to worry. Life will come
along and show us the way."*

**"Most of the time, whether we want to go or
not."**

--Shine

The Cowtown Coliseum

Did you ever dream a little dream? Did you ever
have a "tug" on your spirit that just wouldn't let you
go? I had one, and like we often do with little dreams, I
put it off. Didn't have the time, didn't have the money
– too many things to do. But little dreams have a way
of hanging around on the corners of our mind, just
standing there smiling. And if we listen, if we will be
still and listen, little dreams keep calling to us. *"Come
on,"* whispers our spirit, *"come this way and do this
thing. You know you always wanted to...come on!"*
And someday - someday we say – we are going to, but
we just never get around to actually doing the thing. So

it was with the Fort Worth Rodeo.

The first time I ever laid my eyes on the Cowtown Coliseum, I fell in love. It was after all, located in one of the finest cities in the world, Fort Worth, Texas. Fort Worth, home of the Texas Christian University Horned Frogs, home of one of the few human beings who could strike a golf ball with clear purity and pristine perfection, the place where Ben Hogan lived. The place where Slingin' Sammy Baugh, great Texas calf-roper and legendary quarterback, filled the air with footballs on Saturday afternoons in the glory days of the Southwest Conference. The food at Joe T. Garcia's and Angelo's Barbeque is world class, and after eating far too much of that delicious fare, you can walk down to Ryon's or Leddy's, and find the best western tack and apparel anywhere. Billy Bob's claims to be the world's largest honky-tonk and has the best bull-riding actually inside any beer joint I've ever been to, and it's all in the Stockyards.

The Fort Worth Stockyards sit where the cattle drives came to town over a hundred years ago, and 'til this day, you cannot walk down those old cobblestone streets without thinking the herd is about to run over you. Street musicians, shops, restaurants, and some of the nicest people in the world live and work in the Fort Worth Stockyards, the place where Will Rogers and Teddy Roosevelt came - home of the Cowtown Coliseum, the oldest covered arena in Texas.

If Spielberg or the Disney folks are ever commissioned to do a rodeo movie, to capture the real sights, sounds, smells, and magic of the thing called *rodeo*, I promise you that movie will be filmed in the Cowtown Coliseum. It looks like a Shakespearean stage with brightly lit sets decorated just perfectly to thrill crowds cheerin' for cowboys riding broncs and cowgirls racing around chasin' cans. So many memories there.

She was about twenty. The color of her hair was a perfect match for the red roan she rode. She flew around the barrels, and my, my, did she sit him well. After her run, with a little awe in my voice, I said, "You ride your horse so well."

"Yeah," she laughed flipping that roan hair out of her face. "I ride 'im like I stole him, don't I?" Twenty years ago now. Never saw her again. Still love her.

Standing there thinking about all that, and someone said, "The cutting is about to start over at the Will Rogers... time to go."

As we were filing out, I turned to look at it all just once more. No matter how many times I had done that in the past, just couldn't get enough. The ceiling, the stands, the lights playing on the bucking chutes – just drinking it all in thinking, "Lord, don't let this be the last time," and the little voice said, **"Someday we'll bring Shine here and rope."**

"Yes," I said. "Yes, that's a dream of mine."

That moment became a running joke in my life. At least, once every couple of weeks, someone would ask, "When are we going to Fort Worth?"

"Pretty soon," I would reply. "Pretty soon I'm taking Old Shine out there to the Cowtown Coliseum, and you heel for me, okay?" And then I'd stand there and tell them about that special place in the heart of the Stockyards until they claimed they had to go home. And as they were driving away, I would still be talking, and my last words were always, "It's the oldest covered arena in Texas, you know!"

But you know how it is with dreams. There's just so much to do, and money is always a concern. Besides the horse was never ready, and it was such a long way, and…the days went by, and Shine and I slow-loped after the dairy queens. Then I found myself at Dan's funeral.

Darrell is my traveling partner, and amigo. Dan was his brother-in-law. Dan served his country for twenty-eight years, was a much-decorated soldier in Vietnam, and everybody liked Dan. We had so many good times together. On one occasion, he cooked a burger for me at his trailer at a horse sale in Wyoming. I still wake up in the night thinking about that burger. Best one I ever had.

We laughed about that many times. Pictures of fishing trips, cook-outs, and travels all over the country decorate Sharon and Darrell's home, and in most, there stand Dan and his wife, Barb, taking care of all the guests.

They came from Arizona during Christmas, and after an evening at Darrell's, the next night, I had everyone up to the farm for barbeque. We relived old times like we always did, told the same stories all the wives had heard so many times, and I remember feeling grateful that so many wonderful people have chosen to come into my life. A few days later, we received the news that Dan's brain cancer had returned. In a few weeks, Dan passed away.

I went to the funeral to honor Dan and to be with my friends, Darrell, Sharon, Barb, and Dan's mother, Harriet. The loss, while expected to some degree – no matter how expected, never helps does it – was still

painful to bear. As I sat on the old pew in the little
Methodist Church in the country, the realization came
clearly that life passes so quickly. Just yesterday it
seemed Dan was cooking the world's best burger. In
actual time, it was more like three years ago, but I could
still remember every detail of that soft Wyoming
summer evening.

We went by Darrell's after the service to toast a man
that had served with honor and protected us all for
almost three decades. Later at home, I sat in my barn
looking at the moon, thinking about how important it is
to live our lives, how short our time is, and how grateful
we should be for green grass, clear water, good friends,
and good horses. And just before I dozed off in the
chair, I realized I knew the next place to take Old Shine.
Life had told me.

**"Can I go, Daddy? Will ya taka Boo Man?
Daddy? Daddy? Whassa matta wid him,
Unca Buddy?"**

"He's asleep, son. He had a hard day," said
Buddy. **"Let him alone now, and don't worry --
he'll take you too. You know your daddy don't
go nowhere without you."**

A few days later, three trucks and trailers filled with
horses were bound for that place where they say The
West begins - Fort Worth, Texas. Shine, The Blue Man,
and I were in the lead; Darrell, Sharon, his sister Pat
and husband Mike in the middle; and following behind,
great tripper from Arkansas - my heeler - Johnny
Stevens, and his wife, Paula.

Walking Shine and Blue down the cobblestone
streets right in the middle of old downtown, all I could

235

think was, *"Lord, I love this place!"* Tourists everywhere from England, Germany, Japan, and Czechoslovakia - all with cameras clamoring for a picture of a cowboy and his horse.

"You holda camra, cowboy? Take a pitcha me and wife wit' you pretty hoss?"

And a few steps later, another stopped me with, "I say, old man, we're from England; my name is Hobart Merriwether, and I must say you look smashing. We've never ac-chew-ally been this close to a buckaroo before. How about a picture for me and the missus? Maggie, my dear, the boys back home in the pub will never believe this! Saaayyy…you're not by chance in the 'ro-day-o' are you?"

"Yes," I laughed. "We're in the event called team roping in tonight's performance."

"Best part of the trip, Maggie!" he thundered. "Best bloody part of the trip!"

"Best part. Best part," Maggie tittered, holding her hand over her mouth.

"If you are coming to the show," I said still laughing, "let me tell you how we say that word."

"Oh, I would be so grateful, my good man. Do tell me, old chap."

"Okay, it's 'Ro-dee-o,'" I said growling.

"Is it necessary to make that guttural sound with it?" he asked.

"Absolutely!" I said.

"Do let me try it," he said, bending his knees slightly. And then… "RO-DEE-O!"

"I think you've got it!" I said with real surprise in my voice. "By George, I think *you've got it!"*

"I THINK SO TOO!" he screamed. "Maggie, the

cell phone…hurry! I'm calling the boys in the pub!"
Lord, I love this town.~

Once we arrived at the old mule barn, the stable
manager, an old Mexican man, showed us where the
horses would be stabled. Standing in the stall with
Shine, I felt him pulling and rooting on his halter for
some of the leftover hay in the manger.

"Is this fresh?" I asked him.

"No habla Engles, senor," he smiled.

"Esta' pastura está fresca?" I asked pointing.

"Si, es okay por tu caballo," he said, rubbing
Shine's neck, and smiling. I noticed Shine looking at
him, and I thought that was a good sign. Shine rarely
liked humans, but this old man seemed to have a
calming effect on him, and I was so grateful for that.

"Es un buen caballo…muy precioso," he said
looking at me, him with his old rheumy eyes.

"Si, yo se," I said.

"Yo sabo," he said, smiling again.

I thought that was odd too. How did he know I
thought Shine was precious?

After a bit more small talk, I knew the Shine Man
and my Blue were in good hands with the old
gentleman. "Cuida mi caballos," I said.

"Si, no le hace, Miguel," he smiled.

With that primary concern out of the way, my
attention turned the same serious matters any cowboy
would have the night before the rodeo such as, "How
far is the Stockyards Hotel Bar from here?" And if
you're one of those who look down your nose at such
base behavior, I can tell you why you disapprove…
because you have never been to the Stockyards Hotel
Bar. That's why.

We found it of course – hated to have been the one who tried to stop us from doing so. Seated around the table with friends, I thought about another line C. S. Lewis had penned long ago that described perfectly how I felt at that moment…"There's nothing like sitting around the fire with a glass of port with Christian friends."

That's what we were doing at the moment, except for the fact that beer was being substituted for the port, but I knew what he meant. "Good point, Clive Staples," I thought to myself calling him by both names – like Southern people do – and particularly so after a few beers. Sitting there with my friends, I felt like we were all part of some expectant mountain climbing team gathered to plan tomorrow's ascent. The others were involved in an animated discussion concerning strategy for the next evening's competition. Worries over the short arena, fast cows, and time required to win danced back and forth across the table, occasionally spilling one of the longnecks. Such small matters never deter real cowboys. And for once in my life, I sat there not talking, but just remembering there was no place like Fort Worth, no place like the Stockyards, and no place like this bar. The bar stools aren't even stools, but saddles for goodness sake, and life size buffalo that were running so fast when they crashed into the wall, now only their butt is sticking out …right above the bar. So you tell me…is it me or is it that bar? And for all the fun I was having, I kept thinking about that old man and how Shine seemed to be so comfortable around him. So unlike Shine, and then I remembered, I had forgotten to ask him his name…and how did he know mine?

"Bandy? Bandy Shine?" the old man whispered.

Shine turned to see the stable hand just on the other side of his stall half door, and raising his head, pricked his ears forward. *"Manuel? Is that you?"*

"Es me, amigo. Comó esta?" said the old man, smiling.

"I'm okay, I guess. What on earth are you doin' here?"

"Told you, bro, I'd always be with you. So how you doin'?"

"I'm good. Hay was good. Fresh. I liked it. Bit a chicken on the butt hidin' in it, scared me half to death."

"I know…," laughed Manuel. **"That's Polly. She hangs around the barn here. I told her to hide in the hay. "Couldn't resist since I knew you were coming. She said tell you I put her up to it."** And then Manuel's countenance changed. **"How you doin' Bandy Shine?"** he asked for the third time.

After thinking for a time, Shine said, *"I'm okay, I guess."*

"Miguel bein' good to you?" he asked.

Shine looked beyond Manuel at the cowboys riding past on the street in the dusky twilight just outside. Manuel knew Shine would find answering that question to be difficult. **"Considering his 'trust' issues,"** Manuel thought to himself waiting.

Since horses can't lie, at last Shine said, *"Yes, he's been good to me."*

"Good," said Manuel smiling.

"How'd you know we were gonna be here?" asked Shine, twitching a fly off his back with a single small muscle.

"Tole you, partner, I'd be there helping you. I make it my business to know where my Bandy is. So, what do you think about tomorrow?"

"Being a horse, I don't think much about tomorrow. What about tomorrow?"

"For goodness sake, Bandy, you're at the Cowtown Coliseum. What do you think we're going to do tomorrow night? You're in the show, son. You rope tomorrow night with Miguel, Johnny, and Bailey, the red roan. How do you feel about that? Are you ready?"

Shine's anxiety began to rise, and nervously he said, *"I don't know about that....*

I d-d-don't know if I can handle all this. There's so m-m-any people, and noises, and... depends on the butt bar, and so many...."

"Listen to me, Bandy Shine," said Manuel rubbing Shine's forehead. "Calm down, amigo. We have twenty-four hours, we have plenty of hay and water, Polly will come by and sit on your back, and we'll talk."

"I don't want a chicken on my back, Manuel," sniffed Shine, certain such a thing lacked dignity.

"Okay...okay, she'll just come by and visit. Shine, I need to tell you about the arena and the bar and the barrier."

"Whoa! Hold it! There you go, you're like him...filling up my mind with details, and telling me all sorts of things I don't know, expecting me to remember them, and then getting impatient," said Shine, moving his feet nervously.

"**Shine. Shine,**" Manuel said softly. "**Don't react so negatively. Listen to me. Our dread is always worse than what we are required to face. That's the reason I'm here.**"

"*I-I-I'm not doing this!*" Shine hissed. Manuel realized the horse's control was slipping.

"**Shine!**" Manuel barked. Then quietly said, "**You're not doing your part!**"

His butt now turned to his friend – the ultimate horse insult - Shine remained stubbornly rigid and silent.

"**I can't believe you would turn your butt to me,**" said Manuel with sadness in his voice.

Shine dropped his head and released a long sigh. "*Why am I having to do this?*" he said almost to himself.

Manuel knew when to be sympathetic, and when not to be. Now was not the time. "**Shine!**" he said firmly. "**Turn around and treat me with the same respect I show you!**"

The big gray remained still for a moment, then slowly swung his body with a silky soft grace that belied his twelve hundred pounds and turned to face his friend.

"*What do you mean?*" Shine asked.

"**Even you admit Miguel is trying, Shine. We all know he lacks so much, but he sees that now and has laid his ego aside for you. He cares about you, and he is trying. You said so yourself,**" Manuel paused to let his words sink in.

Shine, with his head hanging low, said nothing.

"**Can you do what he's done?**" asked Manuel. "**He's trying, Shine. Will you do your part and lay your fears aside? Can you help him**

tomorrow night?"

"I don't..." Suddenly Shine stopped, seeing the other... **"Who is that?"**

Manuel turned, looking over his shoulder to see a middle-aged man walking toward them. **"Oh, that's my partner. His first assignment. He had a personal interest and asked if he could come with me. He's okay; we can talk in front of him."**

"Come meet Shine," Manuel said still looking over his shoulder.

As Shine watched his approach, he realized he had seen him before. And as he came alongside Manuel, he said, *"Hello, Shine."*

"I've seen you before," said Shine remembering. **"You're..."**

"Yes, Shine," he laughed. *" I'm Dan."*

The next morning, after checking on and feeding the boys, we hit the Mexican restaurant early for breakfast. Of the too-long-to-list uniquely special things about Fort Worth, the fact that several authentic Mexican restaurants are open for breakfast surely must be in the top three. Scrambled eggs with cayenne peppers, flour tortillas, refried beans, and hot sauce all made their way down each of our gullets, and while Johnny and I planned to exercise the horses, Darrell and Mike Chancy were looking forward to walking around shops and stores in the Stockyards.

After John and I saddled Shine, Blue, and Bailey, his rock hard solid beautiful roan, we headed out of the livery stable, and after only having to cross one busy highway, found ourselves on the Trinity River. The fact that city authorities allow horses to be ridden along that beautiful stretch says as much about that town as any other thing.

Riding Shine and leading Blue by his halter rope – "ponying" it's called - and with Johnny on Bailey, we made our way down the fifteen-mile trail, accompanied by a massive swath of rich green grass, and the Trinity swirling peacefully along at our side. A few great blue herons raised their regal heads, staring with rude surprise at our having interrupted their morning breakfast of tiny shad. And I thought to myself, *"They should have eaten with us."*

None of us talked much on that four-hour ride - Johnny, me, or the horses. We just drank in all the quiet beauty with gratitude, and riding along, I remembered a dream I had long ago. During one of the best times in my life, I had dreamed repeatedly of burying watches, and after puzzling over the meaning of that, the awareness came that I wanted to stop time and spend the rest of my days in this sweet portion of my life. That's the way I felt on the Trinity that day when my friends were with me, and we were all healthy. A time when we had somewhere to go, something to do, and someone to love, and even cowboys know, it just doesn't get much better than that. And Johnny broke all that stillness just by looking at his watch…"We need to head back," he said.

The Thing Called "Rodeo"

I had been sitting on Shine for an eternity. Actually, in real time, more like a little over an hour. The performance had begun promptly at 8 p.m. sharp like all the good ones do. The first events, bareback riding, saddle bronc riding, calf-roping, and barrel racing had gone off without a hitch, but now the clown had a hundred kids in the arena risking their lives for the twenty tied on one calf's button horns. Had a single one broken an arm or leg in that wild melee – truly a highly probable event - that twenty wouldn't have made a dent in the $1,200 the ambulance ride would cost their parents. Such small matters never deter real calf scramblers, and besides, I had a bigger problem than some kid being deformed for life. The team roping was about to start, and I was worried. I had a real problem.

Earlier in the performance, John and I had ridden our horses in with the calf ropers during their event. With our horses standing over to the side with the calf ropers – the great unwashed usually can't tell us apart from calf-ropers - I saw something that made my stomach turn cold. Some thirty minutes later, waiting on Emmet Kelly - who apparently planned on finishing his routine with the kids some time around midnight - I was sitting just outside the back of the arena, and my stomach was even colder. *I had forgotten about the bar and the barrier in the Cowtown Coliseum!*

The little arena in the heart of the Stockyards has charm draped all over it, and one of the most charming aspects involves the head and heel box used for team roping. Very charming indeed to people from England like Hobart and Maggie, whom I now saw sitting in the front row over to my left. Hobart and Maggie wouldn't be so happy if they were contestants and had to actually rope from those charming boxes...which had, in my mind, now become potential death traps.

Directly above the head box – about eighteen inches in fact – is a bar. Not a pipe bar, not a bar made of cold rolled steel, but a bar bar. A bar that sells beer bar. The "roof" as it were, of the head box is the "floor" of the beer bar directly above the roper's head. And when Emmet and the kids made an exit – if they were ever going to – shortly, my head would be a little over a foot from that solid steel floor, and if that wasn't enough, there was something worse. ***"How on earth could you have forgotten that?"*** hissed the little voice.

My hopes and heart fell with a thud on the dirt below me when I saw the cowboys on the chute stretching the rope across the front of the head box…the Halletsville Barrier. How could I have forgotten the little town with so much history of rodeo just east of San Antone? The place where the idea originated to give the roping calf or roping steer a fair shot by allowing them a head start - the place where the "barrier" was born. *"Lord, I'm in trouble here."*

Shine knew all about barriers. He had seen plenty of them. Actually, that was one of his strengths. For all his other issues, Shine never left the box unless you told him to, and if the steer hung a horn on the gate, or stumbled, the slightest check of my hand on the reins would cause Shine to stop instantly. The barrier wasn't the problem. The problem was like all modern day kids, Shine knew all about "electronics," and Shine knew all about electronic barriers – the kind humans and horses couldn't see. But Shine didn't know about Hallettsville Barriers – the kind you could see – the kind made of old fashioned *rope*. *"Lord, I need some help here."*

My stomach was cold because I knew if Shine reared in the slightest, my skull was gonna have a sudden meeting with the bottom of that bar. Then when

I saw the rope barrier going up, and since Shine had never seen one, I knew he would think he had to jump that barrier. When he did, I saw the story in my mind that would appear in the **Fort Worth Star -Telegram** the next day.

"A team roper from Oklahoma was killed during last night's action at the Cowtown Coliseum. Michael Johnson's skull was horribly crushed when his horse reared in terror from the rope barrier used at the oldest covered arena in Texas - because they do things the 'old fashioned way' here – as any idiot would have known. According to his roping partner, great tripper from Arkansas, Johnny Stevens, "He was dead before he hit the ground." Stevens also asked if any one was available to fill in for his dead partner, and rope with him in tonight's performance. He has a really good gray horse you can head on. Interested parties should call 555-2398. And if no one is interested in roping, Stevens commented that he did plan to attend the funeral services for his partner."

"What's the matter? You look pale as a ghost." Johnny said, riding up beside me.

"Huh?…uh, I dunno. You do too, must be the lights. I'm fine."

"You ready?" he asked. "Kids are finally filing out. We'll be up in a minute."

"Ready? Me? I was born ready. Not a care in the world, but…."

"But what?"

"It's just that Shine has never seen a rope barrier, and with that bar over that box, you know…."

"Good Lord!" he said wide eyed. "I see what you mean. If he jumps that barrier, you're…."

"Yeah," I smiled weakly. "I'm in trouble."

"Man," he said, with real concern in his voice. "Okay, I know what to do."

At that moment, I really felt lucky to have Johnny as a friend, because most ropers....

"Here's what we're gonna' do. If Shine does rear - if he does try to jump the barrier – and you do hit your head, *try to get a loop on the steer before you pass out, and that way I can still have heel shot.* And most importantly, we can still have a qualified time - even if you die." And he rode off.

Seen one heeler, you've seen'em all.

Now that we had a plan, I did feel a little better. At long last, I heard the announcer thunder, ***"And now, Ladeeze and Gen-tull-men, a true cowboy event derived from the working ranches of long ago - The Team Roping!"***

I noticed Hobart standing and screaming from the front row like some deranged Chicago Bears fan. He shirt tail was out, and his hair was a mess. Maggie was still seated, fanning herself violently, still tittering with her hand over her mouth, and I could barely make out her words, "Smashing, just so bloody smashing and thrilling!" She snapped so many pictures so fast, I thought her camera had shorted out and was throwing off sparks.

"6.36!" bellowed the announcer.

"What?" I asked Johnny beside me. "What happened?"

"The two kids from Wyoming," he said pointing. I turned to see two flat-bellies riding out of the far end of the arena giving each other high fives.

"They were just a short 6 on their steer. Get your

247

head in the game; we need to rope tough."

Shine didn't seem to be in his normal state of being abnormal. Rather he seemed sort of calm, but he kept looking at the top row of the coliseum, and….

"That's four in a row," Johnny said.

"What?" I asked.

"Those kids first out were 6; now four in a row have been out run. Nobody's thrown a loop since the Wyoming boys. These cattle are blisterin' fast. Get out quick and stick it on him. Don't worry about the ten-second penalty for breaking out, hear me?"

"Y-y-you mean you want me to break out?"

"No, I don't want you to break out. I'm just saying I'd rather you do that than be late. With these cattle, if you're late, we're dead. But even if we break out, and no one else catches, we'll get $500 for second."

"JOHNSON AND STEVENS, OKLAHOMA COWBOYS, NEXT TO GO!"

No time left to think now. No plans to be made. Just do the deed.

Ridin' him in real easy, tried to keep my hands, my butt, and my legs real soft, but most of all, my mind. Big flock of butterflies lifted off the pit of my stomach, and I heard one say, "Can somebody turn up the heat in here?" I love you, Shine Man. I believe in you. Come on now. We need that greatness. I feel him under me, and he's calm - calmer than me in fact - but he's still looking at the top row. Why on earth is he doin' that? Shine? Steer in the chute over here, partner, not the top row. Look this way.

Easy, Shine…one step back…almost…now! I nodded my head. The gate banged, and the steer moved. Wanting him to come smooth, tryin' so hard not to think about my skull, I squeezed his sides like I would a baby bird...and the steer dropped to his knees!

And I had just squeezed the world's most sensitive horse. He couldn't help it. I had told him to move, and when his big wide chest touched that tiny electronic beam, that little shaft of light that you couldn't see screamed like a cruise ship fog horn. The boys at Fort Worth had played it safe...in addition to the rope barrier, they used an electronic one as well. BRRRRRAAAACCCK! We had broken the barrier. Shine stopped like a shot duck.

Then that little demon from hell lying over there on his pseudo-crippled legs turned to us both with a wicked little grin on his face and knew his trick had worked. He knew the big gray was confused, and he knew I was addled. "Works every time," the steer chuckled to himself. "Pretend to fall, they stop, they give up...heh heh." Then he bolted. And without any time ticking off the clock, Shine did too. The steer never gained a single step on him.

Einstein said, "Nothing in the Universe can travel at the speed of light." If Albert roped one steer off the Shine Man, he would say, "Okay...my bad!"

The dirty little steer's once weak and spindly legs had suddenly and miraculously healed, and were now transformed into powerful pistons churning the earth. But he was no match for the thunder rolling right behind him. The big gray train was rolling now. My wits came back somewhere around the middle of the arena, and my focus had that horn wrap buckle smoking, and just as it was about to burst into flames, the force of my loop coming tight around the horns cut off all oxygen. And I heard him coming...HERE'S JOHNNY!

They came around the corner – him and that good
roan – like two crusading knights mad as hell they
hadn't found the Holy Grail, but had just spied it!
And that precious relic was inside the devil's own.
What blasphemy! Bailey's eyes were black shiny
steel, and Johnny's heel loop sounded like a chopper
on a bad day in Nam. With enough force to slice a
four-inch oak sapling clean and level with the
ground, his loop hit that steer in the hock so hard,
this time he really did stumble, but not before John
pantyhosed him - and when he wrapped his dally,
Shine spun like cotton candy on a stick, and the deed
was done.

"8 POINT ZERO FOUR!" boomed the announcer.
"Uh oh!" he added. "Got some bad news for the
Oklahoma boys. Looks like Michael left a little early."

"Thanks for pointin' that out, you Chuck Barris,
Gong Show-looking fat..."

"We'll add ten to that eight for a total time of 18.04
for you boys. Tough luck, but you're still sittin' second
right now."

The little brown motley steer struggled to his feet
and limped off holding his back right leg off the
ground. Just before he went in the stripping chute, he
turned looking back over his withers, and gave Shine
and me one more little evil grin. I rode Shine out the
back of the arena, through the alley, and out under the
clear night sky. I was shaking all over.

Fear drained out, tension spilled on the ground, and
Shine let his out too. I slithered off the side of him, and
put my arms around him, and held his head. For once
he didn't pull away. Letting out a huge sigh of relief,
he just stood there with me for a while. I felt

disappointment for a fleeting time, crushed that I had
ruined our chances by breaking out. Wasn't his fault.
"I tried to stop," he said.
"Oh, Shine..." I squeezed him tighter. *"It wasn't
you. It was me. I cued you to go."*
"But I didn't know he was gonna fall down,"
he said. **"Maybe I ...."**
*"No, no, son, that's just rodeo. We have to draw
good. Just forget about it. You did so wonder...."*
And the announcer's voice came from far away
floating over those old bricks in that town I love. His
words came crawling over those old wooden fences that
had been there so long behind the Cowtown Coliseum -
the oldest covered arena in Texas, you know. I had felt
disappointment for a moment and then realized my
horse had been cat quick, had performed magnificently,
and most of all, the big gray had not been afraid. I had
roped a dirty rotten little scoundrel pretty good for an
old man, and Johnny and Bailey had been right there -
the cavalry to the rescue. And we had a time, and just
as I was thanking the Spirit and the angels for helping
us all so much, they had one more little surprise in
store.
"You can't outgive the wind," said the voice.
So far away he was, but because the speakers are
always turned up to 10 on the dial at all rodeos, I heard
the announcer in a muffled sort of way, but clearly
enough to make out... "...Jenkins brothers from
Wyoming will win the team roping with a time of 6.36
seconds, and with these fast cattle, we had only one
other legal catch...and that from the Oklahoma team of
**Michael Johnson and Johnny Stevens, who will win
second place with their time of 18.04!"** His words

took the longest time to sink in, and as they made their way down - warming my stomach when they landed - the weight of what they meant was too heavy for me. Unable to stand up, I just sat down on those old bricks. Shine put his nose next to my cheek and blew his breath softly on me.

"You okay?" he asked.

"We won second!"

Shine and I realized that neither of us had said that. We both turned to see Johnny sittin' on Old Bailey, grinning from ear to ear.

"How?" I managed to croak, my voice cracking.

"Nobody else caught a steer!" he shouted. Then at the top of his lungs, he reared back on Bailey and shouted to the world, *"I got the only header in Fort Worth smart enough to break out on these Kentucky Derby Wonders!"*

I looked at Shine, and he looked at me - both of us realizing Johnny thought we had left the box early to break the barrier on purpose. "Uh…well, Shine and I thought it was the only chance we had," I said. Shine looked at Johnny and nodded.

"You two boys were right!" he shouted grinning even wider. Then added, "Come on Shine Man, extra grain for you and Bailey…and the beer's on me, 'cause who ever heard of winning money at a rodeo and going home with any of it in your pocket, huh?"

After unsaddling the horses and seeing Johnny deliver on his promise of extra rations, we adjourned to the Stockyards Hotel. There our crew of eight raised our glasses to a good man.

"For Dan," I said.

"For Dan," came the echo from family and friends.

Manuel and Dan sat high in the stands on the top row of the Coliseum watching the last of the crowd file away. **"Man,"** *said Manuel.* **"That was some rodeo, wasn't it?"**

"Just excellent," smiled Dan.

"What were you telling Shine right before they roped?" *asked Manuel.*

"Oh, that? Just told him to have fun and relax. That it was important to come from the box smooth. You know, Miguel's head and all."

"Yeah," *laughed Manuel.* **"It's so hard probably wouldna hurt him much anyway if Shine had tried to jump that barrier."**

"Oh," said Dan, remembering. "I told him about that too...that barrier. I told him it was just like all barriers we think we can't break, but that if he would just have faith in himself - if he would just wade into his fear - the fear would be brushed aside. Like most 'barriers' in life, it really wasn't that much of a barrier after all."

Manuel looked at him for a moment, then said, **"If you can do all that, think you could get the lights?"**

Dan looked around to make sure the stands were empty and smiled as darkness fell softly on the oldest covered arena in Texas.

Calling For The Steer

Chapter Eleven

ABILENE!

And we came home to slow dance with the dairy queens. Even Shine knew their names by now, Hoppy, Slowey, Mopey, Poot Along, and all the rest. And my soul was thrilled to discover more and more every day, the big gray was becoming...bored.

"Okay, for goodness sake, I'm getting it! How 'bout a tango or a rumba? Somethin' with a little Latin spice in it maybe?"

--Shine

I was quite content in my new role as an "old man." Fast becoming an old fellow I once knew who just quietly rode his horse around the arena in big circles – the old man I claimed I would never be, and the one they said had roped a deer – now I was becoming him, and something was happening to me. Something was happening inside me, and all around me, and if I were forced to name the color of the thing, I would have labeled it a *"deep blue."* And this deep blue thing was causing subtle wonders to come to me now, and each one brought a wonderful "lasting" quality along with it that worked with horses on the first day, and each day thereafter. One in particular made me happy the day after setting up camp in my awareness.

Always wondered how that old man could walk, trot, and lope his horse in a circle, or even do figure eights, *and never move his left hand!* No matter how closely I focused on his rein hand, his hand didn't move, and that was so puzzling to me. We all know the horse must be told where to go. That's fairly obvious - even to a seventeen year old. But the old man – Leslie was his name - didn't direct his horse in that fashion. And now when the blue came on me, I could walk, trot, or lope Shine in a big circle, and even ask him to do small figure eights...without moving my left hand.

Had I been able to accomplish such a task at seventeen, my pride would have swelled beyond recognition, but now at fifty-five, possessing the ability only made me feel small that so long a time had to pass before I could do something so simple. To simply "ask" the horse, or "help the horse understand" instead of telling him...like every bad boss had "told" me, never asking, always telling. I often thought the infinite lists of behaviors I needed to reach the horse were simply unattainable, and too many in number to grasp, and that was true. But now in a paradoxical Zen way, I knew something else to be equally true. That all we really need to know about horses will fit neatly into the palm of our hand, and even if we could hold it all, the weight could be so easily managed - indeed, even unnoticeable. Knowledge has no weight.

And one might wonder with good cause, "Why would such an insignificant thing as an old man riding a horse without moving his hand be so important?" There is a reason. A troubling and yet wonderful reason that I sensed at seventeen. Whatever this troubling and wonderful thing was somehow reached into me even at seventeen, something the two people who loved me most – my parents – were unable to do, and yet this "thing" did know how. I wondered how that old man could maneuver his horse around with such *order.* And I think perhaps cowboys – and all that word means – might understand better than any other. Because that old man made me wonder, I began to think about other things like mysticism for example. Though cowboys might not use the word "mysticism," still they ponder....

In the middle of a world where children die, where old Labs get run over, where our young are sent to fight some silly war the oil barons tell us is important, in a world where Ghandi, Martin Luther King, Malcolm X, Anwar Sadat, and Jesus are brutally murdered for having the audacity to suggest that perhaps we should just be good to one another - even though we all live in a world like that - why do all cowboys still have the suspicion – why does the feeling still haunt us that there is an order behind it all? See, we shouldn't feel that way, but we do. If we live in a world that one notable author described as one that could have been better made "by a blind, deaf and dumb idiot," why would cowboys still have a feeling there is an order behind it all? And let me guess...you don't know why you feel that way, but you feel that way too. Why do we still have that suspicion? There's no reason to, but still...we do. The answer to that riddle has something to do with an old man who can ride his horse around the arena in big circles, and even figure eights if he chooses, and cause a seventeen- year -old boy to remember that over thirty years later. And when the seventeen year old transforms to a fifty year old, and he can do it, then he thinks, "Oh, Mr. Leslie could do that because there is an order to it all. I just couldn't see it before." That's why an old stiff- handed man was important...because he understood the order of things.

I thought about those things, the things all cowboys think about, everyday when Old Shine and I spent so much of our valuable time together just loping along beside the dairy queens. And in a short time, I knew where to take him next and where we were going. I didn't know what would happen, but I did know one thing. Where we were headed...there would be no dairy queens.

"Bring him on brother. Bring'em on!"

--Shine

THE BIG TIME

Well, it was for me at least. The big time, I mean. Not the National Finals in Vegas, not even the United States Team Roping Finals in Oklahoma City, but nonetheless, the big time for me. Abilene. We were on our way to the Taylor Expo Center, one of the most outstanding equine facilities in the Southwest and home of the Annual Original Team Roping Finals held each year in July. The next stop of Shine and Miguel's journey would be the place where West Texas mommas taught their daughters how to fry eggs on sidewalks, where the wind snapped trace chains off fences, and where everyone knew how to rope the day they were born. We were headed to Abilene.

The annual roping championships held in the blistering heat of summer would attract over ten thousand participants. For ten days, from 8 a.m. sharp until midnight, the arena would be filled with young hawks who could rope like the wind, with old men who limped along on navicular horses, middle-aged women with stunning ability to rope, and thirteen-year-old boys and twelve-year-old girls unfurling their loops with effortless ease. Each and every one, young and old, male or female, had one thought on their mind. To grind the competition to dust. To win by such a margin, others would never come back because having been so badly beaten, they would know forevermore winning was impossible.

There would be no dairy queens in Abilene. Some of the cattle would be perfect, but a good number would be what all ropers - even the best in the world – dread with a passion, and would as soon never see again. The enemy of great ropers and novices alike, an evil adversary worse than duckers, draggers, head trickers, dead right twisters, and goring hookers were being trucked and trailered this very moment, to be unloaded shortly in large numbers, and waiting when we arrived in west Texas. The pens at Abilene would be filled with the evil ones...*runners!*

Regardless of one's status in the roping world or level of ability, one foundation principle is that to rope well, every roper must reach his or her spot – that ideal location from which to throw your loop. While it is true that horses can outrun steers, it's also true that if given a head start, some steers can make a roper's life – and his or her horse - miserable. And if roping horses frequented mental health clinics, surely the initial intake diagnosis chart would read, *"The patient is suffering from severe anxiety as a result of repeated mental trauma caused by roping runners!"*

Comparative psychologists, those who study animals and extrapolate findings to humans, contend that horses are slow learners. But they also inform us that while the horse takes ample time to learn a thing, once he learns, his memory is extremely "sticky." The horse has amazing powers of retention. My time with Shine had taught me that once he learned the game of roping, he had a "sticky" dread of one thing more than any other. He was afraid of being outrun.

Mutual Co-Development

What an awkward phrase. Mutual Co-Development? But not so awkward as the word "training." What a perfectly awful word "training" is, and such a liar.

When ropers start a horse, things seem to go rather smoothly in the beginning. Soon however, after repeating a number of runs, the horse begins to act out, engaging in all sorts of what some would call "silly" behaviors. This acting out is frequently interpreted by the rider as misbehavior, as the horse being "ornery," and intentional disobedience. The rider's response is anger, frustration, punishment, and swift implementation of the Eleventh Commandment.

What if we viewed the horse's behavior from another perspective?

"Impossible for red-neck horse trainers! They are only interested in the world through their eyes. A view limited to 'This sumbuck is bein' hard headed!' If only they could see things from mine."

--Shine

Blaming the horse is one option, but such an inferior method when compared to seeking answers to a few questions. Such as... from where in the horse's psyche does such misbehavior originate? What is the etiological root cause of acting out behavior, and why do symptoms manifest themselves in the manner displayed to the world? Is it willful rebellion on the part of the horse – is he a spoiled recalcitrant child stubbornly refusing to cooperate?

"No."

--Shine

Because of a powerful memory and an intense desire to please, the horse soon comes to know what is about to happen in the ensuing run. When the rope horse enters the box – even before entering – he knows the steer plans to leave with all haste. Since the horse understands his duty – to reach the spot as quickly as possible - every fiber of his body is straining to comply with his master's wishes. Anxiety builds with each successive run, and his internal "rubber band" stretches tighter and tighter. Excessive tension builds to such a degree the horse cannot contain the energy in his mind. The energy boils over and spills out into the world, and we interpret that as misbehavior, or intentional disobedience, and our answer is often to punish the horse. Yet when the human suffering from severe trauma or post-war stress syndrome cracks and falls sobbing to his knees, few of us would consider saying, "What that sumbuck needs is a good spurrin'!"

Sadly, there had been days in my life when my answers to acting out problems involved similar thinking. But now because of hundreds of hours on Shine's back, and information gained from truly knowledgeable horsemen, I viewed the chain of events as a grand whole rather than a few specific, undesirable, isolated segments of "bad horse behavior," and both Shine and I were the better for it. That's when I ceased to use the word "training." What a perfectly awful word, and a liar. Mutual co-development is awkward phrase, but not a liar. It means the better the human gets, the better the horse gets. Who is training whom? And whatever Shine and I had learned by mutual co-development, where we were going...we would need every ounce of what we had learned, to be better than we had ever been. We were headed to a special place.

The Promised Land

All those things were on my mind when we finally made Abilene. I turned the big rig into the vast parking area outside the Expo Center, and with haste in my step - as quickly as possible - let the boys out of the trailer. Blue and Shine were only too happy to stretch their legs after riding nine hours, with only one rest stop about half way in between southeastern Oklahoma and west Texas. We headed down to the large covered arena,

which I was relieved to see empty. Inside, I unsnapped
their halters and turned them loose. Like two fourth
graders on a field trip to the big city, the now strikingly
similar matched pair of grays stared in wonder at the
vast facility. Then, looking exactly like a hitched
team, walked slowly in unison around the perimeter of
the pen, gawking at the ceiling, looking at the lights,
smelling the fresh arena sand, and inspecting both the
head and heel boxes with an intense and methodical
scrutiny. After assuring themselves they were safe, they
suddenly wheeled, ran and bucked for a time, finally
kneeling and falling on their back to indulge themselves
in a refreshing sand bath. Regaining their feet, both
shook themselves violently, almost disappearing in the
resulting dust storm.

**"Man, dat was fun Shine Man, dat wassa
lotta fun. Iss issa big place. Me and you
and daddy gonna wope here?"**

"This is a big place," said Shine, using a
pleasant tone for once in his life. In spite of himself,
the big gray was enjoying the surroundings just as much
as Blue. *"I guess we'll rope tomorrow and the
next day maybe."* Noticing the hundreds of steers
in the outside pens just beyond the shade of arena roof,
Shine said, *"Those must be the cattle. Buncha'
long bony dudes, aren't they? Man, they look
fast."*

**"Well, we know one thing 'bout'em, don't
we, Shine Man?"**

"We do? What's that?"

**"Some of'em might outrun da Shine Man,
but can't none of'em outrunda Boo Man!"** and

with that, nipped Shine painfully on the butt, wheeled, and tore away laughing.

"Why you little..." screamed Shine, as he took off in hot pursuit.

I watched the horses run and play for a while, observing Blue as always picking a fight with Shine, and then began the long walk to the trailer for grain and hay. Turning back to look at them, I thought about Gary Cooper playing Lou Gerhig in that old movie, when he said he was, "...the luckiest man on earth." I knew how he felt.

Once the boys were stabled, and the feeding and watering were done, I began to pitch camp – always my favorite part of going to ropings. I unfurled the canopy on the side of the trailer to provide some nice shade, set up tables, retrieved my small barbeque pit and propane stove from the side compartments. After unfolding and setting up the chairs, I'm home sweet home.

The evening menu would feature "Burgers Miguel," a delightful assemblage of highly seasoned patties - rather thin, slightly smoky - and a bit rare, coupled with extra sharp cheese, homegrown tomatoes, and a brilliantly royal purple onion. Side dishes included Dr. Bakin' Beans, a delicious concoction of my own creation - too little known in my great state sadly - consisting of canned baked beans, the maple-flavored kind - aided and abetted by a little ketchup, Worchestershire, and brown sugar. To round out the haute cuisine, chips would be offered as the remaining side. Two candy bars for dessert would finish off the evening nicely, all presented and consumed al fresco. The horse's stalls were clearly visible about ten feet behind me, and we had made the four hundred-mile trip without incident and in fine fashion. And sitting there in the twilight with my two best friends, it occurred to me actually...I was a bit luckier than Lou Gherig.

The Blue Man

My feet hit the floor at 4 a.m. I remembered this was Friday morning and reached over to turn off the alarm set for 4:30. Like always, I was early. Had breakfast at the café - fed and watered - had more coffee. The boys were saddled and ready to go at 6 a.m. sharp. The roping would begin at 8, and two slow hours of warm-up would fill the time. Riding Shine and ponying Blue alongside, we headed to the massive open pasture behind the covered arena. Walking, then trotting, then loping, we stretched, limbered up, got all the kinks out, and even ran a bit. When I saw just a hint of perspiration at the base of their ears, I let them walk, as much to relax me as them. Both were focused, both were ready, and I wished so badly that I was.

Looking from the pasture warm-up area, I could see the parking lot. Wide, expansive, and empty the afternoon before, it was now jammed packed with trucks and horse trailers - a sea of people - and more would be coming. The roping would last ten days, and the Johnson Farms Team would have to make our mark in the first four of those days because the approximate $1,500 I had spent on entry fees, gas, and food was gone, and the two hundred-dollar bills left in my billfold would be just enough to get us home. I had entered twelve times with twelve different heelers. Some were old friends, some were blind dates, and to my knowledge, all were the type of ropers that would show up on time, not be drunk, and not fall off his or her horse. Always a good sign.

I withdrew the folded paper from the front left pocket of my jeans. The first line of the computer print-out mailed to me earlier read, *Michael Johnson - 112*. And below that, *Heeler: Elgin Brown*. The first team would be called to rope at 8 a.m. Estimating a little less than a minute for each roping team, I was fairly certain the number 112 would be called somewhere around half past nine. I looked at my watch and the time was 7 – two more hours. *"Blue?"* I said to him. He turned his pretty head and stared with his big black eyes....

"You call me, Poppa?"

"I did, son. Let's you and me start us off. We'll see how the cattle run."

"Good choice, Poppa. I'moan tell'ya right now, you always needta wope ona Boo Man,'cause Shine, he don't even weally like to wope, but if he does, he likesta go second. 'Cause even his old bony butt know da Boo Man issa bad motascooter! Ain't no cow in West Texas outrun da Boo Man. Good choice, Poppa. Always go widda Boo Man.

Tying Shine in the open area under the announcer's stand, I knew he could see both Blue and me at all times. The head box was only some thirty feet from where he would be stationed most of the morning. As some horses do, Shine seemed to be strongly affected by "separation anxiety." As long as he could see us, he would stand quietly content and not bother anyone. If he couldn't, he became highly agitated, pawed, and nickered without ceasing until one of us came into view. Also, his location would allow him to hear the

opening of the "air chute" used at this particular roping
to release the cattle. I wanted him to hear it hundreds
of times.

Announcers, time keepers, and the arena crew
worked their way through the first one hundred teams.
As I looked at my watch, I saw the face read 9:30.
"Pretty close to being on time," I thought to myself,
also thinking the people who worked this event were
only one-tenth of the way through their day. Some
one thousand teams would rope today, and the labor
required by all involved was backbreaking. And then I
heard, ***"Team Number 112 will be next. Michael
Johnson and Elgin Brown. When you're ready,
boys."***

Noticing Elgin and his big buckskin had already
assumed their position in the heel box, I rode Little
Blue into the header's side and turned to face the steer
and open arena. Quickly going through my checklist,
I made sure my butt, feet, legs, upper body, hands, and
mind were consciously relaxed. Glancing up to see if
the flagger - the arena time keeper - was in position, I
saw that he was. I looked out into the arena to make
sure the previous team had cleared, only then did I turn
my attention to the steer. He was standing straight, his
horns were medium size and perfect for the standard
loop I normally built. That "pre-shot routine" took no
more than five to six seconds, and with one last glance
at Elgin - who was staring a hole in me - I nodded. The
steer came hard and clean, and the Blue Man came right
with him.

You know, it's hard to rope a steer with tears in your
eyes, but I had done that very thing on this blue colt so
many times. During so many roping runs while riding

Blue, the only conscious thought coursing through my brain was, *"Thank you, Lord, for giving me such a fine horse."* The little guy I raised from a pup – who wasn't so little anymore weighing 1,100 pounds and standing fifteen hands – just tried so hard on every single run of his life. He tried just as diligently in the practice pen as he did at the big show. Blessed with mediocre talent, a distinct lack of speed, and only meager athletic ability, Blue's great strength was he didn't know all that and didn't believe it for a second. He thought he was truly the greatest roping horse that ever lived. He didn't believe that – he *knew* it. Full of confidence, and having been given what Sam Snead called the greatest gift – intense desire – at only five years of age, the dapple blue colt - colored like an old pair of jeans - had turned into the best of all things...a willing partner.

With Blue churning his heart out, he reached the spot about halfway down the pen. **"Get him, Dad! Get him! Boo Man gotcha dere, Daddy. Nail him!"**

Not wanting Coach Darrell barking from the inner recesses of my mind, I threw my loop with enough force to knock the steer's horns off and watched as it sailed nicely around both. Pulling my slack tight, I was in no rush dallying, and when we were in good position, I eased Blue to the left. Always what cowboys call "soft in the horn," Little Blue smoothly pulled the steer around what ropers call the "corner" to set him up for the heeler. Elgin was right there at the turn, and after two swings to make sure, released his big heel loop and scooped him up by both back feet. The flagger's hand went down, the announcer said, ***"There's a nice run for Johnson and Elgin, and they'll be...a clean 9.3 on their first one."***

Following the steer to the stripping chute at the other end, Blue pranced and hopped with excitement. Turning his head from side to side staring at the spectators, I knew he was happy.

"Ass what I'm talkin' bout! Me and my Daddy! WE BAD! I'm talkin' 'bout bad now! West Texas bony butt longhorn think he gonna outrunda Boo Man? My Daddy gotta wope, and he's ridin' da Boo Man, and yall's bony ass over dere thinkin' you outrunda Boo Man? Not gon' happen! Da Boo Man can't be outrun. Da Boo Man outrunna cheetah! Cheetah wouldn' even have a chance. Ass how bad I am! I'm da Boo Man, and I got it all!"

The segment of the roping we were in was referred to as a "rotation." Normally, about one hundred teams make up a rotation, and after all have roped, those who catch their first steer are allowed to continue. The ropings are called "progressive," meaning if you miss you're out. But since Elgin and I were clean on our first one, we now waited for our name to be called for the second steer - to be in the "second go"- and that was most likely some thirty minutes away. Taking a moment to check on Shine - he was fine - I tried to relax and find a way to combat what all ropers deal with… endless waiting.

Perhaps twenty-five minutes later, Elgin and I were once again in position and remarkably repeated our first run almost step for step. Now the tension began to build. Now we had qualified for the "third go," and if we could just repeat runs one and two, we had a chance to win the rotation – which paid $1,000 dollars – and even better to qualify for the "short go," or "finals" as they were called, where the big money waited. With some 1,200 teams in this particular roping, all paying some $80 per roper - $160 per team, the pot of money in that short–go promised to be sizeable indeed.

Some thirty minutes later, Blue and I - along with Elgin and his buckskin - were in hot pursuit once again. Little Blue put me right there, and I threw my loop with good force…and I split the horns! Caught the right one, but not the left one. Sick, mad, discouraged and depressed, I turned to Elgin when we rode outside, and said, "Elgin, you don't know how sorry I am."

"That's why they call it "team-roping," Miguel," he said smiling. "You wanted it just as bad as I did, I know that. Shake it off and don't worry about it, won't be the last time it happens. Misses gonna keep happening as long as the Lord lets us rope. Will cost you a cold beer though," he laughed. "I'll be by your trailer tonight."

I appreciated Elgin and knew he was right. I didn't want to miss, but I had. And I thought about the horseman, and the roper, my old friend, John.

"Question is... what do you do after you miss?"

--Bronc Fanning

He had taught me the answer. Now I knew what to do after a miss in roping, and you know, it works pretty well in life too. Take all that sick, mad, discouraged depression, wad it up into a ball, and throw it out the window. Then make a note of what you can do to correct your mistake...and go to work.

"We all make mistakes, but you don't have to make the same one twice!"

--Rosie Austin

I had almost two hours before my next run, so I headed to the trailer for some practice on the dummy. Once there, I moved old Jake, the roping dummy, over in some nearby shade and went to work. Thirty minutes later I was wringing wet with sweat and full of confidence. I had split the horns on the money cow - I had caught the right horn, but not the left one. After my sweltering workout, I knew I wouldn't split another steer the entire roping. Because following the good advice of my friends, instead of getting mad, I worked on correcting my mistake and used that mistake to help me win. I threw one hundred loops in that scorching West Texas heat, and on each and every one, I made a pronounced finishing motion to ensure the loop cleared

271

the left horn, and didn't "split" the right and left horns. Toweling myself off, I mounted Blue and the roan slow-loped us the thousand yards back to the arena.

The afternoon ropings were carbon copies of the early morning. Drew some good ones, some bad ones, and while my heelers missed at critical times, none of their misses were as painful as mine had been for Elgin. I made every effort to treat them as he had treated me.

The good news was I roped five more steers and didn't split the horns a single time. The day was done, and Miguel and the Blue man had done well, but not well enough to make the short go to be held on Sunday night. Tomorrow would be Saturday, and tomorrow would be Shine's day to rope…and I was worried about that.

Shine on Shine Man

Once again, my feet hit the floor at 4 a.m. The knot in my stomach woke me up. I was worried about the big gray. Didn't know if he could handle this. Under no illusions about me, I knew my level of roping. Some people would consider this venue small time, but a total of twelve hundred teams didn't seem small to me. And even though he held so much less fear inside now as compared to before, I could still feel some. I knew he had a knot in his stomach too, and if things went bad, that knot would grow. Four more steers remained. I had roped eight of my twelve on Blue knowing he could not only handle that many, but would thrive on it. Roping created energy in Blue. I also knew he would be a pill when he found out he was on the bench for the rest of the roping. Seemed best not to mention that to him at the moment, so I headed for breakfast.

After too much coffee, I saddled both Shine and Blue, and we repeated our early dawn warm-up, and just as I expected, Blue was an awful pain. As we ponied around the pasture, he jumped, he nipped, he pulled away, danced sideways, tried to outrun Shine, and made a complete nuisance of himself in every imaginable way. That caused my nervousness and irritation to rise, unsettling me even more. Shine had been calm at daylight, but now he picked up on my queasy uneasiness. In the process, he began to prance and snort in an open pasture with no one there. I could only imagine what his mental state would be in front of a thousand people, loud air chutes, and runners. I remembered fresh cattle would be coming today. When I thought about that, Shine felt my thought, and began prancing harder.

My numbers were 498, 662, 882, and 1011. Some good news and some bad. The runs were evenly spaced - none back to back - so that was good. But they were spread over a long day, two in the morning, two in the afternoon, and that meant a great deal of waiting. Considering my current mental state - that was bad. My mental instability was about to worsen. My jagged nerves were about to be sliced to pieces.

Arriving early at the empty arena, I planned to continue Shine's warm-up in the actual surroundings where he would be competing. I tied Blue under the announcer's stand, mounted Shine, and rode to the far end. Something in me said, "Uh oh," and I turned back to look for Blue...*and he was gone!*

Houdini couldn't disappear as fast as this horse could vanish. On many occasions, I had given serious

consideration to the possibility that Blue had been in
the Navy in a former life because his knowledge of
knots was just staggering. This horse could get out of
a straight-jacket. Sure enough, even though I had tied
Blue securely - believe me, I knew his tendencies - one
minute he was there, and the next he was gone. Visions
of semi's brakes screeching, screams, and a dead horse
filled my mind.

I kicked Shine – yes, I committed the great sin – but
it didn't matter. He was already running as hard as he
could when I kicked him. He knew Blue was gone, and
he wanted to find our partner just as badly as I did.

With the wind tearing my eyes, Shine was covering
a huge amount of ground in a very short time. After
about five minutes of sick dread, made worse by the
high speed we were traveling, we saw him grazing in
a ditch some five hundred yards to the southwest, not
twenty yards from the open highway. If he walked out
into that highway, I knew I would never be the same.
And Shine said, ***"Michael! Hold on!"*** If Blue had
started to the busy four-lane at that instant, Shine would
have still arrived in time to cut him off. We slowed as
we approached.

"Blue?" I called softly. "Come on now, son. Come
over here to Poppa...."

**"Oh, it's ya'll. Well, da Boo Man don'
need no company. Ya'll just go do ya wopin'.
Whatever ya'll got planned, jus' go 'head and
do it, 'cause I got lots to do my own self."**

"Blue!" I barked at him sharply, hoping something
would work. "Come on; it's almost 8; the roping is
about to start."

"You gotta horse to wope on.. Bony

cwanky ass mental case, but you gotta
horse. You don' wanna ride da Boo Man,
ride dat fool. I'm iss gon' live out here in
West Texas by myself. Get me a job herdin'
cows. Never did like wopin' anyway."

Blue turned to look at the cars and trucks whizzing
past. He seemed flighty and agitated. I thought I might
be sick. I slowly dismounted Shine.

"Blue, don't." It was Shine. **"Blue, stop this
foolishness, and let Michael have your halter
rope."** Blue stared. I began a purposeful stride right
to him. Not fast, but as if we were just in the arena at
home. As I approached, he dropped his head, and for
just a moment, I thought he might turn and bolt...but
he didn't. I came within reach of the halter rope, and
without rushing, closed my fingers around it with a
death grip. If he bolted now, he would kill us both, and
that was fine with me.

"I'm thinking about killing you," I said to him
through gritted teeth.

**"Well, go ahead, Daddy, but den you
won't have no good horse to wope on."**

Shaking all the way, we rode back to the coliseum.

The roping had been under way for thirty minutes
or more. My number was 492, and when I heard the
announcer say, "450, be ready," I breathed a huge sigh
of relief. I had at least a few minutes to collect myself
and prepare for the first steer.

I tied Blue with the same knot they use on the
gold door at Fort Knox, and still I fretted. I spent the
remaining time with Shine outside in the sun and the
wind, and tried to concentrate.

My heeler for the first steer was a kid from western

Oklahoma named Bubba Farley. I had been pleased
with all my heelers so far. Elgin had done a great
job, and I had missed the money cow for him. Cindy
Thomas had caught two above the hocks, and she
threw the same loop on our third one, only to watch
him somehow wiggle out of it. "I can't throw it any
better than that," she said after the run. "Just wasn't
our time," she added shrugging her shoulders. I agreed,
she had executed perfectly, and for some reason, it just
wasn't our time. All the rest had performed in much the
same fashion, but as team ropers say, "We just couldn't
get anything going." While all my heelers had roped
well, not one was a match for Bubba - my first partner
with Shine. Bubba could heel.

Attending a western Oklahoma college on a rodeo
scholarship, Bubba could snap up two feet with the best
of them. He was twenty-three years old, looked like
James Dean, and was as gracious, well-mannered, and
courteous as a young man could be. I admired that of
course, but the important thing in a man is...*can he heel
or not?* And Bubba could throw a dart through a
swinging tire hangin' in a tree... from fifty yards away.
Bubba could heel, and he was sittin' right across from
me, 'cause they had just called Number 492!

Shine had actually been calm as he entered the box,
and without the slightest "stickiness" when he turned,
now stood calmly facing the steer. *"Are you ready,
Shine Man?"* I asked him.

"Shhh," he said. **"I'm focused."** And taking
that as a good sign, I nodded. And then...I made a
mistake. I didn't squeeze Shine. My bad.

Watching the few previous cattle, I had noticed
that several ropers had broken the barrier because

when the gate opened, as many as the last five steers
had hesitated. The steers just didn't come. With my
good heeler over there, I didn't want to burden us with
a ten-second penalty, so I waited just a moment to
cue Shine, but I hadn't planned on drawing Lighting
Billy. The steer was almost a quarter way down the pen
when Shine said, ***"Now? Can we go now! Think I
might start running after him now?"***

"That would be good," I said. And he fired his
engines. Till this day, I still don't believe it. The steer
had us hopelessly beaten, a true runner if there ever was
one, but I was riding a true runner. Somehow the horse
had his nose almost in position before we reached the
mid-point of the long pen, and I raised my loop... and
now we were almost out of room. The steer began to
angle right, heading toward the freedom of the stripping
chute, and just before he went in, my rope fit snugly
around his horns. This time I did rush the dally, and for
once in my life, got smooth away with it. Somehow -
even though he was at full speed - Shine twisted his
body and avoided slamming into the fence, and in the
same motion, began an easy controlled pull to the left.
And I was so proud of him, but I also knew... we were
done for.

The steer now had about twenty-five feet of my
thirty-foot rope out and was running wild like some big
striper in Lake Texhoma. I didn't know many heelers
that could make a shot like that. And then I
remembered I did know a couple, and one of them was
right behind me. Bubba's bow snapped his arrow, and
just like that, Old Speed Demon had his two back legs
pulled out from under him, and Shine – unbelievably -
was still focused, and twirled to a face without adding a

half second to our time. And then I heard…

"Johnson and Farley are clean on their first one with a 10.0 flat."

Stunned, I just sat there. Bubba came riding up, and as he coiled his rope, said, "Man, Mr. Mike, that gray horse can *run!*" I didn't hate it when he called me that.

"Uh, yeah…he's pretty fast. W-w-we've been w-w-working together a long time, and uh…w-w-we've both gotten b-b-better," I said, still in a daze.

"Come on," he said, "We need to get out of the way." I realized the next team was still sitting in the box waiting on us to clear the arena, and we quickly made our exit.

Once outside, Bubba said, "Good job there, partner, on reaching out to catch that one."

Wincing, I said, "Yeah, uh…well, I actually made a mistake on that. I held Shine in there too long and let the steer get too big a jump."

"Must not'a been too big a jump," Bubba said smiling and looking down at Shine. "That gray horse caught him. That fellow can run, Mr. Mike!" Then he said, "Same plan in the second go, okay? And in the third, and in the short-go. We're gonna win this thing, Mr. Mike!"

I was liking it more and more when they called me Mr. Mike. After Bubba rode away, I reviewed what had just happened. My horse had entered the box without a single stutter step, and he waited until I cued him to go. After his perfect beginning, I then screwed, blued, and tattooed him by making him wait too long. He overcame what should have been a fatal mistake and caught the fastest steer in Abilene and handled the blatant idiot like a dream, even having the presence of mind not only to avoid charging into the fence, but faced perfectly, and now… wasn't even breathing hard. I looked at him… *"Shine, how did you just do what you did?"*

"Focus," he said.

I looked at him again. Even though it was late morning now, I could clearly see it. He had a glow about him, and I knew what it was…it was that *greatness* coming out. And he wasn't done, not by a long shot. He was about to let that greatness come spilling out all over…all over everywhere.

Forty minutes later, Bubba was staring a hole in me from the heel box. Our second go steer was in the chute. The Oklahoma Kid had his pistol cocked, and he was ready. The chute man had his eyes locked on me, and I said, "Anytime…."

And this time, I didn't hold Shine in the box, but just after seeing the tip of steer's left horn around the gate, I squeezed the big gray's sides. We were out, and the barrier didn't buzz, and I felt hope. Then, I realized this second steer could outrun the first one. His tail was straight up in the air and about to burst into flames from the friction created by his speed. And to his credit, he took Shine halfway down the pen before my arrow hit home. Bubba's finished him off. Fumbling my dally just a bit cost us a second or two, but that bitter taste was sweetened when the announcer said, *"Johnson and Farley add another clean 10.0 to their first one, now 20.0 on two."* Shine had performed Act II - Scene II, better than in the early morning show.

And the tension began to build. Now we were eligible for the third go, and if we could just repeat steps one and two, we would most likely win the rotation, split one thousand dollars, and be eligible for the short-go…where the big money waited. And all I could think about was split horns.

During the thirty plus minutes we waited for our third steer, I spent the time washing the failure image of the earlier miss from my memory, replacing it with mental pictures of my right arm sweeping my loop over both the steer's horns. In my mind, my hand came so completely from right to left as my swing finished, my hand gently bumped Shine's neck. I roped the third steer once a minute while we waited, and when he came into the chute, I had roped him thirty times without a flaw. All I had to do was rope him once more in the real world. Just rope him one more time. And I hoped for a little luck.

Bubba and I had managed to get by two really bad steers. While they didn't duck or dodge – at least, they were honest – they were just so fast. We had drawn two in a row that ropers called "eliminators," and maybe we were due for a good one. I knew the pens held a fair share of runners, but after having two that could win first and second in a foot race against all the rest, surely now we wouldn't draw another one. I just had a hunch we had a good chance for a medium steer, and I hoped my hunch was right. It wasn't.

The people in the stands were stone silent as I rode into the box for the third and final steer. Everyone knew if we could manage to stop the clock, Johnson and Farley would win the rotation and be in superb shape for the finals. I executed my pre-shot routine in the normal five to six seconds and was conscious of Shine's calmness. *"Can you give me one more?"* I asked him. Shine did not respond. I called for the steer....

We were out clean, and the big horse was giving me everything he had. And the third steer was faster than the first two. *"Jeez..."* I thought disgustedly. *"How could we draw three runners...how could I draw the three fastest steers in my life, all in a row?"* And I did something I had never done, I squeezed Shine a second time. An instant later, I felt the thing called *awe*. Shine began to run faster. *Shine had a second gear!* The steer was already half way down the pen, and Shine was a good four lengths back, but I suppose the Shine Man felt that lost causes are truly the only ones worth fighting for. By the time, we reached the three quarter mark, the big gray hound was stretched low to the ground, destroying the earth behind him as he ran, sending huge chunks flying in his wake. Without believing such a thing possible, I realized Shine had reached the spot, and I only had a few feet left. I roped the steer. Shine slid, and Bubba fired....

"Here's something you don't see too often, folks. Johnson and Farley add one more ten flat to their string. And their total time of thirty on three will be good enough to win the rotation, and one thousand dollars! And right now, they are sitting first for tomorrow night's finals."

I turned to look back down the arena, and I could see it everywhere. Lying on the arena floor, hanging from the lights, some shining on people's clothes, most of it on my jeans, and some on my hands. Sparkling and shining, shimmering in the light.... Shine's greatness had come pouring out.

"They're wrong, you're right. They're wrong, you're right," the little voice laughed, and kept repeating the

phrase over and over inside my mind. I felt the thing called joy.

"That horse can run, Mr. Mike!" Bubba shouted, holding his hand high in the air, and I tried to reach his hand, but could not. Too drained. He lowered his, and slapped mine. Almost knocked me off Shine, but I didn't care. I slid from the saddle down Shine's side and hugged his neck. He was breathing hard, but not from fear, but rather the greatest performance of his life. There was no fear in him, and the joy swelled. I knew the tears would be coming soon, and I really needed to get out of there, but now the people were rushing to the area just outside the rear of the arena.

"Man, that gray is something!" said a stranger.

"Well done, Miguel!" said Elgin, slapping me on the back.

"Horses like that just natural born to do it," said one old man. "Am I right, son?" he asked. "He just took to it natural like, didn't he?"

"Yes," I said weakly. "He was always a natural."

"Can I pet Shine, Mister?" a little boy asked.

"Sure you can, son. You can sit on him if you want."

"Oh," said his mother, reaching for her purse. "Let me get a picture! Get up there, William. You can take this to show and tell."

And they kept coming. Talking about the great Shine, and how fast he was, and how beautiful he was, and how great he was. And I just stood there, letting it all wash over me. What was I gonna do? Leave them standing there? Champions don't act like that.

The rest of the day was a dream. I had roped three more times with other heelers in different rotations,

caught two and missed one that ducked right, but that's
team roping...you have to draw good. We just didn't
get anything going, but we truly enjoyed the day.
Adding the $500 of the thousand I split with Bubba to
my jeans pocket helped too.

The day came to an end, and we unsaddled the
horses and headed to the trailer. Friends came by, and
we relived every step of every run. I cooked supper for
a half-dozen compadres, and just as I was about to take
my first bite, knew I was suddenly going to be sick.
Something inside me said, *"Do you realize what this
means?"* And when I did, I really got sick.

Be Careful What You Pray For

Remember that old line? Can you hear that ringing
sound? Be careful what you pray for. That warning has
become so entrenched in me, whenever I find myself
earnestly desiring a thing, I recoil. *"Be careful,"*
something says. *"You really want that thing? Okay,
but you might get it, and then what will you do?"* No
negative thinking here or feelings of unworthiness
that I don't deserve good things. It's more that when
something you really want comes on you, you should
be mindful to read the small print guarantee that
promises to also bring along much more than you
planned on along. So if you pray for a thing, be careful.
You might get it, and everything that comes with it
- some of which you didn't pray for. And so it was on
this day with Old Shine.

I had returned to the world of roping some ten
to twelve years ago right after that sabbatical in the
woods. I emerged from that time of solitude different.

Notice I didn't necessarily say better, but different. And as a result, I decided to live my life in accord with mythology scholar Joseph Campbell's advice that we should "follow our bliss." Hmmm…that helped me to realize I needed to identify what that bliss was, and I found the answer.

My bliss was to write and to rope. To be a good writer and a good rider. Even though I left the world of rodeo at twenty-five and returned to that world at forty-five, I roped the dummy during all the time I spent imprisoned in the corporate world. But this time when I began again, I approached the world of roping in a different manner.

After awareness came into me that roping was a long-standing passion, now at middle-age, I began to work in earnest. For months, I threw one hundred loops a day at Jake and was surprised my former skills had almost disappeared. But I persevered, and a hundred sore muscles later, some of that skill returned. I managed to secure an old paint horse that like me had lost a step, and he became the best teacher I ever had. He knew so much more about the game than I.

I found mentors, teachers, tutors, coaches, and instructors much farther down the path, but I called to them, and they said what all powerful teachers say, "Come on, we'll show you how." And I did something better this time than I had ever done before…*I listened to them.* I didn't tell them why I couldn't, didn't tell them I was too old, didn't tell them "that won't work for me," didn't tell them "that's not the way I do it" – I didn't tell them anything because I didn't speak. I listened. Then I did what the masters said for an extended period of time and failed countless times. I

never let that bother me in the least. Because I
expected to fail, and each time I did, I made a note
about how to correct that mistake and eventually began
to improve. Eventually, in fact, reaching a level of
roping that surpassed any ability I had at twenty-five.
No boasting here…it's that system I used. If we would
do a thing, there is a functional and effective system
we can employ taught to me by those farther down the
path. And this system really works.

Ask a master, listen to the master - don't talk, do
what the master says for an extended period of time,
and improvement will come. The system works. It's
a dead lock cinch. You might not be a star, but this
system will cause you to twinkle more than you once
did. Here's the proof of the pudding. After all that
effort, work, and endless hours of failure, Shine and I
were sitting first in tomorrow night's finals in Abilene,
Texas. The thing I had prayed for had come on me and
brought so much with it, I now found myself sick at my
stomach. So, be careful what you pray for.

My company left around 9 p.m. And the long night
began. I couldn't sit still, couldn't drink beer, couldn't
eat, and couldn't sleep. After the joy subsided – and
it never completely would – I began to realize my
position. Tomorrow at 6 p.m., some fifteen hours from
now, Shine and I would ride in the box, and if we could
manage just to rope the steer – just get a reasonable
time in the books by roping one steer – at the other
end of the arena there would be two saddles, two horse
trailers, and a suitcase. And in that suitcase rested…
$10,000 dollars!

The knot tightened as I began to tally the figures.
The saddles retailed for $2,500 each, the trailers for

$7,500 each, and the ten grand...well, that was ten grand. If we roped the steer, Bubba and I would split a potential twenty thousand. I just couldn't believe it, but the knot actually tightened more. I tried to get some sleep, but to no avail. I woke at 4 a.m. again naturally, and begged my mind and body for much needed rest. *"I need to be fresh,"* I said. ***"Are you crazy?"*** came the reply, ***"We can't sleep; we need to get up and fret and pace all day!"***

The day crawled by. I looked at my watch at 9 a.m. Twelve hours to go. Right then and there, I decided to stop torturing myself and made a solemn promise not to look at the time again until I was sure it was around noon, and somehow I managed to do that. Quite proud of myself for having the discipline to not glance at my watch every ten minutes, I looked again. My watch read 9:10. "Great," I fumed. "Now my danged watch quits on me." A friend rode by the trailer at that moment, and I said, "Do you know what time it is?" He looked at his watch, and said, "About 9 sharp." Great, now time had decided to go backwards.

I had just about decided to give up the ghost when company happened by...Bubba's daddy. Charley was a big, barrel-chested man, who had spent his life in the coaching profession. Like all coaches, Charley said everything really loud, and he always said it twice. "Hey!" he boomed. "Hey!" he boomed again. "You and my boy got'em! Great job! Great job! Now, let's talk strategy...we need to talk about strategy!" No sleep, a busted watch, and now Charley. Just what I needed. "I'll fix us some coffee," I said.

"Coffee hell! Coffee? Son, we need to start drinking beer right now. Need to be loose. Need to be loose come showtime."

"Coffee, Charley. I'm not drinking beer before the roping."

"There's your problem right there!" he thundered. "There's your problem! You're tight! You're tight, son!"

"And nearing deafness," I thought.

"Let me tell you the strategy I got worked out here, Miguel. I can put you at ease. Here's the deal. Here's the deal...."

Charley leaned over real serious like, and I could tell he had already hit the beer.

"There's only one unknown variable here, Miguel. Only one unknown variable."

"Only one unknown variable?" I repeated just because it seemed like fun.

"Only one unknown variable. Only one unknown variable...."

"And that is....?"

"Whether you gon' catch that head or not, boy!" Charley hissed.

"Thanks, Charley. I hadn't even thought of that."

"WELL!" he bellowed. "You need to think about that, son. You need to think about that!"

"Yes," I said with a sigh, feeling a hundred years old. "I guess...."

"Now listen to me, Miguel. Listen to me. My boy don't miss. We know he's gifted, always has been gifted. My boy don't miss. So...the only unknown variable here is whether you gon' catch 'at damn head or not! That's what I'm sayin'. Whether you can stand the pressure or not, you know what I mean, son?"

"Well, I think...."

"Don't – I'm talkin' 'bout don't let a bunch of people come by here today and put all sorts of pressure on you 'bout how you're too old, you ain't never been in a situation like this, and how anybody else would fold up like a house of cards if they was sittin' first, and so on. What I'm sayin,' son, is don' let these loud mouths get you all worked up. Are you with me? ARE YOU WITH ME?"

"I'm with…."

"And one other thing. When ya'll rope tonight, down 'nare at the other end of the 'rena, there's gon' be two saddles – nice saddles son, nice saddles – two trailers, and $10,000 dollars in a suitcase! Did you know that, Miguel? Did you know that, son? That right there's what I'm asking you here today."

"I did know…."

"And I'm gonna tell you son, and I'm not ashamed of it. Me and Mildred…we need that money. It ain't rained in sixty-six days where we live, we got no hay, and we got no wheat. We need that money. My boy don't miss, Miguel. So all I'm sayin' is I just want you to think about one thing today. Will you do that for me? Will you just do that one thing for me here today, son?"

"Anything, Charley."

"Just remember, Miguel." And Charley leaned forward again, and in a low voice, said, "There's only one unknown variable here."

The Call

Apparently, my watch had made an internal decision to start working again. The time was now 3 p.m. Three hours to go, but now, thank the Lord, I had something to do. I threw a few loops at Old Jake and put on a fresh undershirt. I saddled both horses and began the long trek to the big pasture behind the coliseum. Blue was on better behavior than normal, and Shine seemed strangely calm. And I had a suspicion why.

For three days, Shine had been saddled, and while in the shade, he had been saddled for some twelve hours each of those days. He ran hard and roped a number of steers yesterday, and all that plus the scorching heat had to have taken something out of him. His edge was off. Fatigue played a role in his calm demeanor. I wasn't the slightest bit worried that he was too much so, just relieved that some of his normal tension and energy had been released from standing on that hot West Texas sand. He was tired in the right way.

We warmed-up with our normal routine, and I felt somewhat better until my eyes made their way to the north end of the arena, and I saw the shiny new trailers. Couldn't see the saddles or the suitcase, but I knew they were there. The knot tightened again.

The more I rode Shine, the more the tension increased. Couldn't shake negative pictures. My mind was filled with duckers, stumblers, barrier buzzers, weak spaghetti loops, and split horns. Tried to breathe. Couldn't do it. And Shine began to prance. *"I need some help here, Lord."* Some ten minutes later, we were still warming-up, and I was still choking like a dog when the cell phone rang from my jeans pocket...it was Earl. "Michael? Michael, can you hear me?"

"Yes, is this *Earl?*" knowing it had to be someone who just sounded like Earl. The caller couldn't be Earl because....

"Yeah, it's Earl. How you doin'?"

I wanted to tell him the truth, but I certainly

couldn't do that. So instead, I said, "Uh…well, I'm okay I guess."

"Okay? You and Shine are the high team back, and you're just okay? Lord, son, what does it take to make you happy?" And that hit home.

"No," I said, "Really, I'm doing well…."

"Man, high team back on Old Shine. I heard the good news, so I had to call. That's something. I'm proud for you and Shine. How did my grandson do?"

My voice was about to crack, but I managed to say, "He did well, Earl. You would have been proud of Little Blue."

"Always have," he said. "Always have. We did a good job with him, didn't we?"

And then my voice did leave. Finally, I said, "We did, Earl."

"Okay…." he said sounding like he was about to hang up, and I interrupted, "Earl! Earl?"

"What? What? I'm still here."

"Question is how are you?"

"I'm doing okay, Michael. I really am. No news on a heart yet, but me and Mary are hoping. I'll let you know the minute we hear anything. Hell of a note, ain't it? Somebody has to die for me to live. So I can get a new heart…."

"Earl, if you get one, can you try to find a 'soft' one, this time?" I asked.

At that crack, he began to laugh loudly, and that made tears appear on my face without warning. But he didn't know that.

"Can you get a softer one this time, you old buzzard?" I shouted into the phone.

"Yes," he laughed. "Yes, I'll tell'em to give me a

softer one this time. Listen, I'll let you go. You and Shine kick their butts. I said a little prayer for both of you."

And he was gone. And I sat out there on Shine in that West Texas wind, holding Blue by his halter rope...

"Was'at my Grandaddy Earl?" Blue asked.

"Yes, son, it was."

"How he doin' Poppa?"

"They're still waiting," I said. *"They will call if they hear anything."*

"Oh...," said Blue.

I looked at my watch. 5 p.m. One hour to go. I turned Shine and Blue toward the arena in the distance. Riding across the big open field, I thought about what had just happened. I was so nervous about the coming events, I had called for help. I didn't expect the reply to come so soon, and I certainly didn't expect the Divine to use Earl to return the call, but he was an excellent choice - he had returned the call within ten minutes. Earl, who at the moment, was lying in a hospital in Dallas, Texas, waiting for a heart from somebody who had to die so Earl could live. And Earl called me to help me with my problem. My big problem. Whether I caught a steer or not. Whether I won $10,000 dollars are not. And if I did, it wouldn't be enough money; I'd just spend it. And if I didn't win and never had it, then I wouldn't miss it. My big problem. Earl had one too.

If Earl didn't get a heart transplant soon, he would never leave that hospital. Earl would never see his horses again. Earl would never walk across the earth on his farm again. Never drink coffee at the Redland Country Store again. Chances were good Earl would never step into the sunshine again, and Earl had called me to help me with *my* problem. I couldn't cure his, but he had cured mine. *"Thank you for the help, Lord,"* I said to the wind. We arrived at the back of the coliseum. I wasn't nervous anymore.

Earl

The Finals

The time had come. Well, at least it was coming in about two minutes. The stands were full, and strangely quiet. The announcer was welcoming the crowd with his introduction....

"Welcome Ladies and Gentleman, and children of all ages. Tonight's performance will begin shortly. We'll see the finals for this year's Number Five Roping held here in the beautiful Taylor Expo Center in Abilene. And what a roping it's been! Some twelve hundred participants began three days ago, and now that number has been reduced to the final thirty with the best time on three steers. And now we are set to go....

We will begin with the team having the best time on three steers, and that's an even 30.0 flat. The first team out this evening will be the Oklahoma team of Michael Johnson and Bubba Farley. Anytime you're ready, boys!"

I rode Shine into the box. He turned to face the steer with a smooth and silky grace. The pre-shot routine clicked off in my mind. The steer was standing straight. Head up, him with his big high horns, just perfect to split. I smiled to myself.

"Here we go, Earl," I thought, and nodded. The gates swung open slowly, and the steer began his slow exit, and Shine did the same. Everything slowed down. I had all the time in the world. In slow motion, stretching out long and low, the big gray was letting the greatness come now, all of it coming. So clearly, I could hear his gentle breathing, and feel the strength

of his muscles generating effortless speed, and hear his hooves hitting the arena floor like the sound of distant thunder. With a mind of its own, my loop began to spin with a slow and easy twirl. I could hear the powerful torque even in this slow time. With a mind of its own, on the second revolution, the rope decided we were in just the right spot and made the decision to fly. The loop hit the base of the steer's right horn and began a slow curl, first clearing the left horn by a foot, then beginning a leisurely journey across the steer's withers. We had caught the steer in the first quarter of the arena. My dally snapped the trap, and Shine moved like a cloud to the left. We were less than four seconds now. The steer – made in Heaven – seemed to be enjoying the ride and was more than pleased to accompany us across the arena floor. He hopped along like a rocking horse, holding both back legs up just a bit to do what he could to make the heeler's job easier…and Bubba's rope never even touched him on any part of his body.

The Oklahoma Kid had missed.

For once in his life, the Oklahoma Kid had thrown a blank.

Time blistered back to reality. Suddenly, we were back in the world where everyone else lives. And for a moment, I felt deep despair, and the voice said, **"Be careful what you pray for. Be careful what you pray for. You never prayed to win. You never prayed to win. You prayed only that the horse not be afraid. Look at him."**

And Shine stood still facing the steer just as stunned as everyone else, and there was no fear in him. *"Yes,"* I said. *"Thank you. Thank you. He's not afraid. I'm not sad."*

"Bubba?" I called to him. With an ashen gray face,

294

the reality of what had happened sinking in now, his eyes met mine, and he said, "Huh? W-w-hat?"

"Bubba, we need to move. The second high team is waiting."

In a daze, Bubba looked back to see the number two team waiting patiently. He began to ride to the side, and I called to him again, "Bubba. We need to go out the back, son."

"Oh...uh...yeah," he said.

Once outside the arena, Bubba slid off his horse, and I knew he was going to be sick. He eased down on his hands and knees, and I turned my face away. The other cowboys standing there moved slowly away to avoid embarrassing him. I heard him gag, and he wiped his mouth and mumbled something. "Bubba, you okay?" I asked.

"I'm just so sorry, Mr. Mike," he said in a voice I could barely hear.

I didn't mind that he called me that at all. "Bubba, it's okay. That's just team roping. Shine and I wouldn't be here if you hadn't caught those three runners. Bubba, it's okay...."

He spit again and wiped the back of his hand across his mouth, and said, "You know it's not okay. But most of all, I would like to apologize to that "Stick" you're ridin.' That horse has greatness in him."

"What did he call me?" asked Shine. **"He called me a 'stick'? What does that mean?"**

"It means you're a good one," I said. *"He means you're something special."*

"Oh. Well...okay then."

"I'm okay," Bubba sputtered. "I think I just need to be by myself for a while."

"Sure, Bubba," I said. "Thank you for roping with me." And I rode out the back. Just as I turned past a building some one hundred feet away, Charley came tearing around the corner and almost ran into me.

"Good God!" he screamed. "I thought the finals started at 7; have you roped?"

"No, they started at 6," I said, "and yes, we have roped, but Charley…."

"DID YOU CATCH?" he yelled.

"Charley, I …."

"I ASKED YOU DID YOU CATCH?" He screamed this time.

"I did, Charley."

He spun and tore away, and as he disappeared around the building, I heard him shouting at the top of his lungs, *Mildred, Mildred! Honey! Honey! We done won $10,000 dollars!"*

I didn't have the heart to ride after him and tell him what happened. Besides, when he found out, he would just find a way to blame me. And I understood that. He loved that boy.

The Post Game Show

To my surprise, Blue was still under the announcer's stand where I left him, and for once in his life, he had remained tied. Along with my two tired friends, we made our way across the super-heated vast pavement parking lot and headed to the trailer and stalls. When we arrived, there was not a dry thread or hair on any of us. They were hungry and even more thirsty. After they slurped down two buckets of water each, I prepared their dinner and began to arrange the fixings for mine while they had theirs.

I planned once again to go with "Burgers de Miguel" for the evening's fare. That menu item always really impressed dinner guests until the dinner guests learned I prepared the same entrée every night. After Miguel burgers three or four nights in a row, the crowd tended to thin out. Seen one dinner guest, you've seen'em all.

While the grill was heating up, I let the boys out to graze. Kept their halter ropes long and untied, so they would step on them if they wandered off, and to insure I could catch them easily. But since it was so late in the day and so peaceful, I didn't think they would wander too far. I had a feeling they wanted to talk. And since I was pretty sure none of my buddies would be coming by – in light of the day's events, the reason being people don't visit much when you lose – I welcomed the company of my two good horses. After all, they were what every roper dreams of...a good pair.

"Well, I guess we're done, boys." I said from my lawn chair. The West Texas dusk was purple and hauntingly beautiful, and miracle of miracles, the wind in that wild country had decided to hold her breath for once.

"How'd I do, Poppa? Wuz you proud of da' Boo Man?" Blue mumbled with a mouth full of grass.

"Just really good, son. Just really good," I said. "But you didn't ask me how Shine and I did."

"Lemme' tell you sumpin,' Poppa. Da Boo Man ain't never gon' have the slightest interest in how my Daddy did wopin' on some udder horse, you know what I mean, Poppa?"

"I'll tell you, I've never been more surprised in my life than when that kid missed those heels," Shine said chewing. At that moment, I knew something good had happened. Shine was talking with us, and he wanted to be part of our world. And he continued, **"He's the best heeler I ever pulled a steer for. Every time he came to the horn, on some of the worst and wildest cattle we've ever roped, Michael, that kid never jerked me once. How did that happen? What caused him to miss?"**

Trying as hard as I could to act like Shine and I had these sorts of informal conversations all the time, I said, *"That's just team roping, partner. Just wasn't our day."*

"You know what?" he said. **"I'll bet you a bale of alfalfa if we had drawn another one of those wicked snakes we drew the first three rounds, he would have roped him, and Blue and I would be smelling around in that new trailer right now, what do you bet?"**

"I bet you're right," I said.

"My Daddy says, 'Wopers always miss da perfect cow.' Das what my Daddy says, and ya'll hadda perfect cow."

"I thought you weren't watching," said Shine.

"Well...," Blue said, looking away, then admitting, **"I saw a wittle bit of it."**

"I'm happy with what we did, and glad we came," I said.

"Me too, Poppa, you wope on da Boo Man all time, we wudda won fust place."

And there was silence for a time, and Shine said, **"I'm glad we came too."**

The next morning - a crisp starched shirt of a Sunday morning - we headed home to Oklahoma.

Chapter Twelve

RIDIN' IN NEW COUNTRY

Stole that line from Larry McMurtry. In *Lonesome Dove*, Gus says, "There ain't nothing better than ridin' a fresh horse in new country." I now knew how Gus felt. Both Blue and Shine were fresh, and even though we were in our familiar arena at home, we were covering new ground. We were riding in a new world. In the old days, if Shine had performed as he had in Abilene, at this moment I would be driving ninety miles an hour to the next one so I could win more money ridin' my "stick." But not now. Now I knew how important it was to maintain his engine. Now I would not be guilty of driving him until we ran him so long and so hard, we completely depleted his big engine of oil and blew that big motor of his sky high. Now in this new country, I knew what Shine needed…more slow dancing with the dairy queens.

"Oh, good grief!"

--Shine

Michael Johnson

And Blue needed the same thing.

"Oh, good gwief!"

--Blue

Whether they wanted to or not, the best thing for the boys would be to unwind their spring as much as possible. To let their rubber band relax until no tension remained and not be tight by any measurement on the most sensitive scale. They were tired after the almost thousand-mile trip, had lost weight during the oven-hot five days, and needed to decompress. Long early morning rides in woods would be good, as would running ten to twenty jerseys through the box, and not roping or even chasing a single one from horseback, but rather only to "score" the steers, asking the horses to just stand and do nothing. And that's what we did – for a week. We just took it easy, and the medicine worked well. The boys were calm, and in the best shape of their life, both physically, and more importantly...mentally.

Backsliding

"Humans do it...why can't horses?"

--Shine

A couple of weeks later, we were on our way to South Carolina. Bronc had called and offered a most attractive invitation. "Come and see me," he had said.

"Load up the boys and bring your rope and an appetite. We'll cook, talk, visit with friends, and I have some sixty steers. We'll rope all day and talk all night."

302

And we were on our way.

The long two-day trip was finally done when we arrived on the South Carolina mountaintop…literally. The farm and ranch were actually located at the crest of a huge earthrise, and the prettiest thing about the whole place was the wide spacious arena filled with deep soft sand. Complete with an electronic steer chute requiring no human to load or release steers – that task handily accomplished by the small electronic device Bronc had tied to his belt – we roped all day and spent the cool evenings in conversations with topics ranging from horses and horsemen to recipes for Boston Butt and the sauce of course, to favorite writers, best stories ever – read or heard – and defending passive voice in literature agreeing that indeed, on some occasions, we both preferred it. Having formerly owned a newspaper, Bronc is an excellent writer. Our days involved much less verbal sparring.

During the day, Bronc either sat on his horse, occasionally heeling for me, or spent the rest of the time sitting on the fence watching me like a hawk on every run. I knew my longtime coach well enough to know he rarely spoke when instructing. Bronc followed the axiom of St. Francis who said, *"Teach always, and when necessary, use words."* Bronc didn't talk much during class.

A disgusted look over his shoulder meant "No." A nod so small you could hardly see it meant "Yes." And every time I missed a steer and asked him for the explanation as to why – what I had done wrong – his answer became monotonously repetitious… "Position," he would bark. "There are three facets to good roping," he said, beginning one of his mini-lectures. "And those

three facets are...position, position, position!" And
then silence would drift all around the mountain, broken
only by the soft opening swish of the electronic chute
gate.

Some time late in the second day, I roped a steer,
and after pulling my slack, and moving to dally, I
"waved it off," meaning I flipped the loop off the steer's
horns.

"Why do I do that?" I asked. "What causes me to
wave it off like that?" I had put the question to so many
ropers and had received so many varied answers. But I
knew the master would know *the* answer, and I waited.

"Come with me," he said hopping off the fence. We
left the horses tied in the arena and headed to the barn.
Once there, Bronc set the roping dummy in the middle
of the barn walkway, and looking at his watch, said,
"It's 5 p.m. now. Rope this dummy until 7, and the
entire time, I want you to work on waving it off. I'll go
start dinner. Come eat in a couple of hours."

I knew better than to argue with the master, so I
began. Two hours later, I walked onto the front porch
of his farmhouse. He was seated outside under the
covered front porch with his boots up on a rustic, small
cedar coffee table.

"How did you do?" he asked.

"I can't wave it off the dummy!" I said with
frustration. "I tried for two hours, and I couldn't wave
it off a single time. That exercise didn't help me one
bit, all that effort, and I didn't wave it off one time!"

"Why do you think that is?" he asked.

"Because I couldn't wave it off!" I almost shouted.
"I was right there in the proper posi...." I stood there
for thirty seconds, and then realized I was really mad.

"Why didn't you just tell me that instead of making me rope the dummy for two hours?"

"I've been telling you about 'position' for two whole days, and obviously the message wasn't getting through. Just thought I would try a different approach."

"I have an approach I would like to try. I would like to pop you in the eye!"

"Okay, but you ain't gonna get no barbeque," he laughed.

I was mad, but the new approach worked. I didn't wave my loop off another steer.

Tunica

We roped hard for three days, alternating horses, working on fundamentals, bad cows, and...position. At the end of the time, Bronc said, "I think you're ready. Let's go to Mississippi."

I was thrilled. Bronc thought I was ready to rope with him in Tunica, which might not be the big time, but you could sure get up on top of your truck and see the big time from there. Tunica...A U.S. Roping! Pretty big time to me.

We arrived the night before, and since we helped the producers of the event wrap some three hundred steers with protective head wraps, they offered to let us run them through and rope them all. Such practice the night before was invaluable.

I began on Blue. The steers were fast, but as always the colt tried his heart out, and we managed to rope his set – at the far end – but the Blue Man caught them all. Then I mounted Shine. He was spectacular. Bronc would later comment, "That horse has an instrument panel full of lights – and we don't know what they all do yet." That moment was the highlight of my trip. The low point would be coming shortly.

"Ain't that just like life?"

--Shine

Because of the fast cattle, Bronc suggested I go with Shine when the official roping competition began. I would head on Shine in the Number 12 Roping, and Bronc would be my first heeler.

"I luv Bonk Fanin, but he's w'ong. He's w'ong. He's w'ong!"

--Little Blue

As the roping began, I was over-nervous again. Thought I had whipped that demon, but this was Tunica, with Bronc Fanning over there in the heel box. Every eye in that massive coliseum would be on us – well, actually on him – because everybody always stopped what they were doing to watch Bronc Fanning when his name was called. And I rode Shine into the box, and ...*he wouldn't turn around!* My nerves cracked and fell on the head box dirt floor.

I jerked him, I pulled him, I begged him, and at last, he turned just a bit, and I nodded knowing the steer would be lighting fast, and he was...if lightning could trot.

We draw three world record holders in Abilene, then, in Tunica, draw an arthritic cripple that couldn't outrun Milton Berle. Just one simple question here; is that fair?

Shine jumped on top of him, and I pulled the reins
- far too severely – in an effort to keep him back. That
harsh jerk slammed the bit against the roof of his
mouth, and he went straight up in the air. We repeated
that "porpoise breeding a whale maneuver" down the
arena two more times – much to the delight of the
crowd, who now understood the great Bronc Fanning
was only being kind when he consented to rope with his
handicapped friend, Miguel. And I missed the steer.

Never more disgusted in my life, I rode out the
back. I intended to reach the trailer, load up, and leave
before being seen. But just prior to escaping, I heard
Bronc say, "That was my fault. I should have had you
ride Blue."

**"Takes a big man to admit when he's
w'ong, and Bonk Fanin knows he was w'ong.
I luv Bonk Fanin 'cause now he know, "You
always go widda Boo Man!"**

"It wasn't your fault!" I almost spit at him. "It was
mine. I didn't do anything you told me to. I was out of
position."

"Well, that will come with experience. Keep
your head up. You have more steers to rope for other
people."

He was right, I did. I rode Blue for the rest of the
roping and caught all my steers. And that didn't help
my feelings a bit. I was mad at me and disappointed in
me, and I felt the same way about Shine. I thought we
had moved along the path, but I was wrong. The big
gray had reverted to his fear. We weren't that far along
at all.

Michael Johnson

Heartbreak Hotel

You know where that is…down there at the end of lonely street. And that's where I was headed. I had an inkling at the time. The dairy queens had told me. But like we do when we learn some relative is disturbed, I hid that nagging concern from the world. Once again, I hid my true feelings from my friends, from myself, and from my horse. And I had good reason to do so. We had moved down the path. Because of all the progress we had made together and all the greatness he had exuded at Abilene, I denied what I knew to be true. Shine was not well. Shine was still sick, and a part of Shine was still afraid. I felt it in the runs with the dairy queens. And they are such gossips.

"Oh, if I could only tell the story in the sequence that it really happened. He did make improvements in his horsemanship skills, he did give me more time, but if he really had bought the dairy queens when he said he did, things might have been different. And I'm sure he believes it happened the way he said – we all tend to do that – but it didn't happen that way. That's why I backslid. Baptists do it…why can't horses?"

--Shine

Shine had performed magnificently in Abilene, no question about that, but something troubled me even about that. *I didn't know why!* I know that makes me sound picky and impossible to please, and my only defense is that's not why I felt that way. My reason for feeling that way was because he reached a distant plateau too high and far away too quickly…and I didn't know why. Such a strange thing to say for a cowboy who at one time knew he could make a great horse in thirty days; the same cowboy who now knew after five years, his friend was still not well.

Was he a great horse who responded to pressure? Perhaps so, but if so, why then did he revert to fear at Tunica? And why, on some occasions, had I felt that fear in him when we did our slow two-step with the dairy queens? And I had felt that fear. In the softest, most non-threatening environment on the planet – our home court - a planet populated by Hoppy, Mopey, Slowey, and Poot Along…why on some occasions, did the great Shine exhibit fear from such sweet and soft little creatures as these baby jerseys? But he had. And that worried me.

I needed a horse doctor. Not a "Wetamanavarian," as Blue called them – he never could get that word right, been mispronouncing it since he was a baby – but a "horse doctor." They are such people you know, and I knew several. Kenneth Colson is one, and that's where the Shine Man and I were headed.

Horse Doctors

Funny how the Lord puts people close to your hometown just when you need them most, and He had wisely chosen to put Kenneth close to mine. I was able to recognize Kenneth and his credentials because of something a Catholic priest had taught me long ago. And that priest's name was Michael Jamail.

A graduate of Notre Dame he was, and his daddy

owned Jamail's in Houston, a mega-grocery store that also catered and was accustomed to one thousand-seat, one thousand-dollar-per-plate fund raisers for the wheelers and dealers of the elected officials who had aptly named their city bird the "construction crane." I spent time with the Michael in graduate school while we were both earning our doctoral degrees, and I always remembered something he told me long ago.

"Whenever you have a problem in life, and you ask someone for advice," he said, "if they give you a quick answer – if they know the solution to your problem immediately – get away from that person as quickly as you can. They have nothing to offer you. But on the other hand, if you ask someone for help about a particular difficulty you are experiencing, and you know the person has expertise in that area...and that person responds to your question with a puzzled look, and says, "I'm not sure; let's talk about it and find the best solution," stay close to that person for the rest of your days. That person can help you." And that was how I recognized Kenneth Colson, H.D. - Horse Doctor.

"Well, uh...hmmm," were his opening words. Those were the words he used in his response to my almost hour-long soliloquy describing what I had now come to call the "Shine Story," - the title of the movie I knew they would surely someday do about his life.

"So...," I asked him. "After hearing all that, what do you think?"

"Hmmm...," he said again, and I moved a little closer to him.

"Let's watch him, and see what he does," he said. "Then, we'll try to figure out what we could do to help

him the most." And I'm thinking, *"Ray Hunt had Tom
Dorrance. Lord gave me Kenneth Colson. Ray Hunt
ain't got nothing on me."*

Turns out I was right about that. And having said
that, it is truly difficult to describe what Kenneth did
to help both my horse and me so much. But help us he
did. What he didn't do was make a list of what we were
doing right, and what we were doing wrong. He did not
give us any assignments to work on. What he did do
was watch, look, listen, and try to find something that
would help. And I didn't have to tell Kenneth about
Shine's misbehavior; I showed him.

Kenneth's pen is wide and long. His cattle's speeds
are medium slow to slow. The head and heel boxes are
wide and deep, and he insists all visiting ropers take
their time, and be good to their horses. The perfect
place for Shine not to feel threatened and to be at ease.
We loaded the first steer.

"Let's just take it easy here," Kenneth said in a low
voice. "Let's just score this old slow steer." He opened
the gate, and the black steer came so slowly, he failed to
dislodge a single fly on his back. *And Shine reared and
walked out on his back feet!* We tried again, and steer
number two proved to be a photocopy of the first one,
and Shine burst forth with the same totally irrational
fear response, once again rearing and exhibiting intense
anxiety. In a calm voice, Kenneth said, "Hmmmm."

I've had some low points in my life. Times I'd
just as soon not remember, most dealing with failed
relationships with a couple of women I've loved, or
deaths of friends too painful to recall. But that moment
on that day was one of the worst. I knew then beyond
any doubt I had failed in my quest. I had failed to

311

fulfill my spiritual assignment. After all the work, bottom-of-the-valley failures, and peak-of-the-mountain successes, still I had failed. The horse I thought possessed greatness, the one who had roped perhaps a thousand head - in a wide, long, safe pen with slow cows - had betrayed me. The realization came clear. I had been nothing but a fool. I led Shine to the trailer, and unsaddled him. And I knew I would never rope on him again.

For the next few days and weeks, life was tough to live. I tried roping on Blue and Buddy, but even though I wouldn't look at him, I knew the greatest horse I had ever ridden stood alone on the far side of the hill in the pasture, and he wouldn't look at me either. I didn't try to understand it, just tried to live with it, but I couldn't. My mind started talking again. I was in the barn staring at the floor trying to concentrate on the fact that people had real problems, and those with death, cancer, divorce, and those dealing with all the rest of life's curve balls that she can sometimes throw so wickedly, would say, "So you have two horses to rope on, your health and sight, and you can't function?" That made me feel worse. And the little voice said, *"Try again."* I exploded.

Fury just ripped me. If I could just get at this thing, I would choke it to death. Finally, I knew this was no spiritual assignment, just insanity. I was disturbed like some stalker or man who couldn't let go of his wife.

If anyone ever had countless incidents of failures that proved the "time to quit" had arrived, that someone was me, and still the voice spoke. I searched my mind for some...any...mental health professional who might understand. Maybe someone in the clergy.

"No," the voice said. **"Looks like that. Not that. Not crazy. Right. You were right."**

I really can't remember if I cried or not, but I know I just gave up. I gave up on the whole crazy stupid notion and stopped fighting the voice and stopped hoping. I just stopped. I had come to the end.

"No, not the end. Just a stone in the path. Try again," said the voice.

Something in me said, *"Tomorrow. Tomorrow we begin again."* And we did.

When I saddled Shine the next day, he didn't look at me, nor I at him. Neither of us spoke, but there was the slimmest of feelings that while I could never say he "enjoyed" it, I felt he was somehow relieved. We danced with the dairy queens, and he was…medium. Not overjoyed, but without sick fear. We did that for days. My spirits lifted. I could still ride the best horse I ever knew, and if nothing else, I could practice on him. He seemed to be comfortable here at home, and that would provide me with the world's greatest practice horse. He could run fifty or sixty steers and not evidence the slightest fatigue - not that I would ever do that. He was just that strong and possessed that much endurance. Soon, the days transformed to a monotonous sameness, and I knew he was sad. I didn't know how to help him.

"I haven't had much to say in a while, and the reason is I felt just like he did. That period he's talking about was so discouraging and depressing I don't even want to talk about it. He felt I betrayed him. I understand that. He betrayed me.

Michael Johnson

*At Abilene, he was so focused. His entire
attention was on that buckle on the horn wrap
every second we were there. That helped me
so much. He had faith in me, and that gave
me strength. At Tunica, he was fine the night
before when we practiced, and the next night
during the competition, he was nothing but
a jangled mass of raw nerves. I think he was
afraid to miss for Bronc. At Abilene, missing
never entered his mind. At Tunica, that was
the only thing he thought about, and he was
so nervous. I picked up on that because my
internal state is only a reflection of his. If he's
afraid, I am. But I tried to help us.*

*When we went into the box, I just paused. I
didn't get sticky. Instead of just giving me a
second, he slammed me in the mouth insisting
that I turn immediately. That infuriated me,
and I got mad. He got mad, I got mad, and the
run just went downhill from there. I did get too
close to the steer, but I was slowing down; then
he hits me in the mouth again. I did a poor
job, and I'm not blaming him, but I didn't miss
the cow. I can do a lot of things, but I can't
rope. That's his job. He softballed that steer,
the loop split the horns, and the rest is history.
I'm sorry it happened, but it wasn't all me. He
wasn't the only one betrayed. And the incident
at Kenneth's....*

*There are so many things I could say about
that day, but instead of throwing stones, let
me take the blame for that one. I just...I just*

314

*made a mistake. Maybe I was mad, or...I
don't know. I just did something I regret. And
in my defense, ask him if I ever did anything
like that again. When he left me in the pasture
for days, and we didn't rope...every day I saw
him on Blue, and I was no longer part of all
that, something happened during that time. I
missed it all. And I knew we were done. I just
made a mistake, and I regret it. Haven't we all
done that?"*

--Shine

Both lost and confused now, Shine and I mindlessly
trotted alongside the queens. Like some married couple
who had lost their love, we were just going through the
motions. We didn't know what else to do. We didn't
talk much because we didn't know what to talk about.
Both of us had tried everything we knew. Some five
years of highs and lows, and now it seemed I could
only dwell in the valley, and Shine walked along that
deep floor with me. We found ourselves frustrated and
stalled with no wind at our back to move us along. He
had his head down, and mine was down too. And then
something came to help us.

Intuitive Leaps

How do we learn a thing? How do we problem
solve? Scores of books have been written in an attempt
to answer those questions. Most learning theorists,
psychologists, and physiologists have formed a tenuous
consensus – tenuous, because those types rarely agree
on anything - that says, "We learn by trial and error.

We learn by approaching a task, observing what's required, then 'attempting.'" In most cases, our early attempts result in failure. We try again, and if unable to complete the task, we try again. By using this "look, try, fail" approach, the brain gains information, and in successive trials, our mistakes become less frequent. By this "one, two, three…" method, we eventually gain mastery of the desired task, and we can ride the bicycle or work the fraction. We learn by a methodical one, two, three approach. While most in the cognitive field would squirm with this too-simple explanation, they might grudgingly admit, "Well, that's the general idea."

Some however – more radical thinkers - have posed the possibility the brain - at times at least - may learn in a more mysterious and unexplained way. That phenomenon has been given a name by an eclectic group of philosophers, clerics, psychologists, brain physiologists, and other free thinkers throughout history, and many have written – or tried to write - about the "intuitive leap." Hard-nosed researchers in academia turn up their noses at such mysticism, but I do not. I believe in intuitive leaps because one came on me long ago. I had been the recipient of a strange visitor who changed my life.

My academic background had a shine the color of tarnished silver. C's, D's, and F's in middle school, D's and F's in high school, and thirteen consecutive F's in college. The reason for this abject failure was finally explained to me at the age of nineteen by a college graduate student majoring in Psychology. After administering a Wechsler I.Q. test to me in the spring of 1968, he informed me that my intelligence level was slightly below average. *"Well,"*

I thought with relief. *"The mystery is solved."* Yet the mystery was just beginning.

A couple of months after that revelation from the future Dr. Freud, something happened. Something came to help me. I was sitting in an orange chair in my mother's living room on a Tuesday night. The time was perhaps ten minutes before 7 p.m. At that moment, I was lost in a fog. The worst student ever, I simply could not see how any human being could be expected to know about English, Science, Math, History, Biology, and Psychology, all in one day, which is what my current class schedule seemed to be requiring. No wonder I was failing in college - such a task was impossible. At ten minutes after seven, I was an A student.

I'm sure that story would cause one to wonder what happened during those twenty minutes, and almost thirty-five years later, I'm still wondering too. All I know is something came to help me. During that period, my brain switched from the one - two - three method, to the one, two, three...*sixteen* method. My brain just made an intuitive leap. Not that I suddenly knew all the facts about the various subject matters – that would have been nice – but rather something inside explained to me – *"No one expects you to know all the information, but others do expect you to learn the information one fact at a time. The going will be slow and the task arduous, but doable."* That was the leap my brain made. From that day forward, I never made another B, C, D, or F ever again. If that appears boastful, I need to explain I still have the below average I.Q. - I'm using it to write this book.

My point is not to boast, but to struggle to explain that on one occasion in my life, something helped me understand the world just a bit more. That knowledge seemed somehow not in me, but it *came* into me. Why that event happened when it did, I don't know, but I'm sure it did not occur because there is anything special about me. Somehow I know such knowledge is available to us all, yet except for a few small smatterings of insight, I have been unable to call up this source again for decades. Yet it did happen once, and so many years later, a similar event occurred. And this time, the knowledge came to explain Shine.

Dream a Little Dream

My mind was in a state of high agitation. Stressing and fretting over Shine for days, thoughts swirled out of control, and images kept repeating themselves on my internal "mind image" screen. And they were getting on my nerves. I wished they would stop – these mixed images that made no sense. I needed some rest.

Finally one night, close to mental exhaustion, I fell into bed. Tossing and turning, I looked at the bedside clock, and since it said 2:12 a.m., I knew sleep would not come. But something like it did. Not conscious, but not awake – in that place between this world and the other - the images shot, spun, and swirled like comets with tails.

Pictures and people, stop signs, and James Taylor, the great horseman from Lubbock saying, "Rope on him quicker!" Small segments from video clips from great ropers, internal snapshots of Shine walking out on his back feet, mental images of Shine running swift and low and free, with an untroubled spirit. Bronc saying, "The stop sign. The stop sign, do you get it? I told you too much, you're tired. That's why I don't talk much;

people can't take it all in. I know you're tired, but do
you get the stop sign?" Something about how we don't
slam on our brakes right at the stop sign, but we coast
to it. "Yes, I get it," I had said, but I lied. I was sleepy
and wanted to go to bed. I didn't get it. And the images
shot and swirled, and were maddening, and too much,
and then....

They began to come together, with their bright
comet heads melding into one, and their fiery tails
extinguishing, flowing, and falling down into one thing.
Actually, two things...two massive bronze gears with
teeth. One began to click in sync with the other. All
of the teeth were former comets made of Bronc, James
Taylor, videos, and pictures of Shine, but now the images
transformed into teeth on huge gear wheels, and the
wheels moved slowly until all the teeth fit perfectly in the
notches on the wheels, and everything locked into place.
Everything stopped, all having now come into perfect
harmony, and I knew. I saw and understood. Something
had come to help me with Shine.

And I woke up.

I bolted upright in the bed. The clock said 3:33. I
hadn't been asleep that long, but the powerfully lucid
quality of the dream caused me to notice my hands
were shaking. I rose from the bed, dressed, and went
to the barn. Shine was standing just outside. I stood
rubbing his neck for a while, then went back to bed, and
fell into a deep and restful sleep.

"There's something different about him."

--Shine

Michael Johnson

The Making of a Horseman

Not that I am one. A horseman I mean. But I'm
becoming one, and had I known the price - the gut-
twisting – you're a pompous ass fool – bucked off
– stupid mistake-making idiot – humiliated – crying
– pull my soul out through my nose – broken-fingered
price I would be required to pay – I might not have
taken the job in the first place. Like the Duke said in an
old movie once, "There were a helluva lotta things they
didn't tell me when I signed on with this outfit."

"Sprained finger...just sprained."

--Shine

And whatever strides have been made in my
development with horses, because of Darrell, Bronc,
Craig Hamilton, Rosie, Kenneth, and all the others, the
one who taught me the most was the great gray. The
Shine Man has been the best teacher I ever had. And
looking back on the experience, he never quit me. He
did every single thing I asked him to. If I asked him
to be afraid, he was. If I pulled on him during a run,
he would hop up in the air just as I had told him to do.
If I rushed him, and the energy and pressure spilled
over, still he tried again the next day. And finally,
when I began to do what all great teachers do with
great students – that is to just get out of the damn way
– Shine began to shine. And now his mind and mine
have held together for over a year. Shine is no longer
afraid. Still hyper at times as all big motor horses are,
he can act out a bit. But now, I'm more aware that
some prior behavior on my part has cued him to do so.

320

Now I search for *my* error, not his, and he responds so
much better. The better I become at asking my horse to
do a thing, the better he becomes at doing the thing.

In **Pygmalion**, Eliza asks Colonel Pickering, "Do
you know when my real education began?" Then Eliza
explains her transformation really began the day she
arrived at Wimpole Street, and she attributes the miracle
to not how she behaved, but how she was treated. Now
I knew that was also true of roping horses. So many
helped me, and like Eliza, there was a moment when
my real education began. My real education began on
the day Shine came to Johnson Farms.

Since that time, the journey has been full of pain
and heartbreak. I learned I was a fool about horses.
During that time I feared for Earl's life. During that
time I lost my love. She left in the spring. Did my
obsession with Shine cause her departure? I don't
know, but I doubt it helped much. Like the rest of
our time on earth, some days have been difficult to
live through. Yet there has been so much clear joy.
Someone asked me once, "What color is joy?" I know
the answer now. Joy is clear. And I've felt it so many
times during my years with Shine.

I feel a grateful joy for the men and women who
helped me with him. The ones who when I confessed
my ignorance didn't laugh at me but admitted the
same was true about them. And I saw the sadness in
their eyes when they said that. They shared what they
learned with me, and Shine and I are better for it. There
is joy in that.

More joy came on December 1, 2004, when Blue's
granddaddy received a heart. The transplant was
successful, and Earl comes to see his pride and joy

often. When I watch Earl and Little Blue standing together talking, life is so worthwhile. Earl walks on his farm and we go to the Redland Country Store for early morning coffee. There is joy in that.

Finally, because of Shine, one other source of joy came I never thought possible. Since I was young, there has been a deep desire in me and as I grew older, I felt the chances of it ever coming into my life slipping away. I had lost hope that the one thing I always wanted would ever come. I wanted to be part of a healing.

That was the reason I went to school - to learn how to help people. While I loved the experience and my professors, I didn't learn how. During my working life as a psychologist – while some encouraging words may have helped a few – to insert a key into someone's psyche and alleviate suffering? Never happened. The one experience I longed for never came, and I lost hope that it ever would. But it did. It came in Shine.

I was part of healing a living creature after all. Now I know why the Lord sent him to me. Anyone else would have given up on him. I knew so little, I blamed myself instead of the horse. That's what saved him. That is the key to horsemanship.

"It is a confession of poor horsemanship to complain that the horse will not obey. Horses have an almost uncanny way of knowing if a rider is able to require obedience or is just a passenger."

Bob A. Carson – Horse Sense

I was part of healing Shine. There is so much joy in that. The big gray provided a powerful and lasting healing in me as well. Every horse I ever work with in the future will benefit from the lessons taught by Shine. There is joy in that as well.

On the night of the dream, something provided me with an understanding of a substantive number of pieces of information. I knew their implementation would not work the next day, but I knew just as surely in time, they would. And they did.

Parts of the dream were mysterious in a profound way, and some parts explainable – at least to some extent. The pictures and people I saw in the dream state were all either real people or real events I encountered during the past three years. James Taylor was one.

The skilled horseman from Lubbock had on one occasion spent some two hours listening to me rant on about Shine, but unlike most of my other friends, James listened with intense interest. James had been given a similar assignment years earlier with a horse much like Shine. Like me, James knew his horse had tremendous ability, but he had found great difficulty in channeling that energy and talent. After my long speech to him that day, I listened as he shared some solutions he discovered that helped his horse in a very real way.

"Michael," he said. "The key is to rope on him quicker...sooner, I mean. These two horses - mine and yours – from what you've told me, are so alike. Both of them have tremendous ability to get the roper to the spot. That's their strength - so we should let them use that strength. The instant Shine gets you even close to the place you can throw your rope, throw it! Let catching the steer become of secondary importance. We're trying to help your horse here."

His words would prove to be prophetic. After the dream, James' words seeped their way down into me.

During the run, I began to rope much sooner on Shine, and I could feel his welcome appreciation. Such a procedure caused the big gray to relax more than ever. I learned if we could keep his powerful motor from getting over in the red zone, we were both better off. Roping quicker did just that.

And my understanding of Bronc's stop sign analogy became vividly clear in the dream. Apparently my conscious mind - too tired and sleepy to hear - didn't understand, but my subconscious must have been listening very closely. That part of me was not only listening, but understood every word. Bronc was trying to tell me when we approach the steer, if we check the horse – that is, ask him to slow his speed a bit - we should do so gently, and early in the run. We should gently check the horse on the way to the steer, not when we arrive at the spot. Just as we do in a vehicle when approaching a stop sign…we don't slam on the brakes, we coast to that stop sign. The dream clarified his meaning. When I began to execute such maneuvers on Shine, nothing ever helped his roping more.

And so it was with all the images in the dream; so many bits of information came so quickly, and in such a powerful and symbolic way, I woke with a start and knew while there were many rational explanations, part of the experience was beyond the ordinary. Something had come to help me again. And this something had brought simple and ordinary information, but the thing that did the bringing was not ordinary at all. This great and kind intelligence came into me, and used the imagery of spinning wheels and gears to show me the answers had already been given to me. And what brilliant imagery and striking colors the knowledge

324

chose to use - beautiful, powerful, and unforgettable. All I had to do was put the pieces of the puzzle together. This "helper" did just that for me. Whatever it was, I will always be grateful.

"And I will always be grateful as well. Nothing ever helped us more."

--Shine

And sure enough, Shine was not so trusting the first day, nor the second. But as time passed, what the dream had brought was real and lasting. Now the Shine Man has his hand off his knife. He can still snort and prance, but I can tell - as I probe around inside his mind with mine - the fear is gone. I no longer rope for me much anymore; I rope for my horses. If people are drunk and acting stupid at some arena, I make a graceful exit. If the pen is short, and the cows are big, fast, and draggy, I won't ask my horses to risk injury. If the mud is a foot deep, I know I'll have to buy a new rope because after catching the steer, I won't make Shine follow the steer to the other end just to avoid soiling my rope. I'll drop my rope in that mud. I can buy a new rope, but I could never buy another Shine.

Ray Hunt said, "Once you start giving, you won't believe how much you get back." "Giving what?" I had asked. Now I know. When I began giving to Shine, he responded. While I always believed in him so, he had more greatness in him than I imagined. Riding the big gray and Little Blue has resulted in our winning more in the last nine months of my life than I did in the previous fifty-seven years combined.

The proof is inside me. The proof is "look at

me then," and "look at me now." I no longer lie to cowboys to fit in, or lie to my horse, or to myself. I know he's close now, and the way I know is how I feel when we rope. To rope on the Shine Man can be described only as a great privilege. Lord, if I could just describe that. If I could just somehow grab Mother English Language by the throat, hold her down, and make her spit out the words, surely they would be so beautiful and clear. And words I've never heard.

When I'm an old man in a nursing home, I don't think I'll ever be bitter 'cause even if I can't see the television or read a book - as long as my mind holds - I'll think about the great Shine, and my mind will return to the three runs at Abilene he made to take us to the finals. I am proud we made the finals, and the fact that we didn't win the roping really doesn't bother me.

"It bothers him a little."

--Shine

I will always remember those three runs. Three steers that could only be caught by the wind in a spring storm...and I was riding the wind. I never felt so alive. And we did win. We won something priceless. Two in tandem, two in unison, two dancing and becoming one. I never remember cueing him to face on a single steer because I never did. If the steer darted right or left, I never told him to follow. We were one thing – just for a time; we were a mythical thing – a centaur. For a time, we were both better than we really are.

To the best teacher I ever had...I would like to thank the difficult horse who made my life miserable. Because of that difficult horse who made my life so miserable, I am more. Not there yet - just a little closer to the base of the mountain.   I'm still so ignorant - a word meaning lacking knowledge or comprehension. After learning so much from Shine and the others, still I lack knowledge and comprehension of the gift of the thing called the horse. At least I'll always be welcome in the company of great horsemen.

Why did we live through it all? Maybe some Divine Plan? It seemed so at times, and I will always believe it was. And I also know Shine and Blue are good for two things. To rope really well - they can do that - and to break my heart. I love them too much and when we feel that way about something or someone, that's what always happens to our hearts. Some avoid such deep connections with other living creatures to prevent the pain bound to come when we are forced to leave them behind or go on without them. But C. S. Lewis had some memorable words about using that method to avoid pain....

"To love at all is to be vulnerable. Love anything, and your heart will certainly be wrung and possibly be broken. If you want to make sure of keeping it intact, you must give your heart to no one.... Wrap it up carefully round with hobbies and little luxuries; avoid all entanglements; lock it up safe in the casket or coffin of your selfishness. But in that casket – safe, dark, motionless, airless – it will change. It will not be broken; it will become unbreakable, impenetrable, irredeemable.... The only place outside of Heaven where you can be perfectly safe from all the dangers and perturbations of love...is Hell."

--C. S. Lewis

And now I sit here in the early morning in my study looking out at my farm, and at this moment, I can see Shine standing on top of the hill. As it's April, the grass under his feet is such a sparkling green, and the sky behind him is clear and blue. He's older now, almost twelve, and only recently have I become aware his color has changed. He and the small cloud above him are perfectly matched. We've been together seven years – it doesn't seem that long at all. There's some sadness in me as I look for his dapples and realize they are almost gone. Shine is almost white now, and even though older, so much more beautiful to me. I guess that's love, isn't it - when you still love someone no matter what age does to their appearance? And I think to myself, perhaps I haven't completed my spiritual assignment of healing Shine, but I know I didn't fail the class. And inside me now, I know we are both better than we were.

I hope we haven't come to the end, but for now, we will be on our way.

Shine, Michael, LittleBlue,
and The Rowdy Cow Dog

"Come wope widd'us sometime!"

--The Blue Man

Michael & Shine

Bronc Fanning   Craig Hamilton   Earl

Wallace & The Dairy Queens

EPILOGUE

Manuel picked up all the files and folders at once, and then began bumping their bottom edges on his desk top until they aligned. He laid them in a neat and orderly pile on the right side of the small table adjacent to his work area and made ready to begin his journey to the Master's home. The call had come that morning, and he knew he was expected in the late afternoon. Arranging the bandana around his neck, he checked his hat and noticing a dusty smudge on the crown, removed it with the small brush he kept for such occasions. With one last look in the mirror and a good-bye pet for Rowdy, the cow dog, Manuel walked out the front door of his cabin. He looked forward not only to the destination, but to the walk as well. He smiled to himself, remembering such an invitation filled him with fear the first time.

He had been so frightened, he rushed to Maxine, the pretty intake angel he had met when he first came. She listened and then laughed, "Manuel, there's no need to be afraid. The Master simply wants to see you, and the experience will be most pleasant."

And Maxine had been correct. Now as Manuel

Michael Johnson

strode purposefully along, he had no fear whatsoever, but he looked forward to a pleasant conversation with the most pleasant friend he ever had. He smiled again as he saw the beautiful, but modest dwelling on the hill, and remembered again how the first time, he had expected something much more grand. He crossed the small stone bridge, waving to the wood ducks in the pond. Once on the wooden porch, Manuel started to knock and saw the door was open. "Of course," he laughed. "His door is always open."

"Manuel? Is that you?" he heard the Lord ask. "Come in. Come in."

Manuel entered to see the Lord seated behind a large oak desk, with his feet crossed resting on the corner. He wore a faded blue shirt and old comfortable looking jeans. His roughout boots were clean, but obviously used.

"Good to see you my friend," He smiled. "How are our horses?"

"He always calls them 'our' horses," Manuel thought to himself. "They are good, Lord; all are doing well," he said aloud.

"Good, good, you do such a splendid job with them," the Lord said.

They talked for a while, and Manuel found himself relaxed and truly enjoying the interchange. At last, the Lord said, "I want to ask you something, Manuel."

"Yes, Lord?" replied the old man.

The Lord walked to the window behind the desk and looked out for a time. Without turning back to look at Manuel, he said, "This is not intended to alarm you in anyway, but as you know, there will come a time when I will be in need of a horse."

332

Manuel did know, and he saw the sadness in His eyes. On some occasions, the Lord talked about the coming battle, but then, His spirit would lift as he spoke of the victory.

"Again, Manuel, I repeat this is not meant to alarm you. I have no news of any impending events because no man knows the day or the hour. But like any good son, I must be about my Father's business and prepared to do what is asked of me."

"I understand, Lord," said Manuel.

The Lord turned smiling and said, "Manuel, do you know of a special horse I might ride when the time comes? This horse must have great ability, possess all the required skills found in a great heart, and run like the wind. And I prefer him to be white. Do you know of such a horse I might consider, Manuel?"

"Lord, you know all the horses much better than me," said Manuel.

Smiling even more, the Lord said, "I didn't want to influence your choice, old friend. Do you know of such a horse I might consider, Manuel?"

Manuel turned to look out the window. The mother wood duck was swimming slowly across the small pond with four babies in tow. "How beautiful they are," he thought to himself, and then he said...

"I do know of one, Lord," he said. "I do know of one."

"I saw Heaven standing open, and there before me was a white horse, whose rider is called Faithful and True."

-- Revelation 19:11

Michael Johnson

Michael & Buddy

The Rowdy Cow Dog